Tales of a
Sussex Family Farm

Angela Lewell

Tales of a
Sussex Family Farm

"Frithwood," Lee Place, Pulborough.

Life at Frithwood 1949–1997

by

ANGELA M. LERWILL

THE CHOIR PRESS

First published in the United Kingdom in 2023 by
The Choir Press

ISBN 978-1-78963-339-9

It's the past that tells us who we are.
Without it we lose our identity.
Stephen Hawking (1942–2018)

This book is dedicated to
Dorothy Consuelo Lerwill
A wonderful Mother
Teacher and Friend
Who taught me all I know
And set the standards by which I live

Contents

Foreword

An appreciation by Graham Harvey, former Agricultural Story Editor for 'The Archers'

Angela Lerwill's evocation of life on a small, family farm in the second half of the 20th century is, by turns, funny, sad and inspirational. This is no escape-to-the-country idyll. Eking out a living on a few secluded acres deep in the Sussex countryside was always hard, especially in winter, when 'mud would fester, pipes might freeze and newborn lambs die before daybreak'. Under bright summer skies, daily life might seem more tranquil. But the longer days also meant more hours of back-breaking work, especially for the author's parents, Berns and Consuelo.

Their story's told with warmth and affection by Angela, the youngest of their three children. For almost half a century the couple spent their lives nurturing animals and growing crops, while somehow managing to raise a family. This at a time when big-business agriculture – backed by government - was set on sweeping away small mixed farms like theirs and replacing them with large, specialist units, reliant on chemical fertilisers, pesticides and public subsidies. That Berns and Consuelo managed to keep the farm going for so long is a measure of their resourcefulness, determination and sheer love of the land on their own few acres of England.

Angela begins the story with her own first memories from when she was five years old in the early 1960s. She's sitting in the farm's ancient green van with several trays of home-produced eggs stacked on her lap. It's livestock market day in nearby Pulborough and in the back of the van, separated from driver and child passenger by a slatted, wooden partition, are three porker pigs. Selling produce in the local market was essential to the cash-flow of small, mixed farms like theirs. Within a decade the market at Pulborough had gone and the land turned into a car park for London commuters. Just one more blow to small farmers struggling to survive in a countryside being transformed for industrial-scale agriculture.

But there's no bitterness in these tales of a lost England, still less any sentimentality. Life on the land could be tough, perhaps brutal at times. We're not spared details of the distress caused by the castration of male piglets, a practise apparently forced on farmers by butchers who insisted that pork from uncastrated males had an unpleasant taint to it. Then there was the annual killing, plucking and dressing of the Christmas turkeys, a gruelling seasonal marathon that everyone got involved in. Yet to conclude that these grim tasks showed a lack of feeling or humanity would be wrong. When Blanche, the Guernsey house cow was finally sent to slaughter after years of faithful service, we learn that Berns cried himself to sleep that night.

There's a liberal dusting of humour in these country tales, too. The story of Jack, for instance, the runt of a litter of piglets, who was fed daily at the back door to the farmhouse. Finding the door open one day, he ventured into the house. Moving from room to room in search of milk, he finally found his way into the bathroom which was on the ground floor. For some reason the door slammed shut behind him and he was imprisoned. When he was finally released by one of the family several hours later, he seemed to have lost a little of his bravado!

Apart from these moments of sadness and comedy, farm life was mostly about the ceaseless round of routine jobs concerned with the care and welfare of animals, made more difficult at fixed points in the farming calendar, when the great seasonal tasks came around – muck-spreading, lambing, shearing, hay-making, harvesting and turkey dressing. Despite the wide range of farming enterprises, money was always tight. There were compensations, though. There were always foods from the farm to look forward to – seasonal delights like walnuts, field mushrooms, blackberries and soft fruit. Plus there were the year round staples - milk, butter and clotted cream from the house cow, and eggs from the farm hens. For Consuelo there was also the fascination of working in close harmony with nature. The wild flowers around the farm were, for her, a particular delight.

Another consolation of those far-off days on the farm were that family life was intricately bound up with the life of the local community. Angela recalls in detail many of the people whose lives were linked with the family at Frithwood – neighbours, farming friends, past farm workers, even the delivery driver for the local grocery store and the London journalist who, for a time, escaped from the city at weekends to a small caravan parked on the farm. While the constant care of animals meant the Lerwill family had few opportunities to escape the farm, they were part of a closely-knit community, very different from the social isolation felt by many farmers today.

Tales of a Sussex Family Farm is an intimate portrait of a way of life, that for all its hardships, enriched the lives of many in Britain. At the end of World War Two, two-thirds of the country's farms were small, mixed farms like this. The families who ran them were hard-working, self-reliant, and proud of their independence. In the dark days of war they'd helped to feed the nation when starvation became a real possibility. Yet the post-war government believed their kind of farming to be inefficient, an anachronism. Using the bribe of subsidies – something traditional farmers had never wanted – they set Britain on the path to industrialisation with its chemical fertilisers, pesticides, giant machines and animal factories.

Today the error of this policy is plain to see in our eroding soils, vanishing wildlife, polluted rivers and contaminated foods. Angela Lerwill's beautiful and timely book reveals the magnitude of what we've lost.

Preface

Angela is five years old. She is sitting in the old green van in charge of several trays of hens' eggs stacked on her lap. A wooden slatted partition separates her from three porker pigs snuffling through some smelly straw. Outside, her parents are saying their fond farewells. Berns, her father, clambers in beside her and off they go, ascending the small hill in front of the old farmhouse.

Monday mornings mean Pulborough Livestock Market, a regular event in Berns' week. Upon arrival, he relieves Angela of the eggs, and together they guide the pigs towards the weighing scales and into an empty pen. Waiting close by is Mr Joyce, the butcher, Berns' regular vendor. With pleasantries exchanged, the men discuss last week's prices and a deal is struck. The auctioneer is informed of the private sale.

Angela's memories start with this trip to Pulborough Market, an important venue for selling fatstock. However, the momentum of change in British agriculture meant that within ten years, Pulborough Market would be swept away and turned into a car park for London commuters.

This book is about Berns and his wife Consuelo's constant struggle to maintain a farming life more reminiscent of the interwar years than the 1960s. Whilst farmers of old knew their animals and their land like the back of their hands, British agriculture was changing. Small farmers were either being forced off the land or becoming large agri-businesses and slaves to the banks. Outside pressures of government interventions, globalization and greed were gaining momentum. 'Big' became the in-word; big ideas, big machinery, big fields and big borrowing from banks. Even in the 1960s, the Lerwills' way of life was becoming an anachronism.

Introduction

Deep in the Sussex countryside lies a small collection of old buildings called Frithwood. Nestling close to the River Arun, they huddle together tucked under the lee of a modest hill; the old place is secluded and remote even by Sussex standards. Most of its history has been lost, but some of its recent past is captured in this book.

Married on the last day of 1949, Berns and Consuelo Lerwill made Frithwood their home for the next forty-seven years. Like their forebears, they eked out a life working the small acreage supplemented with a few rented fields away from home. Their lives were spent nurturing animals, planting crops and raising a family. The mixed farm, however, always came first.

In the winter, short days partnered with dreary dank conditions challenged both adults and children alike. Mud would fester, pipes might freeze and newborn lambs die before daybreak. In these dim days, it was difficult to remember the tranquil times of summer, when the old place seemed so idyllic. Nevertheless, making a living was always hard work.

With Berns' aspirations being blinkered by poor health, the Great Depression and the Second World War, life was tough. He rarely shelved his worries and hated even the idea of borrowing money. If one could pay one's way, remain independent and proud, that was sufficient.

Early Days

'Love is the absence of judgement.'

14TH DALAI LAMA

Early Biography of Bernard Walter Lerwill

Four days after the Great War (1914–1918) ended, a farmer's wife at Malham Farm, Wisborough Green, realised that she was going into labour. The baby's father was Walter Sidney Lerwill (known as Sidney) and was one of fourteen children who largely grew up at Pallingham Manor.[1] On 15 November 1918, a boy was born named Bernard Walter (known as Berns). He was the fifth of six children born to Sidney and Annie Lerwill,[2] née Elliott.[3]

In 1924, the family moved from Malham to Lee Place Farm about three miles to the southern side of the River Arun. Berns had ash-blond hair and needle-bright blue eyes, but always suffered a delicate constitution and was subsequently spoilt. Like his father, he loved horses and spent much of his childhood with the family pony, sometimes fox hunting alongside his father. He attended Wisborough Green Village School and then, at the age of eleven, travelled to Horsham some twelve miles away, to attend Collyer's Grammar School.

Berns hated school and could not wait to leave when he reached his fifteenth birthday. He returned to Lee Place to help on the family farm, earning the princely sum of ten shillings (50p in today's money) per week and his keep. Encouraged by his father, he kept a horse, a few pigs, rabbits and chickens of his own. During the Second World War, Berns occasionally sold eggs and the odd side of

---

[1] See Appendix A: Family Group Sheet for William Lerwill.

[2] See Appendix B: Family Group Sheet for Walter Sidney Lerwill.

[3] See Appendix C: Family Group Sheet for Thomas Howe Elliott.

pork on the black market, hiding them among apples sent to London by the fruit farmer at Tullens Toat. This was lucrative and Berns once told Angela, his youngest daughter, that he was able to make seven pounds profit on a pig in those days.

Unfortunately, when Berns was twenty-eight, he contracted pneumonia and was sent to the Royal Sussex County Hospital in Brighton. Whilst there, he met an attractive young nurse with jet-black hair called Dorothy Consuelo Neave. Known as Consuelo, never as Connie, the pair courted for two years, marrying in December 1949.

Fortuitously for the couple, the Lee Place Estate had come onto the market in June 1949.[4] Berns bought Frithwood for £3,500 which consisted of 33.5 acres, an Elizabethan farmhouse, Sussex threshing barn, cart shed, hovel and stable.[5] It lay a field away from Berns' childhood home at Lee Place.

The next step was to pay the sitting tenant to vacate the house.

Early Biography of Dorothy Consuelo Lerwill (née Neave)

With a Spanish name like Consuelo, one has to ask why? She was born to English parents who were living and working in Bolivia. Edward Neave had gone to Bolivia in 1911 to help construct the national railway from La Paz to Antofagasta. In 1924, he had married Jessie and the couple remained abroad until returning to England in 1946. They lived in the capital La Paz, where the three Neave children attended a convent school. In 1934, after a sea journey of six weeks, Peter, aged ten, and Consuelo, aged eight, started their boarding school education. Consuelo attended Charters Towers School in Bexhill-on-Sea and Peter attended Brighton Grammar School. Ruth, the youngest child, stayed in Bolivia until 1938, when she joined Consuelo at Charters Towers.

With parents abroad and the Second World War raging in the Atlantic, Consuelo only saw her parents once over the next twelve

---

[4] See Appendix D: Schedule of Sale.

[5] See Appendix E: Geographical Position of Frithwood Farm.

years. Wartime bombing along the south coast meant that schools were being evacuated. Charters Towers moved to Milland Place near Liphook, in Hampshire. Upon successfully completing her school certificates, Consuelo trained as a State Registered Nurse at the Royal Sussex County Hospital in Brighton. After meeting Berns, she worked briefly at Horsham Hospital before marrying.

Ships in the Night

Traditionally, farmers' sons married farmers' daughters. Social events acted as an informal way of youngsters getting to know each other; Young Farmers' Clubs, introduced after the First World War, helped in this field.

Berns and Consuelo however, met via a different route, through a chance meeting in hospital where Berns was a patient. In retrospect, Berns was probably quite envied at the time as not only had he met a handsome young woman who had a profession but also that she had an exotic past. Clearly he had landed on his feet as Consuelo was quite a catch.

Much later on, after selling Frithwood in 1997, Berns told Consuelo that marrying her was the best thing he ever did in his life. This display of love was a rarity for Berns and one that Consuelo cherished.

Marriage and Beyond

In retrospect, Berns and Consuelo's marriage was a bit of a gamble. Not only was Consuelo a total 'townie' but she was used to luxuries such as central heating. Berns' family wondered whether she would be able to cope with a spoilt husband and living in a remote, barely habitable farmhouse. They still had a lot to learn about Consuelo.

Prior to the sale of the estate, Frithwood had been farmed as part of the Lee Place farmstead. Over the years, Berns' father had mixed success in letting the house. However, during the Second World War, with the Blitz raging in London, the old house had been made into a make-do hotel accommodating eight paying guests. Rudimentary plumbing had been cobbled together providing an indoor toilet and bathroom. When Berns and Consuelo returned from their short honeymoon in Cheltenham, the reality of what was ahead must have started to hit home for the young bride. With the excitement of the wedding over and a few supposedly passionate nights it was back to the old, cold farmhouse.

Determination and resourcefulness were all part of Consuelo's DNA and she quickly adapted to her new environment. With no electricity, Tilley lamps for lighting were the order of the day. Pam, Berns' youngest sister, probably taught Consuelo how to manage and fill these as this was one of her regular jobs at Lee Place. Nonchalantly, Consuelo took it in her stride as each challenge arose.

A few years later, an electric generator was installed in the old stable and was mainly used for lighting in the evenings. However, when the cost of fuel rose to half-a-crown (12.5p in today's money) for one night's lighting, Berns decided that it was time to get connected to the mains supply. This was a great move forward and meant that both outdoor and indoor jobs became much easier.

Meanwhile, Consuelo had started decorating their bedroom using over one hundredweight of plaster to stabilise the lath and plaster walls. However, her battle with the old cooking range was not quite so straight forward. Situated in the old scullery, the chimney was not tall enough to let it draw properly. It required the back door being kept open, which was clearly unsatisfactory.

Alongside this frustration, Berns still owned a thoroughbred horse which needed to be exercised regularly as he occasionally went fox hunting. Many dark winter evenings, Consuelo found herself alone in the house as Berns massaged and groomed his horse out in the old stable. With her patience being tested, she finally let rip and told Berns that he should buy a wife and marry his farm! The result of this outpouring was the purchase and installation of a Rayburn cooking range. Consuelo rarely lost her temper, but there were limits even for her.

Getting Started

In order to make a living on such a small acreage, it was clear that more buildings would be needed and those standing would need to be adapted. Berns quickly got busy.

At about the same time the couple married, the prisoner of war (POW) camp at Marringdean Road in Billingshurst was being dismantled and sold off. Berns bought two large sheds. The Nissen hut became the feed shed and the other became known as the battery house, after Berns had a few battery hens for a short time, but was largely used for turkey rearing in later years.[6]

Opposite the Nissen hut, Berns had a row of loose boxes built by Joey Bicknel from Billingshurst. He may also have been responsible for enclosing and partly roofing the yard for overwintering cattle. The old hovel was converted into three versatile pig pens, capable of housing either a sow and litter or a family pen of fattening pigs. These pens and a few old sheds near the pond were the first accommodation for porker pigs.[7]

The laying hens were housed in fold units or night arks on the hill.[8] These arks may have come from Lee Place when the couple married. They housed about twenty-five birds and were mobile, so every few days an iron bar would be used in holes at each end to nudge them forward, giving the birds fresh grass. Fold units were also located below the battery house, some of which were used as a sickbay for pecked or sick turkeys in later years. A number of other small poultry sheds followed.

During these years, farm dispersal sales were quite common, as farmers retired or moved. Auctioneers sent out mailings to farmers detailing livestock and deadstock.[9] Time permitting, Berns would sometimes attend, returning with all manner of things ranging from water tanks and feed troughs to larger pieces of farm machinery.

---

[6] See Appendix F: Layout of Farm Buildings.

[7] Pig production is largely divided into two categories depending on live weight; porker (70 kg), bacon (75–90 kg).

[8] Fold unit or night ark: movable chicken house with wire run.

[9] Deadstock: farm machinery and equipment.

Establishing a Family

Two years after they married, the first of the couple's three children was born in 1951; a son, Hugh. A daughter followed in 1954. However, she went without a name for several weeks. It did not seem to matter what names Consuelo offered to Berns; he rejected them. Eventually, she asked him to suggest some of his own, and reluctantly he offered Rhona, a name of an old girlfriend. In her usual pragmatic manner, Consuelo thought, considered and agreed, and the baby became Rhona Consuelo. The final child, Angela Mary, was born in 1958.

Managing your Man

Over the centuries, any new wife has to consider one thing, how to manage her man. Today, Western women often enter a marriage with an income and car, making them independent. However, in the 1950s, there were countless women, including Consuelo, who were totally dependent on their husbands. Not many women drove at the time, and although Consuelo had two series of lessons, she never took her driving test.

Berns always liked to think that he was the boss and so Consuelo needed to hone her man-management skills, otherwise known as manipulation. Nevertheless, Berns never realised and he often got what he required and she sometimes got what she wanted. An early example of this is how Consuelo got a fence erected around the old house.

Having a garden fence only became important as Hugh started toddling. Consuelo had casually mentioned it a few times to Berns, but nothing had happened. She realised another approach was needed. A while later, Consuelo observed Hugh aimlessly meandering away from the back door towards Lordings Rough. Knowing that he was in no danger as he was in an open field, she deliberately let him wander a fair distance before retrieving him. Later that day, she nonchalantly mentioned Hugh's adventure to Berns. Within a day or two a fence around the old house was being erected.

Working The Land

*A good farmer is nothing more or less
than a handy man with a good sense of humus.*

E. B. WHITE (1899–1985)

This chapter gives a glimpse of the life the family lived alongside their farm animals. Some stories are funny and touching whereas others show the reality of raising animals for slaughter.

Jack the Runt

Unlike lambs, piglets are notoriously difficult to hand-rear. They simply do not like sucking on anything apart from a real teat. Many runts die of starvation. Nevertheless, with great patience and determination, Consuelo raised at least one. He was called Jack. At night, he slept in an old poultry shed amongst plenty of clean straw, but during the day he roamed at will.

Without a garden fence at the time, Jack soon learnt where his milk came from; Consuelo at the back door. His internal clock was brilliant at alerting him to meal times and off he would go in search of his tucker. On one occasion, Jack came to the back door and found it closed. On trotting around to the front of the house he was delighted to see that the front door was open. He ventured indoors. Once through the sitting room, he came to the lobby near the back stairs and the bathroom, where he became imprisoned, as the door banged shut behind him.

A while later, Consuelo found a crestfallen piglet in the bathroom with evidence suggesting he had been trapped for quite some time.

7

The Raging Sow

Even the word castration has an unpleasant ring, and is barbaric. At the time, however, butchers forced farmers to castrate male piglets as they claimed the meat tasted too strong. The method was simple; using a scalpel, two slits were made and the testicles pulled and cut out.

Berns had a sow with a litter housed in one of the old stable pens. The usual procedure was to leave the children in the garden and to let the sow out of her pen, dealing with each male piglet. The sow's freedom came at a cost, as shortly after her release she would hear the most horrendous squeals of her beloved sons being half-butchered. Naturally, she would immediately be on the warpath. It was a potentially volatile situation.

The pen in question had two entrances and thus the marauding sow galumphed around the building trying to gain access. Halfway through the operation, Berns and Consuelo were somehow aware of another human in their midst in the form of a small boy, the Parry's young grandson, Jonathan from Woodlands Farm. This was potentially dangerous as the sow was both big enough and angry enough to kill the small child.

Rarely ruffled, Consuelo swung into action. She told the child firmly but quietly, to keep as still as he could behind the wall. Fortunately, the angle of the sun and the position of the boy were such that the savage sow was unable to see him and she turned tail and went roaring off to the other door, leaving two adults drained of adrenaline and a bewildered child. The crisis was over.

Feeding Pigs

During term time, Consuelo would prepare breakfast for the children and then tackle her farm work. At weekends and holidays, the girls would sometimes help. With a choir of hungry pigs, the party would pass through the garden gate close to the Sussex barn, sometimes pausing to chuck old stale milk or kitchen scraps over the wall into the first pen.

Turning left, away from the Sussex barn, the trio would follow the narrow concrete path towards the old stable, where the concrete came to an abrupt end. At this point, two tanks stood side-by-side; one square (a water tank), the other cylindrical (a corrugated affair) which was used to mix the pig feed.

With no more concrete, one had to pick a safe route up the slight bank towards the Nissen hut where the feed was stored. Consuelo would then take buckets of ground pig meal to the corrugated tank and mix it with water with a large stick and make a porridge-like substance. Angela liked to help by breaking the lumps with her hands but got a bit too ambitious one day and fell into the tank head first. She was quickly marched indoors for a change of clothing.

The boar was always housed nearest to the tanks and often got excited, climbing the gate with his front feet and biting the top rail with his massive teeth in anticipation. The children never got frightened, after all he was just another pig, and when not anxious for his food, loved to be scratched in between the ears by the youngsters.

Once in a Lifetime

The Sussex barn next to the farmhouse was primarily used for storing hay and calf production. Berns kept a number of cows, two or three of which were suckled twice a day in the barn by their own calf, and one or two others. One of these cows was kept primarily to supply milk for the family. She was the house cow and was Berns' darling among the beasts.[10]

There were a number over the years but the family's favourite was called Blanche. She was a Guernsey and had been bought as a calf from the Blanch family at St Andrew's Hill near Billingshurst, specifically to become the family's next house cow. She was gentle and timid, and loved to be with her youngster.

Newly calved cows are often uncomfortable as their udders become gorged with milk. At Frithwood, this often meant that the barn cows

---

[10] House cow: cow kept to provide milk for the farmhouse.

would line up and wait on the concrete path ready to enter the barn. On this occasion, Blanche was standing outside the barn door when Berns saw a large piglet, who was running free at the time, suckling Blanche!

On telling the story to Consuelo, Berns explained that the combination of Blanche being such a placid cow and the young, seemingly intelligent piglet smelling and then noticing where the milk was coming from had culminated in it thinking 'There is a meal in here for me,' and it started sucking at the dripping teat.

It was a once-in-a-lifetime experience.

Milking Time

With trusted stick in hand and dog at heel, Berns would trek the small hill and holler 'Come on.' Nonchalantly, Blanche and her cohorts would raise their heads, eyes twinkling, 'Oh, not that time again.' Moving slowly, they would often detour to the old cast-iron trough near the Nissen hut to quench their thirst, then saunter with swaying udders to the barn, docking at their individual stalls.

Once tethered, the milk bucket and three-legged stool were found. Positioning himself at right angles to Blanche, Berns would nestle his balding head up against her silken orange flank. Methodically, Blanche would 'let down her milk' to Berns' trusted hands.[11]

Hand-milking produces the rhythmic sounds of rain pelting on a tin roof, then as the bucket fills, it gives way to a regular splash-splash. Once completed, Berns would place the bucket on the wall near the side gate.

In a close-by pen, the calves would wait impatiently for their turn to suckle. Once released they would barge and jostle to reach their favourite positions, with Berns acting as referee. Once finished, they would return to their pen to find clean bedding, sweet hay and their water tank replenished.

Untethered, the cows would return to the hill and Berns to the house for his tea.

---

[11] Letting-down milk: cows have the ability to hold their milk.

Blanche Coughs

Berns arrived at the back door covered from head to toe in fresh, warm cow manure. All Consuelo could see were two blue eyes shining out of the streaming green 'porridge'. She knew exactly what it was but wondered how had it happened. Berns, always economic with words, said, 'Blanche coughed.'

In the early summer when grass is high in sugars, cows' manure tends to be wet with a custard-like consistency. Blanche had been waiting at the barn door when Berns had approached from the rear, had coughed and jettisoned manure all over him. He had simply been in the wrong place at the wrong time.

Time to Go

Berns always had a close relationship with the house cow, and this was especially so with Blanche. Calving at about two and a half to three years, Blanche was a stalwart in the Frithwood armoury, providing fresh milk for drinking, making clotted cream and butter for the family, as well as a plethora of calves.

Nevertheless, with a couple of missed artificial insemination attempts to get her back into calf, Berns knew that her days were numbered; no calf, no milk, no life. She continued her life more or less until her final drop of milk from her last lactation; Berns was putting off the deadly deed.[12] Angela remembers observing the old cow in her dotage just prior to market. She was lying on the hill, in front of the farmhouse chewing the cud. It was a warm, September evening and contentment radiated from her face as she soaked in the last of the sun's rays. Little did she know that her time was up.

For several weeks after she went to slaughter, Berns was especially quiet as he came to terms with his betrayal. Years later, Consuelo told Angela that Berns had cried himself to sleep the night that Blanche had been sent to market. Their relationship was special, one that stockmen of years gone by would recognise. It was a

---

[12] Lactation: the production of milk.

partnership between man and beast, one of mutual respect. That was, until she was sent to slaughter. Unfortunately, that is the reality of farming, then and now.

Turkey Breeding

In about May, the broad-breasted turkey hens would start laying eggs due to increasing daylight hours.[13] Once any amorous behaviour was seen, it was time to find the turkey 'saddles'. These simple devices comprised a twelve-inch square of strong canvas with a loop on each side. They were then threaded onto the hens' wings in order to protect their backs whilst being mated.[14]

After collecting the first few eggs, Berns would candle them, to establish their fertility.[15] As fecundity became more established, fertilised eggs were placed in batches into incubators, on a weekly basis over the breeding period. Before incubation however, the eggs needed to be collected.

Usually, Berns collected the eggs after lunch, sometimes assisted by one of the children. When a little older they would go alone, in order to avoid drying-up after lunch. Angela remembers the task well.

The breeding turkeys were usually housed in the middle section of the battery house, and on arriving at the wire gate separating the two sections, one needed to prepare for battle. Stag turkeys in the breeding season are territorial and would fluff up their large tail and primary wing feathers and advance, sometimes quite aggressively if disturbed. Their caruncles would become engorged with blood making them look quite fierce, alongside their floppy snoods.[16] At seven years old, one might come eyeball-to-eyeball with a stag fuelled with

---

[13] By the mid-1970s, most small producers were breeding white commercial turkeys.

[14] Left unsaddled, the hens could easily become badly wounded by constant copulation as the stags gripped the hens' backs using their sharp toes and spurs.

[15] Candling: a simple process using light to establish fertility.

[16] Caruncle: the loose bumpy skin on a stag turkey's head and neck that can be bright red or blue around the face. In the breeding season it becomes engorged with blood.
Snood: the flap of skin that hangs down over a stag turkey's beak.

testosterone; this could be a bit scary even for a farm kid. Fortunately, a suitable implement was at hand; one of Consuelo's old brooms from the house, a bright red one. It was a job that required speed and agility, as one needed to crouch, collect the eggs and keep a beady eye out for any marauding stag that might be approaching, whilst keeping one's trusty broom poised ready to 'hold the line'.

Once collected and candled, it was time to incubate the eggs.[17] Hugh remembers that Berns' first paraffin oil-fired incubator was housed in the egg room in the house (later the kitchen). Other small incubators followed, and a lean-to shed, largely made of cord wood and lined with paper feed sacks, was built onto the old stables.

Berns' ability to expand his turkey business was limited, as each small incubator could only hold about 200 eggs. Turning eggs could take an hour and was usually done after lunch and tea. It was another task that had to be fitted in with other seasonal jobs such as haymaking. The siblings would often help Berns, spending precious time with their father one-to-one.

After several years, Berns took the plunge and had a breeze-block shed built on the west side of the garden to accommodate a large, second-hand semi-automatic incubator capable of holding up to 2,000 eggs at different stages of incubation. This was quite an investment costing £1,000.

Once hatched, the tiny chicks were transferred to the brooder units housed in the far end of the Nissen hut. This was a sort of warm nursery area where they stayed for about a month. After this, they were moved into the loose boxes opposite the corn store and other numerous small sheds, before being placed in larger groups in the pole barns. Some were sold to other farmers.

---

[17] Turkey eggs take about twenty-eight days to hatch.

13

Preparing for Christmas

In the mid-1970s, Christmas turkey production became an important enterprise at Frithwood. Like walking the Camino Way, rearing good turkeys takes planning, patience and persistence.[18] Berns' talents lay in production and rearing, Consuelo's in dispatch.

Forward planning was one of Consuelo's many talents. Bravely, she would combine a family Christmas, alongside dispatching some 1,200 to 1,400 birds. With plastic bags and turkey tags ordered, she would get organised on the domestic front.

The main driver was to buy presents for her children plus about ten nieces and nephews. Armed with her list, she would spend a day Christmas shopping in Horsham. Other autumnal tasks included making the Christmas cake and puddings, and planting hyacinths and other bulbs in bowls ready for Christmas to give to the odd spinster aunt.

With the presents safely hidden, the Christmas correspondence had to be tackled. Consuelo would write to friends and family overseas, then a page or two to enclose with cards, to friends and family not often seen. Eventually, either because of time running out or losing the will to live, she would simply give in and just bundle the cards into their envelopes.

From early October to December, Berns' working day was largely focused on looking after the turkeys. Watering and feeding were big tasks. With no mains water at Frithwood, Berns had to carry buckets of water to nearly every shed. Next was the feed. This had to be physically put into the grinder and then blended in the mixer with the appropriate concentrates to produce a growth ration for the turkeys, and then bagged ready for the next day. As Christmas approached, this took longer as growing birds needed ever-increasing amounts of food, often taking two hours after tea. For Berns and Consuelo, it was a period of arduous and relentless hard slog, hampered by short daylight hours and unremitting mud.

By early November, Berns would collude with other small

---

[18] Camino Way: long-distance pilgrim route in Northern Spain.

producers and settle on his price per pound. Once set, Berns would place advertisements in local newspapers. Butchers, old and new, would be contacted and orders would start coming in. It was 'action stations'!

Turkey Slaughter and Dispatch

The run-up to Christmas at Frithwood was fraught, not with joy and laughter but with stress and slaughter. Turkey plucking was a family business. Even from an early age, the children were never shielded from the realities of killing and plucking poultry, and were encouraged to help. Hugh opted out preferring the school plays, but the girls smelt money and often had plucking targets.

Killing always commenced on 10 December. The breeding turkeys were always the first to be dispatched and were easy to pluck due to their maturity. This, paired with the girls' enthusiasm, often resulted in an unofficial day off school. As the week progressed, their motivation tended to wain as fingers became sore and the novelty sometimes wore off.

Over the fortnight, the youngsters effectively became latchkey kids. Apart from a hearty breakfast and a school lunch, the siblings were left to their own devices. Gradually, the old house got colder and less welcoming, as Consuelo focused on the plucking shed.

Once free of other work, Consuelo would join the men after breakfast. With the counter heaped with corpses, she would process each bird; weighing, tagging, allocating it and then hanging it on a nail in one of the emptied sheds. Peeping inside, one was reminded of a lounge in an old people's home.

Throughout the day, Consuelo would make several visits, often taking out trays of hot drinks for the men. Although Berns would help, his main priority was to keep a constant flow of prepared birds for the pluckers.[19] Often birds were moved in the dark to keep them calm.

---

[19] Turkeys needed to be starved for a day before slaughter in order that they had empty gizzards for keeping purposes.

With turkeys killed and hanging, the next problem was the weather. Cold dry weather was perfect, but frosty nights followed by sun meant that the carcasses would sweat as the temperature varied. This could be a nerve-racking period for Berns, worrying whether the birds would keep until Christmas Day.

Turkey sales fell into three broad categories: private customers, butchers, and livestock auction customers.[20] The last two bought them rough plucked.[21]

Once slaughtered and allocated, the butchers would collect their poultry. Private orders were then double-checked and surplus birds hung separately ready to load for the Christmas fatstock markets.

At the time, there were still a number of livestock markets in Sussex, and Berns usually took turkeys to Haywards Heath, Guildford, Steyning and sometimes Chichester. These markets were essential to dispose of second-grade and surplus birds, and to the overall profitability of the turkey enterprise.

On market day, the birds had to arrive and be entered by a certain time. This involved an early start as other work needed to be completed before loading. If the children had finished school for the term, one would usually accompany Berns, helping to unload and looking out for any theft from the open trailer.

With the volume of turkeys now gone, it was time to prepare private customers' orders. With no cooling facilities, birds could only be dressed a few days before eating, as once the flesh was cut the meat would start deteriorating. Gutting any poultry is not the best of jobs; it is cold, it is physical and it smells. Not keen on the task, Consuelo insisted on equal pay to the men.

In the four days before Christmas, anywhere between 200 and 400 turkeys were trussed for private customers. Consuelo would often truss about half, the rest were done by a couple of men. They worked out of the corn store and Consuelo from the farmhouse scullery. Each site had a leg puller, consisting of a V-shaped holder with a lever that went back, pulling all the ligaments out of the drumstick.

---

[20] Dressed or trussed birds: gutted poultry ready for the oven.

[21] Rough plucked: plucked birds, but not gutted.

In between dealing with customers, Consuelo would tackle her pile of corpses. Normally, this interaction with the outside world would have been welcomed, but with a mountain of dead bodies hidden from view in the back scullery, Consuelo sometimes tired of hearing how busy these 'aliens' were with the build-up to Christmas, as they sipped their tea which hampered her progress. However, ever-conscious of manners and decorum, she just listened and sympathised, nodding sagely to the ebb and flow of the futile conversation.

One Christmas, Angela's English teacher Mrs Windsor came to collect a turkey. Whilst talking to Consuelo in the dining room, she accidentally trod on the family dog and was bitten. She kept quiet, but years afterwards told Angela that she stopped in Northwood to examine her injury. The dog bite had gone right through her slacks and drawn blood.

Meanwhile, Berns was out and about delivering, usually aided by one of the children, whose task it was to mind the vehicle. Deliveries took about three days, finishing by about teatime on Christmas Eve.

On one Christmas Eve, a customer insisted that Berns had a glass of ginger wine. Aged about seven, Angela observed her father sidle behind an armchair, lean over and discreetly pour the wine into his wellington boot. Upon enquiry later, Berns explained it was all he could think of to avoid any embarrassment or becoming ill.

Although Christmas Eve saw the back of the turkeys, Consuelo's work was not complete. After tea, she would busy herself once again with a variety of chores. This included slapping marzipan on the Christmas cake and then the royal icing. This would be closely followed by the last few presents to be wrapped. The size of the Lerwills' Christmas bird was always a mystery as it might be one that was never collected and could weigh anything from a minnow of 10 lb to a whopper of 25 lb. However, with Consuelo's talent for making the best-ever gravy, the family would congregate around the dining table for their Christmas lunch and a tangible, silent sigh of general relief would pervade the air. It would be over for another year.

Focused at Fourteen

One year, Angela aged fourteen desperately needed another saddle for her pony, Satellite. She needed to earn £40 and this meant that she needed to pluck 115 birds. This was to be a challenge both of timing (only one day off school and a single weekend) and whether her right thumb and index finger would last out. This was not all, for every bird plucked by someone else was a turkey less for Angela; it was a question of time. She should not have worried as, ever-focused, she achieved her goal.

The First Farm Dog

Hemp was everything a young farmer and father could want in a dog. He was hard-working, protective and loyal; not dissimilar to his owner, Berns. Like the children, Hemp benefited from a free-range liberalism rarely given to children or dogs these days. As an adult dog, he made his own bed in the Sussex barn at night and was rarely shut in or confined for any length of time.

Berns had acquired Hemp as a puppy from Dennis Marten, a local vet and friend, and like most young animals, the puppy was playful and naughty at times. One morning, following torrential rain, Consuelo went to retrieve the washing off the line. Before her was a mass of shreds, the remnants of her recently completed sewing project, a nightdress. Standing beside her was an excited puppy looking up with his bright eyes and almost mouthing, 'Yes, all my own work.' With her usual pragmatism Consuelo just shrugged it off as just one of those things.

The young dog grew and matured, and his job description widened to embrace child minder, friend, sheepdog and also listener. On warm, sunny days when the children were babies, Consuelo would pop them into the big, old-fashioned pram (protected by a cat net) and put them in the front garden for their nap under the morello cherry tree. As she busied herself indoors, she would look out to see Hemp lying beside the pram, on guard duty protecting its cargo as if it contained the Crown jewels.

Hemp loved to welcome the family home as they returned in the old green van. Having excellent hearing, he would detect the sound vibrations of the ancient vehicle bumping along the track in Northwood and rush to meet the family. They loved to see Hemp's silhouette in the distance, knowing that he was well and wanted them home where they belonged.

Although well-loved, Hemp was not well-disciplined. After all, dogs like people only respond to sound encouragement and training, and without either, Hemp often struggled to meet Berns' expectations. Sadly, Hemp was more used to Berns' bellows than any praise, however, the old dog loved him all the same.

Hemp's main vice was that he hated cats. At one time, the farm hosted five cats: Susan, Ginger, Crackers, Puss William and Snoopy. Their contract was one of meagre rations of bread, milk and scraps in return for ratting duties. Forgetting to pop Hemp into the woodshed prior to lunch could result in a battleground outside the back door.

Ratting with Hemp

One of Hemp's loves was ratting. He changed from a placid loving family pet into a vicious killer with snarled back lips and white fangs. With stock indoors for the winter, the rat population multiplied as they took advantage of the cornucopia of food.

After Christmas turkeys and lambing ewes, the pole barns would lie empty for several months, until Berns had time to muck them out. Using a front-end loader, Berns would excavate the dung, disturbing the colonies of rats that lived in the deep maze of underground tunnels.

Within minutes, there would be an army of rats running in all directions. Hemp would be ready and waiting, encouraged by Berns and the children, egging him on to kill as many as possible. It was a sport which everyone enjoyed ... except the rats and a few mischief of mice.

Just Too Many Rats

One Monday morning at Pulborough Market, Berns got into conversation with his cousin Guy Lerwill. They discussed rat numbers. Both farmers agreed that there was a plague of rats on both farms. Guy told Berns that he had employed a rat catcher, who had baited and collected some 300 corpses, only a third of the rats the catcher anticipated had been killed.

As usual, rat baiting was just part of Berns' winter jobs and his solution was to increase the poison. Unfortunately, this had not been enough, and as turkeys were slaughtered that Christmas and the rats' food supply stopped, the hungry vermin took their revenge and started attacking the breast meat of some of the hanging birds.

On entering the plucking shed one morning, the realisation was stark; several beautiful birds' breasts had been gnawed. Action was needed, and all of the birds hanging in the plucking shed had to be relocated. There were just too many rats.

One Ram, Few Lambs

After a year or two at Frithwood, Berns decided to purchase a few ewes and a ram. As March approached, Berns increased the ewes' feed in anticipation of them delivering a bunch of healthy lambs, but only a few were born. It was a disaster, probably caused by the ram having a low sperm count. It was a year wasted and served as a stark reminder to the young Berns to always have two rams from then on.

The Exhausted Ram

For those of you who are uninitiated in the ways of sheep, it may be useful to explain some bare essentials. Most sheep are seasonal breeders and come into heat when the daylight hours reduce in autumn. Light entering a ewe's brain releases certain hormones resulting in ewes coming into season every sixteen or seventeen days or until they have mated successfully. Unlike cows, who show signs of wanting to mate, called bulling, only rams can detect when ewes are ready to be served.

In order to properly manage the lambing season, rams are generally removed from the flock during the summer. Often, whilst walking in the countryside, one might wonder why a small group of sheep are shading under some leafy glade away from the main flock. These are the rams waiting to be reintroduced to the flock in the autumn. This ensures that lambing is compressed into a manageable time period in early spring.

However, too much of a good thing is bad for anyone, man or beast, as was the case on this particular occasion. As usual, Berns had excluded the rams from the ewes well in advance. The ewes had been flushed on fresh grass in preparation and were ready to be served.[22] Once the children were old enough to understand this coupling process, they loved to be present, as it was hilarious to watch. Rams resembled headless chickens, cavorting round with their nostrils extended and lips turned back (known as flehmening), quickly copulating and then moving swiftly on to the next ewe. After about ten minutes, the Lerwill family would tire and return to other things.

Meanwhile, the rams continued but with less intensity as time went on. On this occasion, the flock was in the field next to the chicken fold units, which Consuelo tended twice a day to feed and collect eggs, and to shut in the hens at night. Whilst tending her chicken the next morning, she spotted a large sheep lying at a strange angle some way away. Immediately Consuelo rushed over to the immobile carcass. It was alive and lying prostrate; a ram exhausted by too much of a good thing. Fortunately, he recovered and continued his duties, albeit at a steadier rate.

Overnight Visitors

Orphaned, weak, or rejected lambs sometimes needed extra help to survive. It was not unusual for Berns to bring the odd lamb indoors for a bit of TLC. The girls would immediately hover around the

---

[22] Flushing: to prepare ewes for mating.

forlorn creatures asking their father as to its sex; ewe lambs could be loved like a dog or cat as they might later become another productive ewe whereas ram lambs only had a one-way ticket to the butcher's block. The children were never under any illusions; life was not always fair for them or other beings.

Upon arrival in the house, the small creatures were lovingly fed as they were often hungry. Instinctively, most sucked freely, quickly grasping the idea that the rubber teat meant survival. Afterwards, they were popped on a hessian sack by the Rayburn in a little alcove of the old inglenook fireplace near to Berns' chair. As they warmed through, they gave off a uniquely baby lamb smell, not unlike a newborn human baby. Sometimes the prostrate body slept, other times it died over night. Nature took its course.

Often the morning would bring great joy as the girls would rush downstairs to see the new project. If still alive, it might be tottering on its ungainly arthritic-looking legs, aimlessly exploring in amongst the dining room chairs. Sometimes, one might try head-butting and suckling the corner of an old cushion, hoping for milk. Once strong enough, Berns would take it back outside to try and reunite it with its mother or else place it in with the other pet lambs, in a special warm pen.

Before the Pole Barns

To produce as many lambs as possible takes good stockmanship and careful management. It is critical that in-lamb ewes are fed correctly, in order that foetal growth is optimised to produce lambs at the right birth weight, thereby reducing any delivery problems and maximising production. This requires a dedicated shepherd, plus his wife.

Usually, the pregnant ewes were overwintered on rented land at Codmore Hill and were checked daily. This winter holiday was no coincidence, as good pasture management requires paddocks to be rested from use at least annually in order to reduce intestinal worm infestation. The ewes would return to Frithwood in the middle of February, ready to lamb in March.

With the ewes back at the farm, Berns would start feeding them an appropriate concentrate, flaked-maize and beet-pulp ration as well as giving them extra hay. Feeding sheep outside, as any shepherd will know, is not the easiest of tasks. Greedy and hungry ewes become fearless of humans, and will insist on rubbing close to anyone carrying, or using a feed bag. This can be a terrible nuisance in wet weather as dry clothing is soon exhausted. Wet clothing was dried out round the Rayburn and the beet-pulp gave off a sweet smell similar to liquorice.

In order to preserve their old clothing, Berns and Consuelo devised an unusual set of over-garments made of large, hessian beet pulp bags, one as an overskirt and the other as a cape, both tied up with baler string. Once togged in this primitive attire, they looked a bit like extras for peasant roles in a *War and Peace* film; the only thing missing was the birch-bark shoes. Many a time, the family laughed as the couple trundled in and out of the house in costume.

Lambing outside requires shelter. Frithwood's ewes were lambed in a field where the sheep could snuggle under a high hedge. Often, however, the young ewes, giving birth for the first time, would lamb anywhere. These young sheep sometimes had an almost comical look on their tilted heads, which emanated a quizzical expression of surprise suggesting, 'Is that wet thing mine?'

Once lambing started, the couple worked tirelessly to save every life. As the month stretched out, Berns and Consuelo became increasingly tired, as checking through the night was often necessary. At the weekends, the children often helped during the day, looking for telltale signs and reporting back. Even at seven or eight years of age, all three offspring were trusty spotters of lone ewes, those behaving strangely or away from the others or obvious signs of a bloody or extended tail end. It was a natural instinct, almost part of the children's DNA.

Once reported back, an adult would attend to decide the course of action. Berns and Consuelo were observant shepherds, preferring patience over stress. However, if help was needed, a bucket, hot water and a towel would be taken and the field hospital quickly spun into action. With Berns holding the ewe's head, Consuelo would put her nursing skills and small hands to good use and often had a successful outcome. The vet was rarely called.

Often, the weather played an important role as to numbers reared. Lambs can survive the cold, but hate cold, wet weather. This particular combination can result in many lambs dying, as they simply lose too much body heat. However, time moved on and eventually the pole barns were constructed and lambing became a lot easier, although the night checks were still necessary.[23]

Moving Sheep

Moving stock to rented ground away from home required planning. In the early days it was still possible to move sheep by foot providing Berns and Consuelo got organised. The best time to avoid traffic on the A29 at Codmore Hill was over a weekend, early in the morning. Even as late as 1973, Consuelo's diary reveals that sheep were moved on Christmas Day morning to avoid the traffic.

Everyone was needed to help with this task. After a hurried breakfast, the family would round up the flock and set off with Hemp, the farm dog. The first obstacle was turning the sheep at a right angle at the top gate, so that the flock could walk along the bridlepath towards Lee Place Lodge. Once the corner was safely navigated, out-runners were sent ahead, one acting as a leader for the flock, and the others to stand in old gateways no longer possessing a gate. Once past the Lodge, the party moved on towards Northwood. The family always hoped that the Mullers' dog, Rex would be shut indoors, as he hated Hemp and tended to bark a lot.

Once past Haybourne and Snape Farm Cottages, the party joined the County Council tarmac road. Another half-mile and the drovers would arrive at Canada Corner on a slight incline, and then on to Blake Wood with Tote Monument on the right. Next, they descended a small hill past Blackgate Farm and the Aylings' bungalow, and another bad bend.

As the party approached the A29, the flock were often driven into

---

[23] Berns then tended to lamb earlier, hoping to catch the Easter trade.

one of the rented fields adjacent to the main road but sometimes the droving continued to Mr Newman's field at Cray Lane.

This part of the journey required nerves of steel. As the flock would need to pass over the railway line at Codmore Hill, Berns had to inform the railway authorities in advance. Once the flock were at the level crossing, he then had to use the railway telephone twice, once before and then after the flock had safely gone over. Sighing with relief, the party then continued the short distance to the field, often disturbing the dogs in Mrs Hobbs' kennels, as they turned the corner into Cray Lane.

It was then time to walk the two and a half miles home.

Sheep Shearing

Finding a sheep shearer was always a challenge. Professional shearing gangs prefer large flocks to maximise their earnings. Over the years, Berns engaged a number of shearers but only the Weeks duo of father and son became regulars.

With the hay depleted in the old Sussex barn by late May, Berns would construct temporary shearing quarters. Sheep hurdles would be erected into one large and one small holding pen, where the hay had been stored. Berns would sweep clean the old brick threshing floor in the centre, ready to receive the fleeces before rolling them into neat bundles and placing them in the wool sacks. With electric extension wires precariously strewn across the area, Berns was ready.

After agreeing a proposed date, the team had to hope for a dry day as the sheep could not be shorn if it was wet. All being well, Berns, Consuelo and Hemp would drive the noisy flock into the barn and wait for the shearers to arrive. After a quick catch-up, the shearing could start.

Rhona and Angela recall rushing home from school on shearing day so they could watch the proceedings. They remember the men in vests wet with sweat as they worked hard to cut through the greasy fleeces, while their father gathered the next few sheep into the smaller holding pen, enabling him to return to rolling the fleeces and tying them into small bundles. These were placed into large wool sheets (large bags) supplied by the Wool Marketing Board, to be collected at some later date.

Let's Play 'Wets'

One Easter holiday Consuelo's mother, Jessie, and sister Ruth were visiting the farm. Lambing had nearly finished and the family had acquired a couple of pet lambs. It was a warm, sunny day so Consuelo suggested that Jessie might like to sit outside and watch the girls playing in the front garden, while she and Ruth prepared the lunch.

Aged about seven and three, the girls had their usual toys strewn around, but soon became bored and decided to play with the pet lambs. They were delighted to see the girls, always associating humans with their milk bottles, so followed them obediently into the garden. Jessie was thrilled to see the girls playing with the lambs, but quickly noticed one had a particularly dirty rear end. Without thinking, she announced that it needed a wash. Immediately, Angela looked towards Rhona and announced, 'Let's play Wets.'

An old seaside bucket was quickly found and filled with water. The unsuspecting lamb was caught and held by Rhona while Angela got the dirty job, not at all fazed by the gluey mess squelching between her small fingers. After all she was a 'wet' and her help was needed. Jessie looked on in amazement. A further suggestion from Jessie involved the nail brush from the bathroom being used to help shift the difficult bits. The job was nearly complete.

Taking a short coffee break, Consuelo and Ruth ventured out into the bright sunlight to find the air full of drama. Consuelo was horrified to find her pink nail brush was being use for such a task and gave her mother a piercing look of disapproval.

Having a Laugh

Sewage disposal was somewhat primitive at Frithwood to put it mildly. Yes, there was an indoor flushing toilet, but one did not ask where it went next. Naturally, all residents including the children knew, and in summer if one was standing in the wrong place, with the wind blowing in the wrong direction, so did other people.

The cesspit was a shallow pond situated on the west side of the house, behind the old barn which had a small elm tree growing in its rich contents. The effluent from the house was largely coaxed out under gravity but this was not possible when the pond was full. This would result in the pipe back-filling and therefore made flushing impossible.

After a bit of persuasion from Consuelo, Berns would locate the night soil implement and proceed to the cesspit. Later, Consuelo just did it herself. First of all, the corrugated iron sheets needed to be removed. Stirring up the old sewage created a terrible smell, which often lasted for several days. Contents were scooped out and left on the grass for natural disposal. For several weeks, the children avoided that side of the house as they were afraid of stepping into something.

On this particular occasion, Berns, for some reason had not put back the sheets of corrugated tin and so the cesspit was open. A half-grown lamb, obviously with a curious disposition, had gone investigating the area and had fallen in. An alert was sent out for Berns. He arrived to find one wet and smelly lamb in the cesspit and an audience of three children, keeling over clutching their stomachs and raucous with laughter waiting for the next instalment.

Undeterred, Berns launched into the disgusting job in hand, grabbing the lamb out of the mire. Still with an audience splitting their sides with laughter, Berns plodded on trying to get off the solids and then washing off the rest with a couple of buckets of water. Berns probably realised that he deserved being the centre of his children's amusement and just kept quiet.

There is a simple lesson to this story, 'Never put off until tomorrow what you can do today.' Funny old thing but Berns never forgot to re-cover the cesspit with corrugated iron sheets again.

Larry the Lamb

One May weekend, Berns and Consuelo had a phone call from their friend in Worthing called John Freeman. He outlined that his teenage son had gone to Steyning Livestock Market and come home with an orphan lamb. John needed a new home for the lamb, especially as it was showing signs of scouring.[24] Could Berns help out?

Berns agreed, providing John could deliver the lamb to the farm as soon as possible, as the lamb's scouring would mean it was probably dehydrated and could die. Later that day, John's fifteen-year-old son arrived on his bicycle with a fruit box strapped on the back containing the poorly creature. The lamb had been named Larry, but was actually female. She had a white face and a pronounced Roman nose suggesting that she was a Cheviot.

Consuelo went immediately into nursing mode and gave Larry a dose of human Dinneford's along with some milk formula.[25] The pampering paid off and within a few months she was mixing with the main flock. Years later, one could always spot Larry, as her big frame made her stand out from the rest of the flock. She lived a long and happy life at the farm, and reared many lambs of her own.

Findon Sheep Fair

Findon, near Worthing, traditionally hosted a sheep fair on the second Saturday of September. If time permitted, the family liked to attend. Often prices were too high for Berns so it was used as an excuse for a day out. In those days, wattle hurdles made of hazel were used to house the sheep.

Consuelo, ever the opportunist, used these excursions to visit her old nursing friend, Sister Theodora, who had become a nun and lived at the Findon Convent. She would telephone in advance and

---

[24] Scouring: agricultural term for animal diarrhoea.
[25] Dinneford's: a human baby medicine for poorly tummies.

arrange to visit in between prayers. On arrival at the fair, Berns proceeded to the sheep pens and Consuelo and the children would go to the convent and take tea.

A few years after Hugh and Rhona had left home, Berns and Angela went to the fair alone, leaving Consuelo at home. Findon Fair had less allure for Consuelo as the convent had closed and her old friend had moved to Lingfield Convent. She decided that as the weather was perfect, she would stay home and start some autumn digging. Berns had a pleasant surprise and prices were within his range. He promptly bought a young Suffolk ram. However, without a trailer how was he to transport the ram home?

Without any further to-do, Berns proceeded to take the seat out of the car behind the driver and make a sort of channel, which was to be used to place the ram. It would be a snug fit. He also instructed Angela that she would need to crouch at one end of the channel gripping the ram round his neck, making sure that he did not try to climb out. It worked, and the three arrived home safely.

It was a journey never to be forgotten. Not only had Angela spent some forty minutes literally head-to-head with a ram, but he had the most appalling halitosis! However, the goal had been achieved, a new ram had been brought safely home.

Bed and Breakfast

Consuelo's bed and breakfast enterprise was probably one of the most profitable ventures at Frithwood. In the 1970s, farmhouse bed and breakfast became very popular and Consuelo's friends, Alma Steele and Pam Luckin, were turning people away. With Hugh and Rhona having left home, Consuelo had three empty bedrooms and decided to take the plunge.

Angela, aged seventeen, remembers that the first guests arrived one evening while Consuelo was on her way back from visiting her mother and sister in Bexhill. Berns was en route to collect Consuelo from Pulborough Station, when Angela took the telephone call. Angela spoke to Pam Luckin and agreed to the booking. It was to be the first of many over the following ten to fifteen years.

Initially, Consuelo ploughed back much of what she earned into soft furnishings. Diary entries from this period, however, suggested that in some lean financial years, this income helped with survival.

Paying guests came from all over the world and from all manner of backgrounds, and this diversity enriched the couple's lives. Although the facilities were still basic, this did not seem to put guests off, as many returned at least once and some returned on a regular basis.

One Dutch couple became friends and visited annually for years. In fact, Consuelo and her sister Ruth went to Holland at least once and had a short holiday with them. Others would come as friends, then return with children of their own, keen to share Frithwood's magic. Some guests came on business. In 1983, Consuelo had two film crews staying, one filming a work by Arnold Bennett and, in the autumn, another covering the Labour Party Conference in Brighton.

In the early days, demand was such that it was not unusual to have a house full of guests, plus some camping in the front garden and visiting family members sleeping in the pale-blue caravan at the top of the hill. On one occasion, Consuelo had ten paying guests overnight.

Looking back, people probably loved Frithwood for its simplicity and Consuelo's warm welcome. For breakfast, she offered home-produced eggs, home-made bread, butter, marmalade and a table thoughtfully adorned with garden posies, which the guests revelled in. Consuelo ran a happy, sharing home and it showed. It was not unusual for Consuelo to receive thank you cards and short letters from guests thanking her for her time and efforts that had enhanced their breaks.

In saying this, one must not forget that not everyone liked what they found at the end of the *yellow brick road*. Consuelo was always forthright and honest about her offer; the road was long and full of potholes, it was a working farm and the house was not a hotel. Nevertheless, people would book and then complain about the smell of pigs, the bumpy track and its length.

On one occasion, a father had booked to bring his two children who had an exeat weekend from boarding school. They arrived in an orange Mercedes car, to deposit their bags. It was apparent that the father was not pleased with what he found. Consuelo showed them their accommodation and served them tea in the sitting room. With confidence, she told the man that it was obvious that this was not what he wanted and suggested returning his deposit and for them to find something more suitable, with no hard feelings. They all looked a bit dumbfounded and a few minutes after Consuelo had returned to the dining room, the daughter, aged about thirteen, knocked on the door. Meekly, she said that they would like to stay and that they were sorry for any offence that they may have caused. Consuelo's motto was always better to be an empty house than an unhappy one. Frithwood was not for everyone.

The worst chore of running a bed and breakfast was the laundry. Many a time in her diaries, Consuelo lists how many sheets and pillowcases that she had laundered. For all this though, most of the bed and breakfast guests were happy and gave Consuelo the company that she needed. Even Berns enjoyed aspects of the business, especially if visitors had some connection to farming.

Struggling Away

'Embrace the glorious mess that you are.'

ELIZABETH GILBERT (1969–)

Lack of money was the common leitmotif at Frithwood.

Bodging and Cobbling

Two expressions often quoted by Consuelo were, *'Necessity is the mother of invention'* and *'Make do and mend'*. These often resulted in a lot of bodging and cobbling as challenges arose and were tackled with a hands-on approach. Aesthetics were never a priority. Affectionately, they were referred to as the struggle factors.

As physical graft occupied most of the daylight hours, heating the old house was a secondary consideration. Whines of 'I am cold Mum' were rarely heard and might not have got much sympathy. Consuelo would probably have advised the said youngster to go upstairs and put on another layer or change into something warmer, or go outside and have a walk before the next meal. One good way of warming oneself up was to saw some logs for the evening ahead.

The dining room with the Rayburn was the only room in the house that was reasonably warm in the winter. Common sense would suggest keeping the Rayburn 'in' overnight using coal, but as this cost money, Consuelo would just chuck a few logs on and hope for the best.

If the fire went out, Consuelo would riddle out the embers to retrieve the half-used bits of coal for the new fire; nothing was to be wasted. Coal was to be respected as saffron might be in a modern kitchen, to be talked about but not used in any great quantity. It was largely reserved for getting the fire started in the mornings if the logs were too damp, or to increase sufficient heat to cook a batch of cakes or a roast dinner.

Bodging and cobbling were extensively used outside around the farm. To be a successful bodger, one needed a basic arsenal of equipment; primary tools consisted of a good quality penknife and copious amounts of baler string. Often, day-to-day bodging required tying things up or lashing things down. This might be securing a gate or shed door or tying a tarpaulin over some bales of hay or straw.

Sometimes, a weight was required to ensure that these were properly secured, for instance against the wind when holding a tarpaulin or for a swollen stable door whose lower half had warped in wet weather and would not allow for the lower bolt to be used. A heavy breeze block slid in front with one's foot sufficed to keep the eager and inquisitive pigs at bay.[26] Once the weather improved and the wooden door had relaxed, normal usage could resume and the bolt could once again be used.

Sheets of corrugated iron were also very useful bodging tools. A sheet of iron with a breeze block on top saved many a bale of hay or straw getting wet overnight. They were also useful for herding pigs to the van or trailer on market day.

Making do or cobbling were also employed to provide alternatives for gates. It is not commonly known but there is a hierarchy in the gate world. At Frithwood, there were largely three orders: firstly, gates on display and in constant use, namely the entrance gate at the top of the hill and the front garden gate; secondly, functional everyday gates; thirdly, inferior barbed wire affairs.

The latter were largely imposters and did not even resemble a gate. From a distance, they would look just like a bit of barbed wire fence, but they could be opened for the periodic movement of farm machinery or livestock. The infrequent access meant that they did not warrant the expense of having a gate of their own. They were affectionately known as poor man's gates.

---

[26] Heavy breeze block, technically known as partition concrete block.

Evolution of the Farm Buildings

During the 1960s and 1970s, there was quite a lot of building work at Frithwood. Fuelled by his growing Christmas turkey business, Berns realised that he needed more shed space. He approached Joe Muller, the farm worker from next door, to see if he would like to help out at weekends. Over the next ten years, Joe repaired and built a whole range of buildings round the farm.[27]

One of the early projects was to build a Dutch barn where there had only previously been a straw stack. This was a Herculean project and probably took about a year to plan and complete. Initially, Berns and Joe had to work out the position of the new barn taking into account the width of the roof struts, allowing plenty of room for tractors and trailers to manoeuvre around the proposed shed. Finally, Berns had to build the last free-standing rick in the exact location of the new barn to aid mounting and installing the cumbersome and heavy roof supports.

Huge holes had to be hand-prepared by Joe and Hugh to eventually house the main props; second-hand telegraph poles. After the pits were dug, the weather turned particularly wet and they partly filled with water, drowning an unsuspecting ewe. Eventually, the hollows dried out and it was time to concrete the telegraph poles in place ready for the roof.

Without a crane, this took a great deal of manpower and a good quantity of rope to haul the struts one by one ascending the 'staircase' of small bales. Each bale step represented a pause and a chance to take a breather before the next heave-ho on the ropes. Potentially, it was insanely dangerous and could have easily gone wrong, but fortunately it did not, and the supports were secured ready for the corrugated tin roof. With the new barn completed, straw could be stowed there, leaving hay to be stored in the old Sussex barn.

The corn store was also built around this time adjacent to the old Nissen hut feed shed. This was useful as it meant Berns could grow

---

[27] See Appendix F: Layout of Farm Buildings.

extra cereals for animal feed. These would then be augered through to the mill and mixer in the Nissen hut saving Berns valuable time as well as effort.[28]

The next sheds to be built were pole barns primarily for turkey production to the west of the Nissen hut.[29] This space had become available, as three pig pens had been destroyed when a large oak tree in the hedge behind fell onto them during a storm. The pole barns boasted good ventilation being open on one side and had feeders which meant that rations could be dispensed from outside the shed, morning and night. These two sheds also doubled as indoor lambing facilities after the New Year.

The last of the big shed projects was to build a new feed shed literally over the old Nissen hut. Leaks had appeared which could not be mended. Again, Joe thought it through and did an excellent job.

Rich in Something

Subtle changes in the weather were the first things to alert the siblings that change was on its way. Early morning river mists would shroud the brooks below Frithwood, giving it an eerie feel, like the marshes in Dickens' *Great Expectations* when Pip met Abel Magwitch. Morning dew lingered and sometimes gave the impression of a light frost as one peeped out of the curtains. Balmy days would then succumb to winds, moderate at first, giving way to howling gusts. The poplar and fir trees at the top of the hill took the full force but the old farmhouse just shrugged her shoulders and hunkered down below the brow, just waiting for all the excitement to settle before going back to sleep.

After the wind, came the inevitable rain and with that the family knew that their old friend would return ... mud. The terra firma did not suddenly transpose from dry to wet, but would mutate with

[28] Auger: A motor-driven Archimedes' screw inside a pipe that takes grain from one place to another.

[29] Some wood came from the demolished railway station at Christ's Hospital.

ungulates over time from hard rock that you could cycle over to a muddy morass. However, no one should be under any illusion that all mud is equal, as in Sussex there are over thirty dialect terms for the stuff; Berns and Consuelo would have known a good many, not by name, but by feel and appearance.

Under Lerwill management, Frithwood was never free of mud in winter. In digging the vegetable garden in autumn, Consuelo might sometimes have the company of *cledgy* mud, which was claggy and sticky and would adhere to her spade. Near the old cherry tree stump near the back door, another mud could be found, *swank* or *gawn*. This mud was a combination of waste water from a broken drainpipe together with garden soil, which made a small boggy patch that was sometimes foul smelling in summer. Although not large enough to action a repair for many years, it was an obstacle to be stepped over en route to climbing over the barbed wire fence next to the cesspit. It was a nuisance but not a nightmare.

Around the farm buildings, other kinds of mud could be found. In the cattle yard next to the Sussex barn, there was *slab* mud. Without a concrete base and suffering from poor drainage, this terrain had the thickest quagmire of mud and dung, especially around the water trough. Next door in the main yard, *gubber* mud could be found, foul-smelling stuff and rich in organic matter. If one dared to explore this area in summer, one might get a nasty surprise. Sometimes, the youngsters would play 'chase' and make the mistake of running up and down the dung heaps, often treading on the dry skin of the *gubber* at the bottom. Footwear would be covered in black, reeking muck and even after a good wash, the pungent whiff lingered.

Outside the front garden gate in winter, a seemingly blameless mud could be found called *smeery*. This was wet, surface mud, which by comparison to others looked quite innocent. However, if one wanted to venture off the farm in winter, wellington boots were essential.

Often Berns overwintered store cattle in the field of four acres near the house. Feeding was easier as he would toss hay and straw over the barbed wire fence, saving himself the ordeal of wading through the *lke* of mud near the gate. This *lke* was a *slob* and often developed into *stodge*. Translated this, reads 'This thick area of mud became like a pudding.'

This might sound bad enough, however, Frithwood mud was never as bad as the mud Angela experienced whilst fox hunting over towards Kirdford, Stroud Green or Bedham woods. These woods had *slab* mud, the thickest of all, and required respect from man and beast. No horse could be expected to gallop through that waterlogged stodge.

The Mechanics of Water Sources

Mains water was never connected during Berns and Consuelo's tenure at Frithwood. Therefore, water could never be taken for granted and warranted respect and conservation, both in the house and on the farm. Different seasons brought different challenges.

In the summer, lack of water was the main problem. This meant that there was less water for pumping to the farm buildings. Fortunately, most animals were turned out in the spring which helped to alleviate the problem. Sometimes, it was a godsend when livestock were away from home as at least these animals benefited from the mains water supply.

In winter, the main worry was frozen pipes. This meant that housed animals sometimes had to wait for their water ration until later in the morning as pipes needed to be thawed. The process was long and laborious and involved detaching hoses and dragging them up the hill. Gravity and sunlight were put to work alongside copious kettles of hot water, used to feed the upper pipe end, in the hope that the ice would melt. It took ages, using precious daylight hours but usually worked.

Sometimes, with sub-zero temperatures, it did not work and the couple would abandon this method as the morning progressed. The alternative was to ferry buckets to animals in every outbuilding using water from the cattle trough near the feed shed, provided that it was not frozen solid. However, Berns was always a stickler for feeding and watering his stock properly, and Angela cannot ever remember a feeding and watering time ever being missed.

Water for domestic use also provided its challenges. It might be useful to outline some basic assumptions: that the well was probably dug when the house was built, and that a cast-iron hand pump had probably been installed over the outdoor well during the Industrial Revolution. From stories that Berns told the children, it would seem that rudimentary plumbing and pumping was probably installed during the Second World War. The ceiling space above the scullery certainly had evidence of this with its hotchpotch of pipes strangely adorning the high ceiling. Finally, pumping water during the Second World War was probably done with a petrol engine as the farm did not have any electricity when the couple married in late 1949.

This pump was situated over the top of the well, just outside the back door. It had no purpose-built cover and in winter was usually shrouded in an array of old hessian sacks, looking more like a corpse from the Battle of Waterloo. All in all, it was a bit of an eyesore. The replacement was placed in the woodshed, which fortunately got rid of this carbuncle.

Once pumped, the water would initially go to a tank in the loft space. However, when this tank needed replacing, it was decided to position the new tank on the upstairs landing, which was marginally warmer. This was a crude affair, basically consisting of the new tank being stacked on top of the old one. It became an indoor feature of sorts. It was only boarded off and properly disguised when Consuelo started her bed and breakfast venture in the mid-1970s. It had a quaint and unique Lerwill feel about it, until one heard the rush of water as it poured into the tank. One can only imagine the reaction of bed and breakfast visitors waking to gushing water outside their bedroom, as the electric pump was switched on.

A Motley Crew of Doors

With the farmhouse dating from the late 1590s, old doors were replaced as and when required. By the time Berns and Consuelo took possession, there was a motley crew of doors that had an evolutionary feel about them. Each had its own secret history and traits. However, they all had one thing in common; they denied excluding draughts as part of their *raison d'être*. They were true libertarians in their world.

The aristocrat of the team was definitely the front entrance. His robustness, size and door furniture meant that he was a boastful chap, barking that he always met guests, received incoming post through his shiny brass letter box and was conversant with the family's business. He was, without doubt, a snob and even bragged about his key.

The key itself was some six inches long and had a most unusually shaped key ward, which did not have common notches and nicks, but had a cut-out which suggested a little girl with no feet. One can only imagine the fun the locksmith might have had in making it. Berns and Consuelo never used the key, too afraid that it might lock but never unlock, leading to another, seemingly unnecessary expense. Far better to leave the key hanging nearby in the lobby for the next forty-plus years, its escutcheon would have to wait for any reunification.

A poor second-in-command was the back door, which had definitely seen better days. He was the workhorse of the community, hard-working but tired after years of service. Even with the Lerwill family, the hard work continued as the old portal helped to lever sinews out of turkey legs at Christmas time, for several years. However, this old soldier's saving grace was the handkerchief-sized window which let much-needed light into the old scullery.

Two portals which might well have been spinster sisters were the old bathroom and sitting room doors. Sharing many similarities, one has to wonder whether they were made at the same time by a slipshod carpenter who took little pride in his work. Unfortunately, the vagaries of time had taken their toll and the old girls often failed to fulfil their original brief, as the winter winds and draughts passed through their shoddy boards. Baths might be rushed and early nights chosen, instead of having a chilly breeze across one's lap or naked body. However, these two were resolute in their determination to keep going, possibly afraid if they relented that the workhouse might beckon. They were true stalwarts.

The only other opening worthy of note was the old stable door on the Sussex barn, which was used at least twice daily by Berns when he milked the house cow. It was old but generally in good order and was highly functional, having large hand-made hinges and a heavy latch, lethal to small hands. The lower door was generally kept shut unless mucking out was in progress. Access was always denied to the farm dog, as he would have frightened the imprisoned beasts. However, the siblings usually had free access unless safety was an issue, at which time they were kept outside along with the dog. It was only then that the door's merits were fully realised as the hole above the lower hinge nearest the ground became an important porthole, essential for an enthusiastic farm dog or nosy child to exercise barn reconnaissance.

Occasional Silences

Disagreements were rare between Berns and Consuelo; it was the 'silences' that were more common. These were most likely to occur around things such as Berns forgetting Consuelo's birthday and rarely buying a card, let alone a present.

As the siblings grew, they took on the role of reminding Berns. Sometimes, he made a special journey to Pulborough to purchase a card. Eventually, it became a bit of a joke as Consuelo was fully aware of the subterfuge. Celebrations like this were anathema to Berns as he just did not see them as important.

The silences might last a day or two, but to the siblings it felt like forever. Mealtimes became an ordeal as Consuelo changed from a chatty, enthusiastic mum into a zombie who was economical with her words, especially towards Berns. Meals became perfunctory and the children dispersed from the table as quickly as possible.

Sometimes, Consuelo used her love of botany to overcome these upsets. In the summer, she might clear away the tea things and then take herself off for a solitary walk, presumably to cool off. Always the opportunist, Consuelo embraced this time to indulge her passion for wild flowers. Picking a few specimens of unfamiliar plants, she would return home to the dining-room table, where she would use her botany books to identify them. All the while Berns sat alone or with the children in the sitting room.

Berns was either too stubborn or unaware, and never deigned to ask her about the problem. The 'war' would continue until Consuelo relented and normal rules of engagement resumed.

Berns was a man of few words and there were six simple words which he felt he could not use to either his wife or children:

'... Well Done ... Please ... Thank You ... Sorry ...'

A Nap with a Difference

Berns' working days involved long hours of physically demanding work and therefore most days he liked to have a nap after lunch. These were usually taken in the old chair next to the Rayburn in the dining room.

From an early age, the children knew that Berns needed his rest and that they had to be quiet. Even if *Listen with Mother* was on the radio, it had to be turned down low so as not to disturb his nap, even if this meant standing on a stool to hear.

Berns would make himself comfortable, while Consuelo busied herself clearing away the lunch dishes, as quietly as possible. A few minutes later, he was presented with a hot drink placed on the wooden arm of the chair.

On this occasion, things looked normal, until Berns noticed that there was something moving in his drink. Bleary-eyed from his nap, he wondered if he was imagining things. Wide awake at this point, he called Consuelo from the scullery and they both peered into the mug in amazement. There were a number of maggots wriggling about, obviously uncomfortable in the hot liquid.

The penny immediately dropped and Consuelo scurried upstairs to investigate. In Hugh's bedroom, she found a jam jar of maggots, meticulously dug out of one of the muck heaps for fishing purposes. The top had become unscrewed allowing some of the maggots to squirm their way through the floorboards and they had dropped into Berns' drink.

Muck Spreading

As day follows night, animals produce dung. With spring emerging, grazing stock would be turned outside onto fresh pasture, leaving behind vast amounts of manure. Time had to be found to clean out the many sheds. Fortunately, it was a flexible job which could be fitted in around more seasonally pressing work, providing the weather was dry.

In the early days, Berns would borrow Boxer, the carthorse and the dung cart from Lee Place. Carting muck is arduous, back-breaking and time-consuming work that might take weeks to complete. Even when Berns bought a tractor, purchasing a muck spreader had to wait until one could be bought at a farm sale at the right price. Until then, he would improvise with a tractor and trailer.

Ideally, manure needs to be well rotted before it is spread on the land, otherwise it de-nitrifies the soil. Therefore, Berns used two methods. The first was for well-rotted muck which was loaded by hand onto the trailer and taken to the field. Then, while the tractor was still creeping along in first gear, Berns would jump off the tractor, mount the trailer and spread the muck off the back of the trailer with a pitchfork. The second was for dung that was too fresh to spread. This was loaded onto the trailer and then dumped into small heaps over a field in rows and left to rot *in situ*, before being spread later by hand. Sometimes the children would help, forking dung from either the moving trailer or the stationary heaps.

Eventually, Berns bought a second-hand muck spreader. It was small and almost Dinky-like with a low trailer area with shallow sides. It worked using belts and chains on the flatbed which gradually took the muck to the spreading mechanism at the rear. Although this meant spreading was made easier, it still had to be loaded by hand.

Loading a spreader is drudgery when working alone, however, with company and a bit of banter, it could be fun. Sometimes at weekends, one or more of the children would help Berns. On one occasion, the gang was filling the spreader outside the old stable. It was a confined space as the heap was stacked along the stable wall, restricting the working space considerably. Angela was about seven or eight years old at the time and was enthusiastically flinging the dung into the wagon when she nearly stabbed Berns in the head with her fork. After being reprimanded, she kept her distance in future and started to appreciate the word 'radius'.

Road Builder

The Lerwills never boasted of having a lane to the farm from Lee Place Lodge as it was a track; the proper lane started at the Lodge. However, even this needed some kind of foundation on which to allow lorries and tractors to pass. With heavy rain, poor drainage and autumn leaves, the old route became a rutted road and suffered from many potholes. Often, these started small and then grew like acne as they spread. Once truck drivers started to complain, Berns knew action was needed as feed lorries were an essential lifeline to the livestock enterprises.

Stone was ordered from a quarry near Chichester. On arrival, the driver would be asked to dump some at the farm, whilst reserving most for the track in the wood. Accompanying the driver to Northwood, Berns would direct the stone to be placed next to the worst potholes and proceed to level it with his shovel. This had to be done immediately, as the track was needed on a near daily basis. On returning home, Berns often looked like an Irish navvy who had lost his gang, tired and exhausted.

Fortunately, spreading the remainder of the rock could be done at a more leisurely pace, when time permitted. Berns would attach the buck rake on the back of the tractor, securing a few bits of corrugated iron to make a platform base and back, and proceed to shovel stone onto the temporary tray.[30] This was then taken to any location suffering from serious mud. The cattle yard around the water trough and boggy gateways were the usual recipients.

At first, the fresh orange substrate looked quite alien but gradually it got churned into the mud, becoming submerged like an

---

[30] Buck rake: farm implement attached to rear of tractor for carrying things.

old ship sinking slowly and sedately. The terra firma it provided did not last long but was welcome all the same.

Procrastinating about the Roof

Looks can often be deceiving and although the old house always appeared to have her lipstick on and her eyebrows plucked, her old bonnet was getting a bit thin. Fortunately though, her chimney had been repointed in the 1960s. By the 1970s, it was obvious that the roof was in need of serious repair, although assessing the true extent of the problem was difficult as there was no roof hatch.

This was soon rectified as Berns and Consuelo bashed out a piece of ceiling along the upstairs corridor and replaced it with a bit of hardboard. With internal and external temperatures often being similar, the primitive portal was in a quandary; whether it should allow cold air upwards into the loft or downwards into the house. Indecision and confusion ruled; the physics were just too difficult.

The hatch proved useful for other things such as removing snow which had blown under the tiles. Before the access was created, the melted snow had left great damp marks on a few of the bedroom ceilings. Consuelo felt that at least with some sort of access she might be able to climb into the roof space and harvest the snow with the coal shovel and bucket to alleviate the problem. She was always good at problem-solving. After getting a bit blasé on one occasion, she accidentally put her foot through their bedroom ceiling.

The state of the roof was continuing to deteriorate and if one looked closely, undulations were becoming noticeable suggesting battens were failing in certain places. Action was needed.

For many years, Consuelo continued to chortle, chivvy and cajole but 'breeze-block' Berns would not budge. It was not that he was not concerned, it was more a matter of money and finding a reputable builder. Unlike many projects where bodging might do, Berns was fully aware that the house roof deserved a decent job which would cost money, a lot of money. From her earliest diaries, Consuelo writes of her worries about the roof. On one gusty night in 1974, the couple moved into the back bedroom temporarily, just in case. In

October 1974, Rhona's first husband Roy spent a day trying to repair the roof in various places. Berns even visited the council to enquire about grants.

Fortunately, Consuelo need not have worried as luck was on her side. One particularly rainy night, Berns happened to go to bed earlier than Consuelo, and on slipping into the bed he found it to be wet. On telling her she simply retorted, 'Now will you do something about the roof?'

This may have been the catalyst that Berns needed. In 1980, the roof was completely renovated probably using some of a small inheritance from Berns' Aunt Dais.

One wonders quite what would have happened if the roof had not been replaced before the Great Storm of 1987.

Rented Land away from Home

In addition to the 33.5 acres at Frithwood, Berns rented bits of land away from home mainly around the Codmore Hill area. Although useful for hay production and grazing animals, they came at a cost; the inconvenience of being away from home and poor fencing. Two fields were rented under formal agreements administered through King & Chasemore, a local auctioneer and land agent. Others were informal private arrangements based on a handshake, and went from year-to-year. Keeping one's word was always important to Berns.

The Codmore Hill field on Cray Lane, adjacent to the railway, was under one such formal agreement and rented from a Mr Newman who lived in Essex. Berns was a tenant for many years and used this ground for growing cereals and latterly for grazing sheep. Over time, the family got to know some of the local inhabitants through their constant visits.

Close to the field lived the Hobbs; Mr Hobbs was a driving instructor and Mrs Hobbs ran a boarding kennel for dogs. Opposite the Hobbs lived Nelly Francis and next to her the Shepherd family who went to school with the Lerwills. Along the road towards Broomershill lived Mrs Spears. Her house was quite large and was surrounded by trees and undergrowth. The siblings had been told that it was haunted which played to their imaginations. Mrs Spears was a strange and mysterious lady who always wore dark glasses, a headscarf, rode a bicycle and never spoke.

Berns also rented several fields at the end of Blackgate Lane. One was called St Richard's Cottages Field and had a number of cottages to its side. One was occupied by a lovely widow called Mrs Gutherie. She was a kind soul and would regularly take Berns a drink when he was making hay and kept an eye on grazing stock.

Opposite St Richard's Field were a few small, boggy fields owned by Mr Coxon. During the 1970s, Berns rented these primarily for sheep grazing. Prior to Mr Coxon buying the property, the old place had been neglected with towering hedges and infilled ditches. The two men came to an agreement; for reinstating the land, Berns would have the grazing rent-free for the first few years.

Close by, Berns also rented two paddocks from a Mr Fowler. Dividing the two fields stood a cottage which the siblings affectionately called Smoky Joe's as it always seemed to have smoke billowing from its chimney.

One of the practical problems of any field away from home was loading animals if they were to be sold. Sometimes this might require an extra journey with hurdles or more man or child power. Occasionally, one or a number of the children would be kept home from school to assist early in the morning. Then Berns would take them on to school in Billingshurst or put Rhona on a later bus, with notes for form teachers from Consuelo explaining the situation.

Other pieces of rented ground that came and went, included some grazing at Westlands Farm from Mr Garbett and Mr Wells in the 1960s. Then, later the field next to North Heath Café, grazing at the Forshaws' and the Henslows' along Pickhurst Lane and some near Snape Farm and Tote in the 1980s from John Parker.

Land at Wisborough Green

'Berns, Berns, the bullocks are out,' Consuelo shouted. Within minutes, the Lerwills were on their way.

The small rented acreage at Wisborough Green was owned by a

retired farmer, Mr Seldon, who lived at Meadow View. He quickly informed Berns of the cattle's whereabouts. The ten bullocks had split into two groups, one was carelessly cavorting in the churchyard, the other was dancing and prancing around the sacred cricket green.

Quickly Berns directed Hugh, aged ten, and Rhona, aged seven, to the graveyard. Meanwhile with the help of a few bewildered onlookers, Berns, Consuelo and Angela tried to steer the other group back towards their field at Great Meadow. By this time the animals were excited and dashed past their field, finally turning left into a garden rushing towards the back. From here, the group jumped several parallel garden fences, denting lawns, and squirting manure in all directions. At one house, an irate woman ventured out bellowing abuse at Berns about the mess on her new gravel driveway and wanting him to remove the dung without taking any of her precious gravel.

Soon the animals were safely back in their field and the family returned to Meadow View for a well-earned drink before returning home.

Fencing away from Home

Adequate fencing, whether at home or away, was essential for both man and beast. One of Berns' sayings was *'Good boundaries make good neighbours.'* Without secure tenure on much of the rented ground, it would have been imprudent for Berns to have invested in permanent fencing.

At Frithwood, fences and hedges were generally kept in good order and were suitable for all kinds of livestock. However, this was not the case with rented land. While cattle need sturdy barriers, sheep are not so demanding.

For Berns, this meant having three or four rolls of pig wire which were kept specifically for temporary fencing.[31] When required, the wire would be loaded in the livestock trailer and taken to the fresh

---

[31] Pig wire: wire livestock fencing fashioned into squares.

pasture. They would then be unrolled and laid out along the perimeter and stood up, forced alongside the existing poor fence or pushed back against the inferior hedge with a foot, and tied in with short pieces of baler string. After this, the flock could be moved into their fresh field.

Over the year, the wire might be moved several times. It was time-consuming but necessary and was just accepted as another struggle factor.

Harvest Time

Harvest time fell into two distinct areas: combining the small acreage of home-grown cereals, and baling bought-in straw from elsewhere. Fortunately, this was usually staggered over August and September.

Berns started growing a few more acres of oats and barley once the turkey enterprise got under way and he had a corn store ready to house it. Often, the Cray Lane field at Codmore Hill and two fields at home were drilled to produce either spring barley or spring oats.

Once the crops were ripe in early August, Berns had to be patient and wait for outside help to come and combine the cereals. Berns was not a naturally patient person and the siblings knew that if the weather looked menacing, it would be wise to keep out of their father's way. The harvest season was a worrying time for Berns, knowing that a bad harvest would increase bought-in feed costs, especially for the turkeys. Farmers have always been slaves to the weather.

One local friend who helped for several years with combining was Robert Myram from Adversane. After finishing his own harvesting, Robert would arrive to help out. His first machine was tiny in comparison with combines today and was pulled by a tractor. It had an equally small hopper and required manual handling into sacks; this was Berns' job. These combines were rapidly superseded by the juggernauts that are prevalent today.

The other task was baling and storing straw ready for bedding the livestock in winter. In the early days, Robert also helped out with baling straw as Berns did not have a baler of his own. As Lee Place and

Northwood no longer carried livestock by the late 1960s, there was always plenty of straw for sale. The usual arrangement was that a buyer would purchase the standing straw and bale and cart it themselves. Any unsold straw at this time was burnt, and sometimes caused hedge damage if the wind changed direction. One year, Joe Muller from Northwood Farm came running over the hill to fetch Berns, as the straw burning in the Lodge Field had got out of control. The flames had jumped from the row of straw and were threatening Frithwood's top hedge.[32] It was a question of all hands on deck.

Once the clouds of dust were sighted or the combine was spotted along the lane, the siblings knew it was time to find their old gloves and head out and help their father. One of Angela's first harvest jobs was to perch on the back of the bale sledge and open its back gate manually after about ten to fifteen bales had been collected. It should have released automatically when Berns yanked on the rope from the tractor but often jammed. One or more helpers would then stack the clumps of bales ready to be collected later by the tractor and trailer gang.

Berns never had a bale grabber and so bales had to be lifted manually from the ground to the trailer. This was not a problem when the load was still low, but, as it grew, lifting the bales became a job for someone with experience and technique. Berns made it look easy; nonchalantly placing his long pitch fork into a bale at just the right position and then using leverage, balance and rhythm to toss it effortlessly onto the top of the load above head height. It was a skill requiring practice.

After her A-levels, Angela remembers one of her teachers, Gordon Smith, coming for tea and helping to load some straw. He watched Berns casually throwing the bales onto the load and had a go. He failed miserably as the weight above his head made him look almost drunk as he ran after the runaway bales.

Depending on the weather, work often continued until nightfall. Once the last trailer was stacked, it was time to get home. Unloading depended on time of day, number of available helpers and the

---

[32] The Crop Residue (Burning) Regulations 1993 effectively banned straw burning.

weather. However, the task became a lot easier once Berns bought a portable electric elevator. This greatly reduced the sheer physical effort required to move bales upwards into the hot and stuffy barns. Nevertheless, it was still hard, relentless work for man and child.

The Old Timer

'Watch out, the rope's coming!' Berns bellowed. With the straw bales stacked high on the trailer, Berns would throw the rope to the youngsters above. Once secured, they were ready to head home from Codmore Hill, some two and a half miles away. Berns would mount the old tractor, revving the engine. Billowing black smoke would dissipate into the fading evening light. With a jerk, they were off.

The first challenge along the lane was the small incline near Blackgate Farm. Cranking the gears in preparation, the old tractor would grumble and splutter, making his feelings known, before they tackled the hill. On reaching the top, the rowdy rooks could be seen returning to their rookery in the ash trees above in silhouette form. This, blended with eerie twilight, added to the children's excitement.

Although not apparently obvious by modern standards, safety was an issue. After all, Berns always told the children to hang on tightly to the rope and was forever shouting, 'Are you still up there?' The main danger came from low-lying tree branches. Often, it was necessary to duck and dive to avoid being scraped off the load. Lying flat and burying one's face in the bales was often the best course of action and added to the drama and anticipation.

At Snape Farm, there was another obstacle, the Scrases' sleeping policemen across the lane.[33] Many a time a few bales were lost, and on one occasion the whole load was shed. Once past Clapper's Pond and Northwood Farm, the party would start to ascend the small hill towards Lee Place Lodge, where the Croom children might still be playing outside with their dogs. With sparks flying in the old workshop, the Lerwills would know that John was working late, repairing some ancient piece of farm machinery ready for collection

[33] Sleeping policemen used for traffic calming.

the next day. At the Lodge, Berns would then turn right, taking the track towards Northwood.

Once through Northwood and Frithwood's top gate, the party would momentarily pause to soak up the view; the monochrome profile of the Wisborough Green skyline and the old farmhouse and buildings in the foreground.

On approaching the house, the open curtains would reveal Consuelo busy preparing a late supper. Moving slowly, the little tractor would edge round to the left and to the back of the Sussex barn. With the quickness of light, the youngsters would climb the barbed wire fence next to the cesspit and rush indoors. Within a short time, the family would assemble to eat supper. Showing off, the youngsters' stories were a litany of half-truth and half-lie as they tried to exaggerate the tales of the journey back home.

It was then a matter of milking the house cow and off to bed. The old timer had done it again.

Police Identity Parade

Vets often acquire numerous animals that would otherwise be destroyed; Dennis Marten, the vet, was no exception. He would often have six to eight dogs romping about in the yard at Gennetts Farm, waiting for new homes. In addition to these dogs, the Martens would have their own collie dogs and would usually breed one litter a year. In 1979, the Martens' dog was called Bryn and was brindle in colour.[34] He was the father to Berns' brindle bitch at the time, called Lassie.

Bryn was a good guard dog around the yard, but on this occasion, he got a little over-zealous and bit someone. The police got involved and organised a dog identity parade. Dennis borrowed Lassie and she was duly identified as the culprit! The police wanted her destroyed. Dennis argued that she was only making up numbers and Berns pleaded her case; Dennis was charged with wasting police time and Berns with possessing a dangerous dog.

Things moved on and a hearing was arranged in the magistrates'

---

[34] Brindle: a brown-and-white collie dog.

court. The first was abandoned as Berns was known to the magistrate. On the second hearing, the magistrate suggested that both parties should *be bound over for a year* as no proper outcome could be reached. Berns was not happy with this as he felt that it suggested he was in the wrong and initially refused, but on realising that Dennis's veterinary licence might be at risk, he relented. It was a strange outcome for loaning a friend a dog for a day.

Life Indoors

'The home should be the treasure chest of living.'

LE CORBUSIER (1888–1965)

Another Day: Berns

Unless it was a particularly busy day, most mornings started with a similar routine. After waking, the couple would lie in their double bed, acknowledge each other and enquire as to how the other had slept. Berns often slept badly due to poor health.

With this civility over, Berns was always the first to rise, anywhere between six and seven o'clock. He would dress in the same order. First the pyjama trousers would be dispensed with and, if it was wintertime, thermal underwear would be quickly pulled on, then the first layer of socks, making sure that they overlapped the bottoms of the long johns, thereby making them draughtproof. Then it was the trousers and braces.

Once secured, it was time to exchange the warm, cosy pyjama jacket for a cold vest, followed by an equally chilly Viyella checked shirt. On top of this, a home-knitted woollen jersey lovingly knitted by Consuelo. Once clad in his slippers, he would pad down the back stairs, towards the kitchen.

Before venturing outside, Berns would drink a mug of cold milk, sometimes making Consuelo a tray of tea. This was not to be expected however, as Berns was of the old school: *'Treat them mean and keep them keen.'*

Another Day: Consuelo

On most days, Consuelo would bundle downstairs and make her own tea, quickly returning upstairs. In the early days it was made with loose tea, and even when Consuelo progressed onto tea bags, it was always made in a pot. In addition to her tray, she would often return with her diary and writing pad.

Once suitably nestled back into her cocoon, she would pour herself a cup and proceed to write her diary from the day before, detailing progress on current farm jobs, completed garden tasks or some family detail. Writing in bed was usually done with her knees up, using them as a sort of easel. If time permitted, she might also write a few lines to her mother and sister who lived in Bexhill. This was a weekly must-do and was rarely missed or skipped.

Upon finishing her second mug of tea, it was time to dress. Like Berns, Consuelo had an established dressing order routine. First of all, pants were threaded up the legs and then the nightdress was hauled over her head, the bra came next and once attached, a vest on top. Consuelo always bought long vests which were tucked well into her knickers. This, she said was to keep her back warm. Socks, trousers and a warm, home-knitted jersey would follow.

With her tray, she would proceed to the bedroom door, place it on the windowsill to draw back the curtain of the west-facing window close by. Savouring the moment, Consuelo would look over the hotchpotch of farm buildings and beyond; East Hilly Field and Green Brooks below Lee Place and Harsfold.

She was ready to start another day.

Standards, Standards

Prior to marriage, Consuelo's life had been influenced by two institutions; boarding school and nursing. Therefore, management of time, routine and discipline were all part of her DNA. In her own mind, she knew exactly what she wanted to achieve on a daily basis both in her domestic domain and, latterly, on the farm.

To those people who knew the couple well, it was obvious where the lines of demarcation lay; Berns' domain was the farm, whereas Consuelo's was the house and garden. Consuelo liked things to be orderly, tidy and efficient. In the garden, she worked tirelessly to adhere to the gardening calendar. In the autumn, she might overwinter delicate plants on windowsills and, weather permitting, dig the vegetable patch ready for spring planting. In the winter, she would plant sweet peas in old toilet roll 'inners'. Summer evenings were largely devoted to this passion, and she might often spend several hours, happily toiling away outside with only the company of a few bats as dusk drew into nightfall. Eventually, befuddled by darkness or hearing Berns call that she had 'done enough,' she would surrender to a milk drink and her bed.

House-wise, she also had high standards, not of material goods, but of adhering to strict guidelines of decorum regarding the spoken word, manners, meals and dress. With such a remote location and visitors being infrequent, Consuelo realised that it would be easy to let things slip. She had seen it happen to other farming friends. She was not having any of that nonsense at Frithwood.

Clean wellington boots and a respectable coat were always required if leaving the farm, even for a walk around Northwood or to Lee Place. Berns never missed a daily shave and always looked presentable whether checking stock away from home or visiting elsewhere. The couple both changed clothes several times daily in order to keep indoors as clean and tidy as possible, saving particular clothing for dirty work. Consuelo used to say that she was lucky as Berns was a clean worker.

Etiquette at mealtimes was also seen as important. Every breakfast, lunch and tea had a tablecloth, mats and appropriate cutlery and crockery set out for all participants. Consuelo usually laid the breakfast table the night before, while waiting for the kettle to boil for filling hot-water bottles or waiting for milk to heat for the supper drinks; she was never a person to waste time. For many years, everyday crockery was an eclectic collection acquired from Alastair, Berns' brother-in-law, who was a china and porcelain buyer for Woolworths for a time. Naturally, visitors merited matching sets.

At mealtimes, the children were asked to *clear the decks* if they happened to be using the dining table. Once assembled, the meal could begin. Portioning out the meat was always Berns' job and he would sometimes ask Consuelo how many meals the joint or casserole had to last. If more than one meal, the siblings knew that second helpings were off. Vegetables were presented in serving dishes for individuals to help themselves. If one took something, one had to eat it; no waste was allowed, after all there were starving children in Africa. With plates charged, the family tucked in to their meal.

Manners were drummed into the siblings from an early age, and were seen as of paramount importance to Consuelo in particular. Swearing was not tolerated and even the odd *damn* and *blast* were frowned upon. Pre-college agricultural students however, often tried Berns' patience and then he would sometimes use the odd expletive, making sure that it was not in Consuelo's earshot. Standards were standards after all.

Priorities, Presents and School Friends

Not many people would have guessed that Berns and Consuelo were a focused couple who knew exactly what they were trying to achieve. Farming at Frithwood was their mission; everything else was secondary, even if it meant that they had to go without.

Berns had what is called topophilia: the love of a place. The whole of his heart was there; he loved the farm, its animals, its buildings, its position and its isolation. He was a man who ploughed his own furrow. However, his love for his way of life could never be questioned. Many a time, Consuelo told the children that animals raised at Frithwood had a good life before slaughter; they were well fed, constantly monitored for injuries or illness, smelt fresh air, saw daylight and often had access to outdoor space for some of their lives.

With a background of poor health, the Great Depression of the late 1920s and the Second World War, Berns' outlook was blinkered. If survival meant carrying on, in an old-fashioned way without excessive borrowing from the bank, that is what he would do to carry on farming. Apart from the cost of the farm, Berns only ever borrowed small amounts of money from the bank just before Christmas to cover turkey feed. Otherwise, it was strictly *'Make do and mend'* all round, indoors and out.

Indoors, Consuelo also ran a tight ship. Her *raison d'être* was not dissimilar to that of Berns; to feed and look after her own 'livestock' as well as she could, on modest means. This meant a hearty menu, utilising home-grown produce wherever possible. With the farm providing some of the meat for the family, Consuelo could supplement this with fruit and vegetables from the back garden.

Consuelo was also resourceful in making presents for the family. She loved knitting and aimed to produce one jersey or cardigan for one of the family each year, whilst watching television on chilly winter evenings. In addition to this, she often knitted mittens and hats for Christmas presents for the numerous nieces and nephews, as well as garments for new babies. Her conquest of Aran knitting was admired by other knitters, who understood its complexities and precision.

Bought presents for the children were another matter. Angela remembers hating the first day back at school after Christmas as friends listed off their presents. Berns and Consuelo were an impecunious couple and never tried to give the siblings what they could not afford. Money was always tight. It was a simple lesson, but a good one. As the children matured, they would often be given a little cash towards the thing they wanted. This way, money was not wasted and the rest could be earned around the farm. There was always plenty of earning potential at Frithwood.

Time was also at a premium and Berns was never a willing taxi driver. Without driving, Consuelo knew that there was little she could do to alleviate this problem. However, her way of overcoming it was to encourage school friends to the farm. She apparently told Berns that this was a good way of getting to know the sort of youngsters the siblings were mixing with and to encourage the right friendships. This was an easy fix, as most children even today love visiting a mixed farm with different animals, a pony to ride and a home-made meal. Many a time, an extra place had to be set at the meal table.

Consuelo's solution worked and the couple got to know a whole range of outsiders over the years, extending their social network and getting a rare glimpse of life outside agriculture.

Berns' Attitude to the Law

Berns saw the top gate as a bit like a portcullis regarding the law. Anybody outside the Frithwood sphere had to obey, but Berns felt that he was a special case and that he could use a 'pick-and-mix' approach. These oversights were not in the league of Robert Maxwell or Lehman Brothers but strictly, they were illegal.

They largely fell into three categories: dealing in cash, ignoring planning regulations, flaunting health and safety rules. Berns' generation had been raised with 'Cash as King' and this attitude was carried on throughout Berns' working life. Cash obtained from some farm-gate sales of eggs, young turkey poults and Christmas birds was kept away from any bank account and tax man, even Consuelo for that matter.

Accrued cash in notes was rolled up and placed in jam jars in strategic locations around the farm buildings for Berns to retrieve at a later date, but was often left too long and became obsolete. Supposedly scared of being caught, Berns did not fancy the job of exchanging the old notes himself. This was a task for college-age offspring, although under strict instructions to avoid banks in Pulborough. The siblings never did work out the logic to this bizarre ritual, it was just one of those things.

Berns also saw gaining building permission for farm buildings as unnecessary. He would have been horrified at the idea of asking for official permission to do something on his land.

Lastly, was the question of Health and Safety which was anathema to Berns. Before attending Harper Adams Agricultural College, Angela was completely ignorant of the legal requirement for a tractor to have a guard over the tractor power take-off (TVO).[35] After all, when Berns was giving her a lift on the back of the tractor, with the TVO shaft rotating at some great speed within inches of her legs, one wonders whether 'Mind the TVO shaft' was sufficient warning.

---

[35] Power take-off: enables a tractor engine to drive other pieces of machinery.

Communications with the Outside World

On a day-to-day basis the phone was often the only means of communication with the outside world. Installed in the 1950s, it meant that Berns could conduct his farming enterprise without having to go to his parents' house at Lee Place to use theirs. It also meant that Consuelo could speak to her family, albeit sparingly.[36] Regular letter writing and walking were the other modes of communication used by Consuelo.

It was fortunate that she was good at letter writing and enjoyed it. She would often have a letter on the go to family and friends. Her style was chatty and a reader who knew the old farm, could easily picture the farming tasks outlined, such as dagging sheep, unloading straw or cutting back nettles under the blackcurrant bushes.[37] Often, letters and stamp money were left in the letter box for the postman to administer.

As well as writing letters, receiving them was an important element in Consuelo's day, especially when Hugh and Angela were overseas. Whilst on her working holiday in Australia for eighteen months, Angela wrote most weeks, as did Hugh while he was in Nigeria and Saudi Arabia. These letters were read, numbered and kept safe. Upon Angela's return to the UK, one of the regular postmen, Dennis, told her how Consuelo's eyes would light up, when he delivered a letter from *Terra Australis*. Phoning Angela in Australia would have been seen as an expense too far; the threesome probably only spoke on the phone half a dozen times over the eighteen-month period.

Phone calls were probably seen as expensive due to the monopoly that the General Post Office had over both the postal and telephone businesses at the time. After numerous reconfigurations, BT was finally established in 1991 and competition finally came to the telephone business. Before that, trunk calls or long-distance calls were seen as expensive luxuries by many people. Therefore, at

---

[36] The first telephone was made from Bakelite and was replaced by a black plastic one in 1974.

[37] Dagging: the removal of mucky wool to prevent fly strike.

Frithwood, all trunk calls had to be rationed and eked out over the month. For many years, Consuelo and her mother took it in turns to ring each other weekly, for a limited time, usually on a Sunday morning.

Using the phone was not taken lightly at Frithwood and all the siblings knew that permission 'had' to be sought and a good reason put forward. Angela remembers many a time being denied access and being told that she would see the named friend at school in the morning. In her teenage years, a couple of 'official' calls were about the weekly ration and even those often had to be cut short. However, with Berns and Consuelo outside a great deal of the time, one could always risk the odd, short call during the afternoon feeding time. The main threat of being caught was if Berns came indoors to collect the afternoon milk bucket. Prior to the 'crime', one needed to check whether the bucket was absent from its stool in the scullery.[38] With no bucket, the coast was clear and an illicit call could be made, but it needed to be kept short.

It was not just the siblings that needed to exercise diligence regarding the telephone, Consuelo also worked on not being found out. Several years after Jane and Michael Joseph moved to Woodlands, Jane asked Angela if Consuelo had a problem with using the phone. Angela immediately knew what Jane was about to say but listened smugly. 'Does your mother have a problem using the phone as sometimes she will chat away merrily and then suddenly cut the call short?' asked Jane. Angela had to explain that her father had come into eyeshot and that Consuelo's feeling of guilt would make her finish the call as soon as possible.

Walking to neighbours was by far the easiest method of keeping in touch. Consuelo would regularly call in to see Joan Croom at Lee Place Lodge at least once a week, usually after lunch. Joan and Consuelo had a strong relationship built on mutual grounds: hard work, challenging menfolk and a shortage of cash. Many cups of tea

---

[38] The milk bucket was placed on an old stool covered with a clean tea towel to prevent cats and flies helping themselves. Usually, Berns would bring in the filled bucket on his way in for breakfast or tea.

were had chortling over these topics which was a release valve for both women. Not many friendships were stronger than the one between Joan and Consuelo.

Bathing at Frithwood

Modern day ablutions are straightforward affairs, just a matter of shutting a door, turning a tap and stripping off. However, bathing at Frithwood usually required negotiations with indoor management. The starting point was always whether there was enough water in the tank from the well, whether it was hot enough and whether it was already earmarked for something else. Once these topics had been covered, a plan and timeline could be devised. However, the bathroom itself needs some introduction.

Berns and Consuelo had inherited what could only be described as a primitive downstairs bathroom. It consisted of a cast-iron bath on legs, a wash basin and a hot-water tank, with a separate toilet in a cubicle next door. The floor was uneven and was made from bricks laid on earth and was damp and cold. The hole taking waste water had never been properly completed and displayed an unusual form of ventilation from below, otherwise known as a draught. If not packed with old rags, the occasional frog would appear bewildered by its new habitat. Although clean, Frithwood's bathroom was not a place to ponder life's great mysteries; better to splash, wash, brush, dry off and vacate as soon as possible.

When the children were small and it was particularly cold, Consuelo sometimes abandoned the bathroom, preferring to wash them in an old tin bath in front of the Rayburn. Preparations included filling numerous kettles and saucepans and laying out a towel in front of the Rayburn as a mat. With nightwear at hand, Consuelo would then process each of the children and dry them off in the warm room, before taking them upstairs to their Arctic bedrooms, where the only solace was a hot-water bottle. However, in the mid-1960s, things started to change for the better.

By this time, Joe Muller, the farm worker from next door, was regularly helping Berns on Sundays with a whole variety of maintenance work, and it was decided that the scullery and bathroom needed a bit of a make-over. A new doorway was knocked out between the scullery and bathroom, and the floors were levelled and laid with linoleum tiles. Once completed, Joe then boxed in the old bath and basin and built a cupboard round the hot water tank with hardboard, making Consuelo's first airing cupboard. The final investment was a pair of new curtains. These were made of towelling and displayed large, white daisies on a black background, which was all the rage in the 1960s. Although still desperately cold in the winter, this was a huge move forward in personal hygiene at Frithwood.

Undoubtedly, the bathroom looked a great deal better, but the old problem of not enough hot water still remained. Although invented, immersion heaters were costly to purchase and expensive to run. Resourceful Consuelo came up with what Baldrick from the *Blackadder* television series would have called 'a cunning plan'. The new twin-tub washing machine, now housed in the bathroom, could be used to heat water for bathing. For years, this laborious procedure was executed by all members of the family except Berns who relied on Consuelo to fill, heat, dispatch and put away the said machine, while he had his bath and walked away.

Literally Bum Gripping

The indoor toilet was situated near the back stairs. It had an old wooden seat without a lid, which was common at the time. However, over many years, and accommodating many bottoms, the seat had unfortunately developed a crack, which pinched one's posterior if one was not too careful. Angela, about five years old at the time, never discussed her method of avoidance. She used the hands-under-the-lap method, upholding the said legs away from the over-zealous crack.

The split began to be discussed, not at mealtimes obviously as this was not a subject for polite conversation, but on a one-to-one basis with Consuelo, along the lines of, 'Mum, when is Dad going to do something about the loo seat?' Eventually, a new black plastic seat and lid were purchased, wrapped in a plastic cover, and this was where they stayed, propped against the toilet wall for many weeks.

In retrospect, Consuelo's frustration must have swelled as she tried to chivvy Berns to tackle the job and had the constant whines from the children about the perishing thing. Eventually, exasperation led Consuelo to tackle the job herself. She gathered what plumbing tools she could find, unwrapped the packaging and read the basic instructions, which seemed perfectly reasonable if one had been dealing with any other toilet.

With trepidation, she tried to yank the old seat from the back of the lavatory. However, this was not as simple as it might seem, as the nuts had corroded and just would not budge. If only she could use a bit more force, she was sure that she would have it cracked; and cracked it did. With a gentle tap of the hammer, the toilet bowl split into two pieces. Looking back, Consuelo probably took a deep breath as she knew that she would have to face Berns, and probably foresaw a minor domestic fracas on the horizon.

Mr Carley, the plumber from Adversane, was contacted and installed the new toilet and seat. The story did not end there however, as a few days later one of the siblings noticed that the toilet was slightly off-centre. It would seem that even professionals have their off-days.

Bronco or Izal, Madam?

Although things had moved on, tersorium and squares of newspaper were no longer used for wiping one's bottom, Frithwood was still in the era of hard toilet paper.[39] Consuelo's mantra was that soft toilet paper clogged the waste pipe to the cesspit and even commented once, that hard toilet paper was better for one's bottom. Leading brands, Bronco and Izal ruled the day, and each member of the family had their own method of enduring the inefficient and uncomfortable material.

[39] Tersorium: a Roman invention to wipe one's bottom using a sponge on a stick. Known as a xylospongium in Greek.

Quite soon after Angela was able to go to the toilet independently, she decided to only use it for defecation, as wiping after urinating was pointless; one's hand returned wet and warm. It was better to give the *derrière* a little shake and if a few drops landed on the seat, let Consuelo deal with it next time she popped in.

The old Scullery-come-Kitchen

Frithwood was probably built at the end of the sixteenth century and its design was known as a three-bay farm or yeoman's house.[40] Following the English Reformation, a great deal of church land was either given as favours or sold off by the Crown and smaller farms established; Frithwood was probably one of these. The layout was simple, with three similar-sized rectangular rooms, side by side. From the front garden, the room to the extreme right would have originally been used for food storage, the middle room with the large inglenook fireplace for cooking and feeding farm labourers, the other for the yeoman's family.

Unlike today, where the kitchen is often said to be the centre of the home, this was not the case at Frithwood. One gets a clue from the interchangeability of the words, kitchen and scullery. The old kitchen-come-scullery faced north, had two small windows and quite a high ceiling as it tucked under the catslide roof.[41] It also had three doors, one of which was the badly fitting back door. On the inner wall were a number of wooden coat pegs, beautifully made by Joe Muller.[42] This is where the mass of outdoor working clothing hung. Beneath this was a large cardboard box, often cut into a sort of tray, sometimes lined with newspaper, which housed the family's wellington boot collection. It was a working hub not a show home.

It was also largely devoid of much kitchen equipment. Apparatus

[40] See Appendix G: Architectural Description of Farmhouse
[41] Catslide roof: a roof that continues below the main eaves height and allows one to have a greater depth of building without increasing the ridge height.
[42] Berns had a number of coats on these pegs, some of which were kept for particular jobs. For example, he had an RAF overcoat and a Second World War pilot's sheepskin jacket which were kept mainly for ploughing.

was sparse: a sink, originally a low, shallow affair, changed to a second-hand Belfast at some point; a free-standing kitchen table; a typical 1950s wall cabinet with sliding doors and opaque glass; a chest of drawers with a tiny free-standing Baby Belling cooker on top; a rudimentary pantry under the stairs; a single-tub washing machine and, eventually, a fridge. With no heating, this was not a space any cook wanted to spend much time in, especially in the winter.

There was some progress, as the old range in the scullery was replaced with a new Rayburn range, installed in the dining room where it could access the big chimney. The only problem was that it looked hideous positioned in the inglenook fireplace. Aesthetics aside, it was practical and provided the heat for cooking, hot water and basic survival.

Phileas Fogg the Fly

In order to appreciate the old farmhouse, you are about to go on a short journey. Inspired by Jules Verne's, *Around the World in Eighty Days* and his character Phileas Fogg, you are to be guided by a fly called Phileas. You are minute.

Hatched earlier in the day from one of the many dung heaps scattered around the farm, your host is already familiar with the terrain. Leaving behind the pungent smell and his innumerable relatives, you glide over the wall separating the farm from Consuelo's summer garden. The contrast is quite extreme, one a smelly farmyard, the other a beautiful garden.

Making a wide circle, Phileas heads for the front door which is open and inviting. Once indoors, you observe that the dining-room door on the right-hand side is ajar and the mellow smell of fresh baking wafts through making your mouth water. In the rectangular room stands an oblong table slightly shifted towards the natural daylight from the window on your right, shrouded by a low, beamed ceiling. You notice the table is covered with two table cloths, the bottom one cloaked by another hiding a bumpy sandwich in between. You assume, correctly, that the tea table has been laid for guests, but covered to keep out Phileas and his sort; such dirty beasts.

To the back, stands a cream-coloured wall dissected by an English cross of stained dark beams. In front of this, to the right is a 1930s roll-top desk, looking a bit worse for wear. Resting on bricks on earth and tended with Cardinal polish, the thin veneer is gently peeling back on its lower edges. On top, there is an Edwardian everlasting calendar boasting 7 July 1968, although this should not be relied upon, with a metal barometer behind. The walls are painted with gloss paint to aid cleaning, as Phileas and his sort frequently leave their calling cards, which Consuelo often cleans off with a wet cloth. The cross beams host an old-fashioned three-pin electric socket: an unintentional, but not unusual Lerwill appendage.

To the left, stands a nineteenth century Bohemian dark sideboard with intricate carvings of wild birds and beasts killed in some gory blood sport, hanging meaninglessly, supposedly adorning the lower doors. On its top, stand two *sentries*, to the right an electric kettle sitting on a metal tray plugged into the socket, to the left a pile of magazines waiting to be sorted by Consuelo and handed on. Turning slightly to the left, you notice a large inglenook fireplace bordered by two well-used armchairs. One, with a faggot oven behind, is strictly for the current dog Fly, who is known to be territorial; the other, for Berns' after-lunch rest. Overhead, a Victorian mantelpiece, displaying a 1940s clock given to the couple by Watts and Sons, the feed merchants from Billingshurst, as a wedding present in 1949.

To the far left, another doorway beckons. This room looks more promising for a possible meal for young Phileas. Its name depends on who you are talking to. To young Angela, it is strictly the tack room, but to most it is and always has been the egg room. A potentially light, draught-free rectangular room, which in 1976 would become the family kitchen. Once surveyed, the journey continues out of the egg room and descends three steps into the scullery, towards the back of the house.

Phileas's flight quickens as he notices the milk bucket mounted on a green stool, enticed by the smell of warm, fresh milk. Fortunately for Phileas, an incoming telephone call has distracted Berns and no tea towel covers the bucket. With dive-bomber precision, Phileas turns and takes a drink, while you hang on for dear life.

Once refreshed, Phileas continues his tour, backtracking to the front door. In the small lobby, he takes care as the space is confined and seemingly dark to the sunny contrast outside. He darts into the sitting room to find guests mingling and a red fly-swat leaning against Consuelo's chair. It is time to make a hasty exit.

The Resourceful Cook

Ask any housewife in the 1950s whether she liked or enjoyed cooking for her family and one would probably get a blank expression of 'What are you talking about?' Food rationing continued until 1954. There were few convenience foods. Cuisine was basic and prepared in the home. However, for those who had experienced shortages during the war, monotony was better than hunger. Fortunately, Consuelo enjoyed cooking and wanted her family to appreciate the joy of country fayre.

Consuelo had learnt to cook at boarding school although quite how remains a mystery as food rationing would have surely curtailed practical cookery lessons. Nevertheless, she was a good, wholesome and prudent cook. Above all, she hated waste.

In addition to cooking for her family, Consuelo liked to grow, gather and preserve as much as possible, enabling her to stretch her modest housekeeping money. This required forethought, time management and sheer hard work to provide a healthy diet for her offspring. Nevertheless, Consuelo was always generous when she had gluts of produce and often took surplus runner beans and other vegetables to the Croom family and other neighbours.

Consuelo's year was divided into different food seasons. In January, she would purchase Seville oranges and make the family's annual marmalade requirement, probably about thirty to fifty jars. As spring gave way to summer, she made copious amounts of jam. Routinely, she might make over 100 jars of strawberry jam, estimating that the family might eat about two jars a week at teatime.

One winter, shortly after Berns and Consuelo married, a lot of trees had been felled on the Brinsbury side of Northwood. In spring, the re-growth of wild flowers included a vast quantity of wild strawberries. Consuelo and sister-in-law Pam picked enough tiny fruits to each make jam.

Consuelo's Strawberry Conserve:

    2 lb strawberries sliced thinly
    2 lb sugar

    * Layer the fruit and sugar in a large bowl.
    * Leave for 24 hours and then boil for 5 minutes.
    * Leave to stand for 48 hours.
    * Bring to the boil.
    * Cook for 10 to 15 minutes
      until setting point has been achieved.
    * Bottle in sterilised jars.

Home-grown raspberries, blackcurrants and loganberries were also used for jam and bottling. Sometimes, extra supplies of blackcurrants and plums would be bought from Eddy Luckin at Orfold Farm near Wisborough Green. In addition, Consuelo also made a little marrow ginger, lemon curd and apricot jam.

As the freezer moved in, bottling moved out. Although the produce still had to be grown, tended and picked, at least the last phase was simplified. Before the chest freezer, most vegetables had to be used fresh or given away, as there were limited ways of preserving them. The inevitable glut of peas gave way to a Frithwood tradition, that of peas being served in a seasoned white sauce on thick toast and eaten at teatime.[43] For children who were used to bread-and-butter teas, this knife-and-fork dish was relished and devoured with gusto. They were a bit sad when the freezer deprived them of this wonderful seasonal treat.

---

[43] In July 1985, Consuelo recorded that she had frozen 10.25 lb of peas and 56 lb of butter.

Chutney was popular with the whole family and was eaten with cold meat and cheese. Apple and tomato chutneys were popular using windfall apples and stubborn green tomatoes which refused to ripen. On chutney-making days, the house would fill with a vinegary smell seeping into every nook and cranny. Consuelo hated the smell. Doors and windows would be kept wide open hoping to rid the house of the pungent fumes.[44]

Then, quite by chance, while glancing through *Farmers Weekly*, she found a recipe for runner bean chutney. This quickly became the family's favourite. Rapidly, Consuelo's new recipe gained fame and numerous copies were shared with family and friends. Often it was simply referred to as Consuelo's Chutney.

Consuelo's Runner Bean Chutney:

2 lb runner beans prepared
1.5 lb onions prepared
1.5 tbsp cornflour and turmeric
1 tsp dry mustard
1.5 pt vinegar
2 lb Demerara sugar
A little salt

* Cook beans in salted water until tender, drain.
* Boil onions in half a pint of vinegar until tender.
* Add nearly all remaining vinegar
  and boil for a further 15 minutes.
* Make a paste with the turmeric and cornflour
  and reserved vinegar and add alongside the sugar.
* Boil for a further 10 minutes
  stirring from time to time until it has thickened.
* Bottle in sterilised jars.
* Keep for a couple of months for the best results.

---

[44] Another dreadful smell that sometimes filled the house was from lambs' lungs, which were boiled for dog food.

In the autumn, Consuelo spent time gathering walnuts and filbert nuts from trees in the farmhouse garden and hazelnuts from unkept hedges on Lordings Rough. In 1991, Consuelo recorded that she had collected 1.5 buckets of filbert nuts alone. They were then dried on old trays and placed on windowsills, often competing with overwintering geraniums, then hoarded away into nets, before shelling and being stored in Kilner jars. Field mushrooms were also gathered from Lordings Rough on a regular basis when in season. In 1996, Consuelo collected 4 lb of mushrooms in one picking, eating some fresh, making soup and freezing some for casseroles. Consuelo's mantra was always 'Waste not, want not.'

Farmhouse Fayre

Cooking was constrained by time and money. Experimentation was somewhat limited but new recipes did creep in especially as the girls started to take an interest in baking. Encouraging her daughters in the joy of food was of paramount importance to Consuelo.

The earliest cooking lessons involved left-over pieces of pastry which the girls would roll out many times, until they were grey and lank. Sometimes, they would use little rolling pins and aprons given to them for presents, feeling quite proud that they were proper cooks. Once baked, the 'pastries' might be presented to Berns at the back door, as trophy dishes, awaiting compliments. Biting into this disgusting hardtack and with an owlish stare from Consuelo, he would give an encouraging word. The girls would beam and giggle, thinking that they had achieved some extraordinary culinary delight, innocent of the truth. Chocolate crispies and other easy-to-cook recipes followed, continually building their confidence in the kitchen. Peppermint creams and coconut ice were popular at Christmas to give away as home-made gifts presented in pretty sweet papers.

Although nearly all the food eaten at the farm was produced from scratch, bread was the exception and was delivered three times a week from a bakery in Worthing until the 1970s. Bread was a staple. Consuming two loaves a day was quite normal. Consuelo did not start making bread seriously until the early 1970s after Angela brought home a few tips from school. Rolls were a particular favourite and presented to paying guests for breakfasts, as well as being enjoyed by the family.

Main meals consisted of lots of roasts, casseroles, stews and pies. Berns did not like reheated meat and so leftover meat was usually eaten cold with baked potatoes. Standby, cheap meals included toad in the hole, liver and onions, sausages, macaroni cheese and breast of lamb stew. Berns often had fish as it was more digestible. Consuelo's signature dishes were definitely her gravy and home-made soups made with turkey or chicken bones. Home-made soup simmering on the Rayburn had a gravitational pull to the hungry youngsters returning from school, who would gobble it up with gusto and often wanted seconds. That was true-love to any hungry child.

Home-made desserts at lunchtime varied from a basic stewed fruit with semolina, ground rice, rice pudding or custard, to a wide variety of fruit crumbles, sponge flans and pies using home-grown loganberries, blackcurrants, raspberries, strawberries, rhubarb, gooseberries, blackberries and apples, topped off with clotted cream. Baked custards decorated with nutmeg were also popular. Angela was never a lover of rhubarb, but loved Consuelo's cobweb pudding, effectively a rhubarb mousse. In the winter, a whole range of pies, steamed sponge puddings, apple dumplings, treacle tarts and spotted dicks might be cooked to bulk out the main meal. Lemon meringue pies, trifles and sponge fruit flans were family favourites and often on the menu for lunch guests.

Bread and cake were the main staples at teatime. Herrings, kippers and melon were treats, although for many weeks in the summer large quantities of home-grown raspberries and strawberries were enjoyed on a near daily basis. Popular teatime recipes included Victoria sponge, plain and fruit buns, fruit cake, chocolate cake, coffee sponge, Australian coconut bar, choux buns, iced Bath buns, scones, hazelnut and peanut cookies, plus many others. Rarely were mass-produced cakes eaten at Frithwood and those that did sneak in came via visitors. Rhona remembers Gwen, Berns' eldest sister, bringing sticky doughnuts on numerous

TALES OF A SUSSEX FAMILY FARM

occasions and Ruth, Consuelo's sister, sometimes bought a plain
Madeira cake from Marks and Spencer.

Clotted Cream

Most new brides today would not want their husband's extended
family living next door or even a field away. However, Berns'
parents were not the interfering kind and just let the newlyweds get
on with their new adventure, only visiting Frithwood when invited.
Nevertheless, Consuelo knew that she and her young family were
always welcome at Lee Place and would often drop in after meeting
the school taxi.

On one of those visits to Lee Place, Berns' father Sidney offered to
show Consuelo how to make clotted cream. With the family
originating from North Devon, this tradition had moved to Sussex
and remained an important culinary treat. This took some
organising. Berns' role was one of buying the right breed of house
cow to provide milk with a high butter fat content and trying to get
the cow to calf at the beginning of the summer. The reasons were that
there would be plenty of milk early in the cow's lactation, that the
high sugar content of the grass would boost the milk and cream
yields, and that cream production would coincide with the soft fruit
season. With the raw materials at her fingertips, it was time for
dairymaid Lerwill to get to work.

The alchemy of cream making began with skimming off the top of
the milk in the bucket. After collecting two or three of these
skimmings, Consuelo would then pour them into a shallow pan and
place it on the top of the Rayburn and scald the milk. The richest
cream rose to the top forming a thick skin that, once cooled, formed
a delectable yellow ambrosian crust. When cooled, this could be
removed; it was then ready to be eaten. At mealtimes, the family
used it as a condiment, sometimes enjoying it at every meal.

Breakfasts saw clotted cream being daubed onto porridge or
cereals and at lunchtime it was spooned onto a variety of puddings.
However, it was at tea that probably most clotted cream was
consumed, often being lusciously spread on bread or scones and

lathered over with one of Consuelo's home-made jams. She also made a range of jellies such as quince, crab apple and blackberry, apple and elderberry. In the summer months, it was partnered with home-grown strawberries and raspberries for many weeks.

The Lerwills valued simple pleasures.

Favourite Sayings and Expressions

Apart from breakfast, most meals were taken together around the dining table. Conversations often centred on the minutiae of daily life. The depth and plethora of these conversations meant that all siblings learnt about farming through osmosis whether they liked it or not. They were, in effect, staff meetings between husband and wife, often deciding what needed to be tackled and in what order; Consuelo's timetable flexing to meet Berns' requirements, rarely the other way round. Often, expressions and sayings were used as a sort of shorthand.[45] In retrospect, it seems a shame that these unique examples of colloquial English will be lost unless recorded.

The Rice Pudding Incident

Rhona and Angela dreaded the new school timetables in September, scheduling domestic science and games lessons on the same day. Practically, it would mean that both girls would have to lug a great deal of stuff to school, which was difficult on their bicycles.

One of Rhona's first cooking forays at the high school was rice pudding. The previous week, Mrs Atkins had given the girls a checklist of things to bring. On discussing the task with Consuelo, it was decided that in addition to the Pyrex dish, a Kilner jar should be taken for bicycle transport purposes.

With the lesson finished, Rhona proceeded to get her Kilner jar ready. Nonplussed, Mrs Atkins just could not comprehend what her pupil was describing; her walk to the Carfax, a forty-minute bus journey and then a two-and-a-half-mile bike ride back to the farm in

---

[45] See Appendix H: Favourite Sayings and Expressions.

the dark. She flatly refused to let Rhona scrape the pudding into the jar.

On arriving back at Blackgate Lane, Rhona used her initiative and proceeded to scoop what she could into the jar and chucked the rest into the hedge. Melanie Croom from Lee Place Lodge stood in amazement as the slop was decanted.

The Slow Creep of Modernity

Modern conveniences came slowly to Frithwood, primarily owing to cost. The first sign of modernity was probably an old battery radio. Until the couple got their own telephone, it was the only communication with the outside world and lived on the oak sideboard in the dining room. It was popular with Consuelo who liked to keep up to date with current affairs, and when in season, cricket and tennis.

Often the radio was on while the family ate their meals, but, when the mantelpiece clock chimed on the hour, the children knew to be quiet as their parents needed to listen to the news and weather forecast. This was particularly important when making hay and baling straw.

Mains electricity was installed in the mid-1950s by Holmes and Cooper from Horsham, a firm owned by Berns' brother-in-law Stanley Swain. However, the farm never had many sockets. This may have been because of cost, limited ideas at the time for the uses of electricity or the availability of parts. The emphasis seemed to be on lighting.

Outdoors, there were a number of electric lights: in the old Sussex barn, Nissen hut, battery house, old stable and in the yard. This meant that precious daylight hours could be used for more pressing work, leaving animal feeding and milking the house cow to be done by electric light if necessary.

Today, it is difficult to envisage a home without electricity. However, imagine it you must. This was the reality at Frithwood where even having a single light bulb in each room was an enormous move forward. One needs to remember that at this time, Consuelo was in her early twenties, was trying to cook with an impossible old range in the scullery, tend temperamental Tilley lamps and cope with all the trials and tribulations of a new baby.

Nevertheless, power points were also a scarcity in the house, with only two upstairs and three downstairs for many years. This meant that large extension leads were necessary for vacuuming upstairs, which was cumbersome and occasionally dangerous. Sometimes, room layouts of furniture were dictated by socket positions and did not always look pleasing to the eye.

One of the first electric gadgets to be acquired was an electric kettle. Prior to this, boiling a kettle on the range or Rayburn might have taken hours. At the time, kettles did not switch off automatically and needed to be manually turned off. Therefore, the first kettle proudly lived on a tray on the sideboard in the dining room, where the teapot could be refilled without Consuelo walking too far. It was practical. When the first kettle needed replacing, Consuelo went strawberry picking near Codmore Hill over several weeks to earn the £20 it cost.[46]

Other electrical appliances followed slowly, often cast-offs from Berns' sister, Nance. As Stan's electrical business prospered, Nance was the lucky recipient of some of the latest household gadgets. Sometimes, Consuelo would inherit some of the older models. Consuelo's first washing machine and vacuum cleaner came via this route. It is difficult to appreciate just how much these new labour-saving appliances must have alleviated the humdrum tedium of household drudgery for thousands of women at the time.

The next two appliances that came to the farmhouse were the fridge and television, in the early to mid-1960s. Prior to having a fridge, a primitive meat cage was hung in the garden from the filbert nut tree in the summer to accommodate perishables such as meat, cheese and butter. It was desperately lacking and often butter would quickly go rancid. The farm's first fridge was won on an Irish Sweepstake. It must have been a godsend to Consuelo trying to feed her growing family without easy access to any shops, the nearest one being at Adversane, a good thirty-minute walk each way.

---

[46] Berns would drop Consuelo off at the strawberry field en route to Pulborough Market.

Frithwood's first television was rented from Radio Rentals and cost about twenty-five shillings a month (£1.25 in today's money). In those days, most televisions were rented, as valves and tubes were unreliable and costly to repair. Angela still remembers vividly the day the television came to the farm. It was wintertime, and she was having tea with her parents in the dining room. However, on this day, she was encouraged to go into the sitting room. She entered, but did not switch on the light, entranced by the open fire that burnt brightly in the grate. Kneeling and warming herself, she wondered why she had been coaxed into a room rarely used. After a few minutes, Consuelo pulled the rope latch on the door, peeped into the darkened room and switched on the light. Angela was amazed at the sight of a large ugly cube sitting on the table near the front window; it was a television.

At last, the sitting room had a purpose and began to be used on a more regular basis. Prior to this, the family tended to use the dining room as it was warmer, had a table for the children to play around, a comfy chair for Berns to read his *Farmers Weekly* and good lighting under which Consuelo could tackle her latest winter knitting project.

Evenings were never quite the same again at Frithwood after the television arrived. Berns would watch horse racing for an hour on Saturday afternoons, work permitting, and the siblings could enjoy the likes of *Blue Peter* and contribute to playground talk without feeling left out. A colour television was bought by Hugh as a present in 1984.

Similarly, the arrival of the first chest deep freezer in the early 1970s radically changed life at the farm. The main advantage was that meals could be more varied. Prior to having the freezer, main meals from October to Christmas revolved around turkey. Growing turkeys can go off their legs and if left in their shed they either become trampled on, or can starve to death. In order to avoid this, Berns would kill the birds so that Consuelo could use the meat for the family.

By Christmas, the whole family including Berns got thoroughly sick of it. They ate roast turkey, turkey casserole, fried turkey, cold turkey and even exotic turkey rissoles on a few occasions. Consuelo even consulted Alma Steele (a friend and turkey farmer's wife) about how to cook disguised turkey dishes. The siblings regularly took turkey and runner bean chutney sandwiches to school for a break-time snack. Hugh sometimes sold his to buy cigarettes. The freezer meant that turkey-tedium could be avoided.

The deep freeze also meant that lambs could be slaughtered and preserved. Sometimes, with orders from friends, a few lambs would be taken to a local abattoir and collected a day or two later. Collecting carcasses and butchering was quite a day. Considerable energy and plenty of plastic bags later, the parcels were boxed ready for collection. The siblings always liked Berns' butchering as his lamb chops were always enormous, unlike Consuelo's which were more modest in size. However, things were not always as they should have been as, on at least one occasion, Berns was sure that at least one of his lambs had been swapped for an old ewe. From then on, Berns requested that the heads were left on the carcasses. Later on, reasonably priced bacon joints were bought from the Horsham Bacon Factory, butchered and frozen.

In addition to this, surplus produce from the kitchen garden could be preserved and used throughout the year. This reduced the time-consuming job of bottling. Previously, Consuelo used a fleet of large Kilner jars which she would sterilise before filling them with all manner of fruit. In order to preserve their colour, these were then stored in the dark walk-in cupboard in Hugh's bedroom (later Angela's bedroom). With the freezer, Consuelo could simply 'bung' them in and forget about them. Overall, the deep freeze was an excellent investment for the family.

The last of the gadgets included an immersion heater, microwave oven and an automatic washing machine bought in the early 1990s.

Modernity was creeping ever closer to Frithwood.

Reversing the Ferguson Tractor

Initially, Berns did not have a tractor at Frithwood but borrowed one of his father's four carthorses for field work. Sometimes, Boxer would stay overnight in the old stable. Unsure of his unfamiliar surroundings, he did not lie down, preferring to rest one leg at a time whilst standing. In the summer, with the bedroom windows open, Consuelo remembered hearing the metallic sound of his shod hooves as the old horse changed legs throughout the night.

Eventually, Berns bought a small grey Ferguson tractor. In the 1950s, many small farms had at least one. When not in use in the winter, it was sometimes parked with its bonnet just under cover in the cart shed at the front of the house. This gave it some protection from the cold weather.

On one occasion, Berns got onto the tractor and had just put it into reverse. Fortuitously, he looked over his shoulder. Standing behind one of the large back wheels was young Hugh, aged about three, innocently looking skywards towards his father. Ever the inquisitive toddler, he had escaped from the fenced garden to have an adventure of his own. Someone, possibly the postman, had not secured the garden gate properly. Winded by the realisation of what might have been, one can imagine Berns dismounting the tractor and giving Hugh an unusually tight hug of utter relief.

The Old Green Van

The van was used mainly to transport pigs and lambs to various markets, but most commonly to Pulborough Livestock Market on Monday mornings.

The medium-sized vehicle had two seats in the front with a wooden, slatted barrier behind that prevented livestock escaping. Straw would be placed in the back, and then the animals were manhandled into the van for dispatch. However, this van was also used to transport the children.

The siblings knew nothing else so would climb into the back hoping that it had been recently mucked out. A few hessian sacks acted as something clean to sit upon and were kept handy in the cart shed. With outings a rarity or avoiding a soaking getting to the taxi or school bus, the youngsters were not too bothered and just accepted that it was part of living at Frithwood.

Nevertheless, when Berns bought a car in the mid-1960s, the

children were delighted. Thighs could be united with a plastic car seat instead of pig dung.

Comparing Livestock

Rhona, the couple's second child, was born on 16 August 1954, the day after her cousin Lyn Wardrop. Effectively the two girls were the same age. One can only imagine Consuelo and Flo, Berns' third sister, chuckling together on the telephone about the coincidence of conceiving at the same time.

The following year, there was a family party. Until then, Consuelo was aware Rhona was a delicate baby but was horrified to see that baby Lyn was enormous compared with Rhona.

On the journey home, Consuelo instructed Berns that the next morning they must take Rhona to the doctor's surgery for an examination as she was so worried. Consuelo was assured by Doctor Pepper that, although small, Rhona was perfectly formed and was doing well.

Advice from Madge

Eric Lerwill was Berns' first cousin and in 1947 he married a young widow called Madge. The four newlyweds got on well and would occasionally socialise together. Madge was an intelligent woman and, aware that Consuelo was willing, gave her some sensible advice, not to learn how to milk the house cow. Consuelo never officially learnt, but when Berns was in hospital, she would take up the challenge on a temporary basis.

'Trouble at Mill'

After seeing Berns off to Pulborough Market on a Monday morning, Consuelo would often tackle the laundry. Twin-tub washing machines used the water multiple times and so there was a strict etiquette for one's wash, starting with whites and finishing with socks and soiled clothing. Sorted clothes on the scullery floor resembled a road map of the morning ahead.

On this occasion, things went well until Consuelo placed her hand into the gyrating spinner to find one of her fingers attached by a mere thread. Quickly grabbing a hand towel, she instinctively angled the finger back into place and crudely wrapped her hand, while rushing to the telephone.

The first Berns knew about it was when someone came bursting into the Station Café looking for him. They briefly explained that Consuelo had rung King & Chasemore's office. Panic-stricken, Berns returned home.

On arriving, he found Consuelo as white as a sheet, nursing her arm and a bit fuddled and pallid. They quickly fled to hospital where her finger was saved.

An Unwelcome Visitor

As the wisteria matured at the front of the old farmhouse, it formed a swirling network of winding branches which meandered over the warm sandstone walls. This was an ideal climbing frame for any cat. Crackers took full advantage of this, using the open window as her own exclusive entrance, although she was quite aware that it was strictly out of bounds. However, undeterred she continued; she would simply climb the wisteria, pass through Berns and Consuelo's bedroom, slink down the stairs, meow and be let into the dining room, ignoring any reprimands from Consuelo.

On this day, she had obviously caught a young rat and taken it into the bedroom, played with it and let it loose, unbeknown to Berns and Consuelo. During the following night, Berns thought that he felt something scampering across the double bed or was he dreaming? He turned over and slept on.

Later that morning, while Consuelo was upstairs making the bed, she noticed a young rat skittering across the room; Berns had been right.

Best Presents

For a while, Angela worked for a company called Norprint International in Boston, Lincolnshire. Although only twenty-four, she had a company car and made the most of it at weekends. One week, when Angela rang home, Consuelo said that Berns was in bed with a bad back and was feeling quite low.

After finishing work on the Friday afternoon, Angela decided to drive the four hours home. She found Berns in bed, but cold to the core, even though he had a hot-water bottle.

The next morning, Angela went to Horsham and bought her parents an electric blanket. It proved to be the best gift that she ever bought them. Ever proud Berns offered to pay for it; he was funny like that. Naturally, Angela declined.

A Funny Observation

One Christmas, while Angela was at the farm, the couple's five-year-old granddaughter, Alice came to stay for a few days. On this particular day, Angela suggested a trip out after lunch. Consuelo said that she would like to visit her old nursing friend Sister Theodora, who lived at Lingfield Convent in East Sussex, following the closure of Findon Convent. The phone call was made and a plan was hatched.

After an early lunch and leaving Berns in his cosy armchair, the two women and the little girl set off. They arrived in good time and were greeted by an elderly nun stooped with age, and ushered to a sitting room with the table laid for tea. Shortly afterwards, Sister Theodora entered, and the two old friends immediately re-acquainted and started chatting. Angela and one or two elderly nuns, equally withered with time, tried to amuse Alice, whilst eating the odd mouthful of cake and gulping some tea. Ever conscious of the convent's strict regime, the threesome departed and returned home having enjoyed their visit.

No more was thought of the trip, until Alice was asked what she had most enjoyed about her Christmas holiday. She simply said, 'Visiting the dwarfs with Grandma.'

Consuelo's Diary Writing

In the early 1970s, Consuelo decided she would keep a diary and rarely skipped or missed an entry. They largely reported farm, family and garden activities, plus weather conditions with the occasional mention of a national or international event.

Her style was factual, direct with little fuss or use of adjectives. They reflected the sort of woman she was; pragmatic, no-nonsense and matter-of-fact.

Here are a few examples:

> 17 January 1974:
> *Made 17 lb marmalade.*
>
> 26 March 1974:
> *Onion sets upset as cats think that they are marbles.*
> *Little rascals.*
>
> 12 August 1976:
> *Berns has sold 1,400 turkey poults to date.*
>
> 22 August 1977:
> *Nearly a wheelbarrow load of onions/shallots harvested.*
>
> 29 February 1985:
> *Cleaned windows and dipped out the cesspit.*
>
> 20 September 1991:
> *1.5 buckets of filbert nuts picked.*
> *Still lots of hazelnuts on the Rough.*
>
> 26 August 1994:
> *Picked 34 cucumbers to date.*
>
> 23 June 1996:
> *David (Francis) fixed up to help Keith Ward*
> *whose man died baling last week.*

After all, she had much to do and little time to waste idling and pondering over mere words.

Consuelo's Front Garden

Imagine a rectangle a little smaller than a tennis court made from two halves of lawn bisected by a central brick path leading to a black front door. Each square is bordered with an L-shaped flower bed. The one on the left follows the garden wall to the cart shed and then abruptly turns away from you, along the back wall of the hovel, coming to a halt near a small gate leading to the Sussex barn and the farmyard. On the right, the border follows the Wealden sandstone wall which dwindles after about twenty feet, near a prunus tree. The border then turns towards the house, stopping a few feet away to allow for access round to the back door. Nearby is the site of the old morello tree, sadly lost to a storm in the early 1960s. Along the front of the house are two other borders acting like a foot warmer, hiding an old lady's ankles for decency's sake. The scene is set.

Immediately to the right of the front door is a majestic wisteria which covers the front of the house, benefiting from its southerly aspect. This was given to Consuelo by her mother when Angela was four years old in 1962. In the spring, sky-blue grape hyacinths adorn the back row while wallflowers are towards the front on both sides. On a sunny spring day, the perfume is quite exquisite. On each side of the front door stand two planted terracotta pots; these had been egg crocks and had come from Lee Place.[47] In spring, they were planted with forget-me-nots and pansies, often Maggie Mott (Consuelo's favourite) and, in summer, with busy lizzies, geraniums and lobelia. To the left of the front door, an inherited forsythia grows producing yellow flowers in early spring. On the far end of the other side of the front door, an old-fashioned pink rose called Albertine thrives, producing a flush of pink flowers in early June. Consuelo grew this from a cutting of an old rose at the garden gate of Lee Place Farmhouse, a loving reminder of Berns' parents.

---

[47] Egg crocks: large, wide-rimmed earthenware pots used for preserving eggs in the past.

The border to the left of the garden gate has an eclectic mix of perennial plants, some dating back to a wedding-present box of plants given to the couple by Berns' Auntie Violet and Uncle Felix. The yellow flat-topped *Achillea eupatorium* is just one example. A large red broom plant dominates the border. This was given to Consuelo by her mother who probably bought it at one of the many church bazaars and plant sales she loved to attend. In the corner, a large bachelor's button or *Kerria japonica 'Pleniflora'* thrives in the damp dark space, bringing joy with its small bushy, yellow flowers. Close to the wall, a patch of lily of the valley, a deep-red peony, musk and Canterbury bells fill the space with ease. Following round, the heleniums in the hovel border offer a lovely show of autumnal colours in September and early October, especially in early morning when the sun from the east shows off their vibrancy. On the corner, a blue Veronica shines through. Assorted hollyhocks and delphiniums give the border added interest and status.

To the other side of the garden gate, the L-shaped border gives rise to a number of roses, lupins, London's pride, purple frith, pinks, daffodils given to Consuelo by sister-in-law Nance and Rhona, and annuals lovingly raised by Consuelo. In the corner stands a deep-purple prunus tree some twenty to thirty feet high. Behind this border lies a piece of grass under-planted in places with snowdrops and daffodils, and three medium-sized Bramley apple trees. There is also a young cedar tree given to them by Angela for their silver wedding anniversary in 1974, the Year of the Tree. And still further, a large, mature walnut and filbert nut tree.

There is no hint of low maintenance here, only the rewards of hard graft.

Spinning and Dyeing

In the late 1980s, Consuelo became interested in spinning and dyeing wool. This had resulted from meeting with a friend called Betty Sawyer, who had set up an informal monthly spinning group. Using some of her bed and breakfast money, Consuelo bought a wheel of her own and joined the group in 1988.

Initial projects used home fleeces and were spun in natural colours, then the odd Jacob fleece was bought for browns and blacks. Consuelo bought a Castlemilk Moorit ewe that was crossed with a Shetland ram, owned by a neighbour.[48] This cross resulted in lovely soft fleeces. Despite looking a bit odd in the flock, this primitive ewe seemed happy enough.

As butter goes with bread, spinning goes with dyeing; one interest naturally tumbled into another. Books were borrowed and study commenced. Early on, Consuelo decided that she would only use natural dyes, remembering her childhood memories in Bolivia of the indigenous people spinning and dyeing. Special plants were sourced and grown specifically, including woad for blue, madder for pale brown and orange. Onion skins and green walnut husks were also used. Being terribly practical, it is more than likely Consuelo might have experimented with human urine as a mordant.[49]

On balmy summer days in between haymaking and harvest time, Consuelo could be found outside the back door and in the scullery cooking various concoctions of dyes, some of which smelt revolting. It was a modern-day witch's den, with old saucepans of steaming brews and lingering mordants. Contented in her work, she beavered away, happy to learn something new and useful. Consuelo was never frivolous with her efforts.

Over time, the projects became more advanced. Her most adventurous challenge was probably adapting a Kaffe Fassett pattern for a jacket for Angela in autumn hues in 1990. It was made from hexagons consisting of three diamonds, and together they gave a three-dimensional design. Angela still has the jacket today and keeps it well away from prying moths. It is a modern-day heirloom.

---

[48] Castlemilk Moorit is an ancient breed of sheep.

[49] Mordant: a dye fixative.

Neighbours and Others

The only reward of virtue is virtue;
the only way to have a friend is to be one.

RALPH WALDO EMMERSON (1803–1882)

Paid Help

Paid help over the years largely fell into three categories; full-time men, youngsters, part-time helpers. Sometimes, contractors and friends helped out especially at harvest time. Appreciation was sometimes offered through sustenance.

The first man Berns employed was John Croom who lived at Lee Place Lodge. However, John did not stay long as he had a large family to support and ambitions of his own. He decided to become an agricultural engineer, training with SCATS in Billingshurst, and then he established his own agricultural repair business based from home.[50] His skills were a godsend to lots of small farmers, like Berns who would drag their old tackle to John's for repairs.

Berns then employed George Ascot who lived at the farm in the far end of the Nissen hut, before it became the brooder house. He was a religious man and always had Sunday mornings off to attend church in Wisborough Green. After a while, George decided to train as a White Father and went to Tanzania to work as a missionary. Nevertheless, communication continued through letters at Christmas and the occasional visit when he was home on leave.

By this time, the Paynter family had moved into Sunwood along the lane from Woodlands Farm to Adversane. Although the Paynter siblings (Topsy, Timmy and Maddy) were older than the Lerwill children, the two families got on well. However, after Mr Paynter died quite unexpectedly, the family moved to Newpound, just north

---

[50] SCATS: Southern Counties Agricultural Trading Society.

of Wisborough Green. This did not deter Maddy from her plan of working for Berns at Frithwood after leaving school.

Maddy's bicycle journey took about forty minutes each way, cutting through Harsfold. She was not only capable, but was responsible and took her work seriously. On one occasion, Consuelo reminisced that Maddy had left work for the day and got about halfway home and wondered whether she had turned the hosepipe off, so she turned round and came back to check. Her diligence was admirable.

After a while, however, Mrs Paynter announced that Maddy needed a proper career. She trained as a groom, eventually working for David Waites at Malham Farm, near Wisborough Green, who was Field Master with the Chiddingfold and Leconfield Hunt for many years.

After Maddy, came a succession of pre-college students. Prior to attending agricultural college, most youngsters had to work on a farm for about a year to gain practical experience. Julian was the first and was the most memorable. At sixteen, he came to work for Berns during the severe winter of 1962/63. Even from the start, it was obvious that Julian had a lot about him and that he was likely to have a good future ahead of him. He came well equipped for life in the country with a fishing rod, shotgun and motorbike. He fitted in well with the family and was hero-worshipped by all three children. Other students followed with less success, until Berns decided they were more trouble than they were worth.

Consuelo replaced the paid full-time worker, and was largely responsible for the laying hens, pigs and helping with all manner of work requiring another pair of hands. By this time, Angela was older and just tagged along.

Fortunately, by the 1970s, Berns happened to come across a lovely chap called Toddy Rough. Initially, Toddy came to pluck turkeys at Christmas, but was soon helping Berns on a weekly basis fitting in hours around his night maintenance job with British Rail. He had worked on a farm in his youth and loved the countryside. He was a great asset and helped Berns for the next twelve to fifteen years. Following poor health, he died in 1989 and was sorely missed.

After the Great Storm of 1987, Joey Bicknel returned to Frithwood repairing and rebuilding a number of outbuildings as well as doing farm work. David Francis was the last part-time helper.

The Croom Family

Luckily, Consuelo had an outgoing personality and easily made friends. This was a huge advantage as without a driving licence, she simply knocked on doors as new people moved in and struck up new friendships. This is how she met Joan Croom.

Joan Croom lived at Lee Place Lodge with her husband John, her mother-in-law and a large family of children: Melanie, Robert, Andrew, Nicolas and Sarah. Angela remembers old Mrs Croom having a bit of a Somerset accent and greeting her with, 'Hello, little maid.' Like Consuelo, Joan was a well-educated young woman with plenty about her and the two women quickly became kindred spirits. With children of similar ages, they had plenty in common.

Most weekends and school holidays, the two sets of children spent countless hours roaming the countryside and having fun together. The oldest four children, Hugh, Rhona, Melanie and Robert, formed a pact and over several holidays spent many days building camps in Northwood. The younger siblings were seen to be too young to join in and were left at home.

The first such camp was called First Tree Fort. This was situated in the corner of Northwood at the bottom of the track from Lee Place Lodge. The track had been constructed from the debris of bombed houses during the Second World War. In 1942, Canadian soldiers camped in Northwood ready for the 'big push' and needed a road for access. The children's camp was formed by an ivy-clad tree, which had fallen against another that had broken its fall over the stream. The children had great fun climbing the sloping tree and, once the top was reached, it offered a panoramic view of any advancing *enemies*.

The other camp was called Crow Castle. It was in a central position in the wood and was basically a huge beech tree which had fallen during a storm. It provided a wonderful natural playground and hiding place, and the children spent most of one Easter holiday at 'The Fort.' Unfortunately, the midges proved too tiresome during the summer holiday and the fort was largely abandoned.

Practical things such as climbing trees did not always come naturally to Rhona and so she asked for Melanie's help. She soon mastered her fear. One of her favourite trees was the old morello cherry tree in the back garden at the farm. From the bird's-eye view, she had a panoramic view of her world. Sadly, Angela was denied this pleasure as the old tree blew down in the mid-1960s.

The Crooms lived at Lee Place Lodge for fifteen years before moving to Devon in the 1970s. Even after forty-odd years, the families still keep in touch and are very fond of each other.

Miss Kathleen Elwin

Following a disastrous poultry venture at Snape Farm in the early 1960s, the farm was divided and sold off in two lots. The farmhouse, buildings, farm cottage and seven acres were in one lot and bought by Miss Elwin. The second lot of land was amalgamated with Tote Farm, next door.

Born in 1906, Miss Elwin was very much a woman of her time and had obviously come from quite a well-to-do background. Looking back, one can only suppose that she had been born at the wrong time, as the Great War 1914–1918 probably impinged on any marriage prospects and then the Second World War severely affected her later life. Although she rarely spoke about her past, she did tell Angela that she worked as a plotter during the Second World War, presumably attached to the Women's Auxiliary Air Force.

From the outset, it was quite apparent that the middle-aged Miss Elwin had independent means and had bought Snape Farm so she could regularly ride to hounds with the Chiddingfold and Leconfield, and Crawley and Horsham Hunts. Usually she would hunt two, if not three times a week, made possible by a full-time groom who lived in, and a cleaning lady who lived in the farm cottage. The farmhouse was modernised and wooden loose boxes erected, effectively making a second yard, sandwiched between the old barn and the house with a chicken run in the corner.

Miss Elwin's hunting routine continued for many years, until old age and employing a good groom became too difficult. Old horses were put out to grass and Miss Elwin's interest changed direction from horses to dogs. She got involved in breeding and showing Australian terriers, and regularly attended the Crufts Dog Show for a number of years. Angela and Consuelo kept in contact sometimes helping with little errands and the dogs. In her late teens, Angela took Miss Elwin to see the school play, *Oh, What a Lovely War!* which she enjoyed.

Eventually, these pleasures shrank away and Miss Elwin's world became her home at Snape and its surrounds. Consuelo continued to pop in and sometimes invited her for lunch. With declining health, her nephew eventually moved her to a care home in Steyning where she saw out the rest of her life. By 1991, Snape had been sold.

Occasionally, Consuelo would arrange to visit her, taking bunches of primroses or flowers from the garden. Consuelo always remembered Miss Elwin's past kindnesses.

Matty the Tramp

Matty was difficult to age. The vagaries of time had taken their toll on the seemingly old man. Prior to Frithwood, he had visited the Lerwill family at Lee Place. The first the family would know about his arrival was when he descended the hill in a grey billowing mac tied round his torso. He would then have a few words with Berns and deposit his meagre belongings in the Nissen hut, staying in the far end where George Ascot had lived. For the next few days, this was Matty's home.

In exchange for a bit of work around the farm, the couple provided him with three meals a day, eaten on a tray in his temporary abode. As one can imagine, Matty was a loner and preferred his own company. Sometimes Consuelo would leave out a few items of Berns' old clothing, but rarely, if ever, were they accepted. After a few nights, Matty would melt away under the cover of darkness, presumably to plod on to another sympathetic farmer. Rumour had it that his trampings had started after an unhappy love affair.

Mr Alan Dugdale

Mr Dugdale was one of the original teachers at the Weald School in Billingshurst and mostly taught biology and rural studies. He and his wife lived in a bungalow at the crossroads at the end of Blackgate Lane at Codmore Hill, nearly opposite the bus stop. In the mornings, numerous children would observe the devoted couple in their goodbye ritual. Mr Dugdale would start his Morris Minor car, whilst Mrs Dugdale would open the drive gates and wave him goodbye. The children would laugh and giggle as they watched the routine uncurl day after day, almost as though the couple were completely oblivious of their audience.

Over the years, the Lerwills and the Dugdales got to know each other, as Mr Dugdale taught both Hugh and Angela. Sadly, his wife died early in her fifties leaving her bereft husband behind. Shortly afterwards, he decided to move and bought a house opposite the primary school in Billingshurst, which made life a bit easier over the last few years of his teaching career.

Consuelo was always a compassionate person and after Mrs Dugdale died, she would sometimes ask the widower over to the farm. On one occasion, she asked him if he would like to look at the bird's nest orchids in Northwood. It was a warm, balmy summer evening, and after Berns and Angela had declined the invitation, Consuelo and Mr Dugdale set off. Angela, who was about seventeen at the time, remembers Berns opening the sitting room door in quite a fluster, asking where they were and what they were up to? Angela had not knowingly ever seen her father jealous before and after reassuring him, quietly smiled at the ridiculous idea of what he was suggesting.

Unfortunately, Mr Dugdale died in 1977 while Angela was attending Harper Adams. She found him to be an avuncular character who had a good heart and a willing ear.

Mr Bruce Bastin

Angela always liked to keep in touch with her friends and, after leaving the Weald, a few teachers were added to the list. Bruce was one of Angela's favourite teachers and she had the greatest respect for him. They wrote regularly to each other whilst she was in Australia and he encouraged her to make the most of her adventure.

At this time, Bruce lived at Roffey and, after Angela returned from Australia, a routine evolved. Whilst visiting the farm, Angela would telephone Bruce and arrange a day for him to call. On arrival, they would go for a walk with Bruce's Old English sheepdog, Fungus, and then return to one of Consuelo's teas.

On one of the last occasions Bruce came to the farm, he brought a lady friend with him. Angela immediately liked Diana and felt she was just what Bruce needed. She was warm, friendly, intelligent and had a good sense of humour. The threesome walked over to Wisborough Green church and arrived back in time for tea.

Eventually, Bruce and Diana married and went to live in Bexhill. Angela still telephones and occasionally calls in when visiting Consuelo's sister, Ruth.

Recently, it came to light that prior to meeting Diana, Bruce felt a bit uncomfortable in Berns' company. In retrospect, he was probably a bit suspicious of a single, older man taking an interest in his young daughter.

Angela's Visit to Roffey

Prior to moving to Bexhill, Bruce lived in a large old house converted into flats. One day, Angela happened to be in the area and just arrived unannounced, suitably clad wearing hot pants. These were short shorts which were very fashionable at the time. Waltzing along the path, she noticed Bruce at the front door, obviously saying goodbye to a male friend. Thinking nothing of it at the time, she just barged in and said her formal hello to her old teacher. The fellow left, but years later, Bruce told Angela that his friend never believed him, when he told him that Angela was just an old pupil from the Weald.

Mr Dennis Marten

Apart from being of average height and build, there was nothing average about Dennis Marten. He had a distinctive look with unusual features. Dennis wore gold-rimmed glasses and his dark eyes screamed with natural intelligence. His jet-black hair was well cut and had a natural wave caressed into place with Brylcreem, resembling the tiny waves on a beach that finally dissipate to nothing. Regardless of setting, he was a dapper dresser, often fashioning a cheroot cigar, a bow tie, and in winter, a camel-coloured coat; its colour matching that of his Rolls-Royce which he owned towards the end of his life.

Dennis was originally from London and had been introduced to Sussex by Harry Laker, Berns' old school friend who lived at Streele Farm, near Billingshurst. They had met at London University in the 1940s, whilst studying Veterinary Science. After qualifying, Dennis settled in West Sussex where he met and married Berns' cousin Betty Lerwill.[51] The couple had a daughter, Angela and two sons, Roger and Danny and lived at Gennetts Farm, near North Heath. Sadly, the marriage did not last and Betty moved away to Lancashire to start a new life whilst Dennis remained at Gennetts.

Dennis was not a conventional James Herriot type of vet and had a number of business interests. He largely split his time between farming, veterinary work and acting as a cattle dealer at local livestock markets in West Sussex. Dennis was a man of many parts, some of which remained an enigma.

Dennis could never be described as a gregarious type, much preferring his own company; essentially, he was a loner. Reserved and self-reliant, he seemed reluctant to talk about his youth or wider family. He approached life in a calculated, contemplative and considered manner.

At market, one would see him seemingly chortling calmly with his apparent chums, leaning over the rails of the sales ring whilst surveying the constant stream of cattle coming in and out. He would nonchalantly glimpse upon the beasts and nod to the auctioneer if bidding. Within seconds, he would deduce whether a beast offered

---

[51] Betty grew up at Northwood Farm.

potential profit or should be left well alone. He was also good at judging people and often circumnavigated around those with whom he had no rapport.

For whatever reason, Dennis seemed to take a bit of a shine to Berns and over the years was supportive to the family. In the early days at Frithwood, Dennis rarely if ever, sent a veterinary bill, and then later he lent Berns scaffolding when the roof of the house was being replaced. Simon Lerwill remembered Dennis always having a boot full of veterinary supplies, which he would let farmers buy at reasonable prices.[52]

Dennis was also a natural teacher and was able to explain difficult things simply. On one occasion, Angela had just arrived home from college to find that Dennis had been summoned to look at a sow with mastitis. As usual, she immediately went out to see him. He told her what the problem was and the amount of antibiotic he was going to give the pig. Unbeknown to Angela, this was going to prove useful in the future.

On returning to college, Angela had an oral examination with the Principal, Mr Harris. The exam was difficult to prepare for and was a bit like pot luck, as students were required to arrive at a given location at a certain time, but questioning could be on any aspect of farming; Angela's time was three fifteen in the afternoon at the piggery. Leaning over a gate, the middle-aged man and the young woman discussed pig ailments. Angela soon veered the conversation round to mastitis and the possible cure, to the minutiae of dosage and frequency. Mr Harris seemed surprised that a marketing and business student had such in-depth knowledge and told her as much.

At around this time, Dennis had acquired a lion cub called Cassius. The lion had belonged to Mr Noye who lived in a caravan in the Billingshurst area. Mr Noye's business involved supplying exotic animals to the circus trade, but after Cassius escaped a couple of times from the caravan, Mr Noye decided that he wanted to get rid of him; hence he came to Gennetts. While Cassius was still a cub, Roger

---

[52] Simon Lerwill was Guy Lerwill's second son by his second marriage to Margaret.

would sometimes take him for walks on a lead, surprising all and sundry. In the meantime, a special pen was constructed.

Visiting the lion became one of those things Angela did whilst she was home with friends from college. A simple telephone call and the party were on their way to Gennetts. On arrival, Dennis or one of the boys would accompany the group to the enclosure. Cassius had an unsocial habit of spraying visitors, so it was always best to keep well away from his cage. Friends were always dumbfounded, but it made for a memorable visit to the depths of West Sussex. Apparently, Simon Lerwill did the same, visiting the lion from time to time.

Word got round that Dennis was an exotic animal vet and was approached by Drusillas Park near Brighton to do work for them. Roger, described how his father had to do research on the particular exotic animal before his visits. This reputation also led to Dennis acquiring a puma called Lindsey.

Simon Lerwill recalled when Lindsey first arrived at the farm. He and Danny had just got back from the pub. The two young men pulled up in the yard parking behind Dennis's cattle lorry. Before going into the house, Danny asked Simon to guess what was in the back of the lorry. Nonplussed, Simon watched the back tailgate plummet as Danny pulled the ropes and through the slatted loading gates two green eyes appeared; it was Lindsey the puma. Lindsey effectively replaced Cassius and lived out the next five to six years at Gennetts. There was never a dull moment with Dennis in charge.

Miss Nelly Francis

Nelly Francis was not an obvious choice for looking after three children under ten. After all, she was in her mid-sixties, a spinster and appeared to barely earn enough to keep herself on her small-holding near Cray Lane railway crossing.

Nevertheless, when her niece presented her with three children to look after, she gave them a loving and stable home. She may have been short of money but she was never short of love.

Nelly's house and few farm buildings were old and tumbledown, and largely held together by a blanket of ivy. Although humble,

Nelly kept the house spotless and there was always a warm welcome for anyone visiting.

Miss Wiggins, the head teacher at North Heath School, was very supportive of Nelly. This was particularly important when the authorities wanted to take the children into care. Miss Wiggins argued that Nelly's love far outweighed any material goods. Fortunately, on this occasion common sense prevailed.

The children, Pamela, Charles and David were a similar age to Angela and attended the same schools. All three matured and went on to be a credit to Nelly's love and devotion.

Mr Roy Theobald

Roy Theobald was Rhona's first husband. They met when Rhona was sixteen and married when she was eighteen. Roy had grown up in Bookham and the couple lived in Dorking, then Mid Holmwood. Roy was essentially a country boy at heart and loved coming to the farm and helping with all manner of jobs.

Often, the couple would arrive either for the day or weekend and Roy would disappear, carrying on with something he had started last time or being directed by Berns or Consuelo to something new. Consuelo often mentioned Roy's support and help in her diaries. He was practical and loved nothing better than burying himself under a bonnet of an old oily tractor or car.

He was also good to Angela. Many a time, Roy and Rhona would detour to collect Angela from a night out with friends before visiting the farm. On one occasion, they collected Angela from the Well Diggers pub near Petworth after an evening of carol singing with the Ebernoe Young Farmers.

Even when Angela had left home, she always knew that she was welcome at Mid Holmwood, where there was a meal and a bed for the night. Many a time she would stay there when working in London, whilst running her own business, Lerwill Associates from Gloucestershire.[53]

Roy was a kind and gentle person who always put others first.

---

[53] Lerwill Associates: a small market research business specialising in the printing industry.

Mrs Annora Esther Osmarston

After old Mr Osmarston died in 1972, the two sons, Henry and Miles, placed their mother in a care home. Their old Edwardian house, The Elms in Wisborough Green, stood in a time warp devoid of humans, but bursting with their ageing possessions. Breathing in the dank smell of old horsehair and mustiness, Angela was reminded of an Agatha Christie novel. Nevertheless, things were about to change for the old lady.

Desperately unhappy, it was decided that Mrs Osmarston would return to The Elms and live in one of the cottages (called Stills), previously built for a gardener or chauffeur. In due course, a full-time housekeeper, Joan, was employed and moved into the adjoining cottage, but she would need that inconvenient thing called *time off*. This is where Angela came into the story.

Having completed her A-levels, Angela was looking for any work that was honest, paid more than Berns and was accessible by bicycle. After a few weeks, she had successfully secured a part-time job from Miles Osmarston to help look after his mother during the summer holidays. Day-to-day duties were supposed to be discussed between Joan and Angela, however, Miles liked to meddle in minutiae.

Miles and his family lived on the outskirts of London and he would pop in regularly to monitor the situation. Over the forthcoming weeks, and talking with Joan and Mrs Osmarston, Angela pieced together that Miles was probably the son who had been a bit of a disappointment and had not had a proper career. His forte was fussing, fretting and flapping.

On one occasion, Angela had returned in the early evening to prepare Mrs Osmarston's supper, when Miles arrived. He found his mother and Angela at the dining-room table, each tucking into a boiled egg and toast. The next day, he telephoned Angela at Frithwood, to say that eating supper with his mother had not been part of their arrangement and that if she wanted to continue this, he would have to deduct 70p for each supper. Miles seemed unable or unwilling to appreciate that his mother needed and wanted the company.

Apart from these minor interruptions and annoyances, Angela (aged eighteen) enjoyed helping Mrs Osmarston (aged nearly eighty). They would quietly chat over a cup of tea after lunch before Mrs Osmarston had her rest and Angela would depart to either cycle home or go on to another part-time job.

Angela fondly remembers some of the topics they talked about. One involved an oil painting which hung in the small sitting room. The subject was a little girl in Victorian dress, with a big floppy hat, sitting on a swing. Although the picture was quite small, the frame surrounding the image was chunky and garishly decorated with gold gilt. Angela studied the painting looking for a signature, thinking that it looked like a Manet. Knowing that she was no art historian, she felt she did not want to ask and look foolish. One day however, while taking a cup of tea with Mrs Osmarston she could not hold back any longer and blurted out, 'Is that painting by Manet?' Mrs Osmarston nonchalantly confirmed that indeed it was and that sometimes it went on loan to various London exhibitions.

On another occasion, Mrs Osmarston asked Angela what she intended to do with her afternoon. Angela replied that she planned to go horse riding. Mrs Osmarston asked if Angela would be grooming her pony herself. She felt that this was a strange question. Who else would groom her pony? The reason behind Mrs Osmarston's quizzing soon became apparent. She explained that although she had ridden as a youngster, she had never been allowed to groom her pony, as this was not a job for a young lady but one for the groom.

The conversation continued and Angela mentioned that she might ride to Haybarn. Quick as a flash, the old lady asked if the old bridge over the river was still standing. Angela explained that the bridge had long since gone, washed away by floodwater but that the support posts were still visible when the water level was low enough. Mrs Osmarston smiled and explained that even in her youth, the bridge had been in bad order and that when using it with a pony and trap, someone had to lead the pony over it so as to avoid the holes in its wooden base.

As the old lady had only recently returned to Wisborough Green from the care home, she sometimes remembered old possessions in the big house and requested that they should be found and brought to her. Quite often, Joan delegated this task to Angela. These excursions were like a journey back in time, with everything covered in dust sheets. Entrusted with a large set of keys, she would set off to explore. Often these forays took longer than necessary as Angela immersed herself in the cornucopia of Edwardian treasures. Once, Mrs Osmarston asked whether she had entered via the back door through the scullery.

Angela had noticed the scullery; it was a small, dingy, dark space with only a small window above eye level, furnished with a low-sided sink and taps positioned quite high up the wall, presumably to allow large pans to be washed. Mrs Osmarston asked whether Angela had noticed the high plate rack above the sink. The old lady said that once, she had been in the kitchen when she noticed that the plate rack looked awkwardly high for the short scullery maid. She asked the girl if she found the plate rack too high. The maid replied 'Oh yes, mam, sometimes I chucks them up there, and sometimes they goes in and sometimes they don't.' Angela and the old lady both laughed.

In retrospect, Angela wishes that she had made notes of her various conversations with this wonderful old lady, a true relic of the Edwardian era.

The Steele Family

Although Berns and Consuelo lived at Frithwood for many years, their circle of true friends could be counted on one hand. The Steele family were one such example and farmed at West Chiltington. They rented a property from West Sussex County Council and were essentially dairy farmers.

Mac Steele had a dimple on his chin which always reminded Angela of Kirk Douglas, the Hollywood actor. In Angela's young eyes, Mac was a star, as he always took an active interest in her life and had a great sense of humour. He was a busy, intelligent and capable man, but always had time for others and was an active member of the West Chiltington Parish Council and the National Farmers' Union for a number of years.

Alma, Mac's wife, was a friendly, outgoing woman with an excellent brain, a brilliant cook and was highly motivated. She had been a land girl during the Second World War and had met Mac on a blind date. As Consuelo was to Berns, so Alma was to Mac; a bedrock of support and encouragement. With her entrepreneurial skills, she quickly realised that their old farmhouse could be turned into a business venture. Consequently, she established a thriving farmhouse bed and breakfast business, well before it became popular, which she ran for many years.

The couple had three boys (Alex, Duncan and Matthew) who were all slightly younger than the three Lerwill siblings. During the long winter months, the two families sometimes spent the evening together, enjoying a cold supper alongside tea and coffee. Alcohol was rarely offered and never to the children.

On these occasions, the youngsters would bundle upstairs into Hugh's den and chat away the hours while the adults chortled over farm issues downstairs around the log fire. However, Matthew was a funny little boy with lots of energy and was sometimes shut out of Hugh's pad, as he was thought to be a bit of a nuisance. On one occasion, his frustration resulted in him head-butting the softboard wall next to Hugh's bedroom door, making quite a dent. On admitting his crime to Consuelo in the kitchen, she agreed not to tell his parents on condition that he came downstairs and calmed down. One can just imagine Consuelo bending to Matthew's height and saying, 'Let's say no more about it.'

As the older siblings matured and left home, only Angela and Matthew remained at school and their friendship deepened. The two adolescents always had plenty to talk about regarding family secrets and current antics. Often, the pair would have a laugh at their parents' expense but only in a loving, knowing way.

Contact intensified during the 1970s when Alma would pass on bed and breakfast leads to Consuelo, and Mac bought hens' eggs from Berns to sell at their farm gate. In retrospect, this was particularly important to Consuelo. She was deeply missing Joan

Croom's company from the Lodge at Lee Place as they had moved to Devon by this time. Geographically isolated and with new, wealthier and younger neighbours, local residents were changing.

Years rolled by and the two widows ended their lives living in bungalows less than a mile apart in West Chiltington. Today, the younger generations still keep in touch, happy that they had shared such a rich patchwork of childhood memories.

The Luckin Family

The Luckins farmed at Orfold Farm just outside Wisborough Green on the A272 to Billingshurst, a short distance from the Lerwills. They were a strange family with lots of eccentricities. Berns and Eddie had met at school and had been friends for many years.

Eddie was not too bothered about his appearance and, although tidy, was a bit rough around the edges. Angela remembers that, whereas Berns would always shave sufficiently below his collar line to be tidy around his shirt collar, Eddie's collar line sometimes revealed a forest of hair trying to escape. Eddie usually wore a brown serge coat over his workwear which also looked a bit quaint. Presumably, this was to help keep clean while working on the farm.

From time to time, Berns bought cereals and feed potatoes from Eddie. Cereals would usually be delivered by tractor and trailer load, whereas Berns usually collected feed potatoes in the van or estate car. Settling up was usually done in a social setting, combining business with pleasure and sharing a coffee and a catch-up. In later years, Berns and Consuelo would sometimes have lunch at Orfold.

Pam was demure and meek as Eddie was not. She had come to Sussex from the London area during the Second World War as a land girl and married Eddie a year or two before Berns and Consuelo. They lived in the rambling farmhouse with old Mrs Luckin and their two children, Vivien and John. Mrs Luckin senior had always been involved in the farm accounts and records, and it appeared that she was quite domineering. Consuelo and Pam became good friends and would sometimes chat on the phone. However, walking over to Orfold to visit her was something else.

Eddie was territorial and hated anyone crossing his land even on designated footpaths. Paths were frequently barred and barbed wire strapped round gateposts with 'keep out' signs. Nevertheless, this did not deter Consuelo as she would simply telephone ahead and seek permission. This saved any potential embarrassment as Eddie was known to rant and rave at intruders from afar. Sadly, Pam only once walked over to see Consuelo at Frithwood. She was a shy person.

Hugh seemed to have more success in infiltrating the Orfold bastion as he and John became friends in their young teenage years, whilst attending the Weald School. The boys would often watch television on Saturday afternoons while Vivien canoodled with her boyfriend on the sofa. They also tackled the sparrow population with their air guns. Many a weekend, the boys would be together.

Unlike the Lerwill siblings who went to school regularly, John often took days off to help Eddie. By the time John left school at sixteen, the boys were starting to drift apart as their futures started to diverge. John left school and went back on the farm to help full-time, whereas Hugh stayed on to take A-levels.

John was always cocky and regularly called Berns by his first name which was unheard of at the time; etiquette demanded formal address. Gradually, John's eccentricities developed and as his hair got longer at the sides, it appeared to become thinner on top. To counterbalance this, he took to constantly wearing a cowboy hat. The Lerwills even joked as to whether he wore it in bed. He also used to sport a large sheath knife in a leather case, which he strapped to his right leg like a gun-runner in the Midwest. He reminded Angela of some of the actors in *The Beverly Hillbillies* television programme in the 1960s.

Prior to the Wey and Arun Canal Trust being formed in 1970, Eddie sold Orfold Aqueduct to the river authority for £1, thinking that he had rid himself of a liability. However, once Eddie knew the Trust's plan, he was horrified at the prospect of people tramping over his land and promptly filled in his section of the canal. He was adamant that no canal restoration would happen on his watch. However, strangers were about to get even closer to Eddie … in the house.

During the early 1970s, farmhouse bed and breakfast had become increasingly popular. Orfold's old farmhouse was well-suited to this as it was only a short distance off the main road, was the first building on the drive and was divided into two halves. The oldest part was at the back and used by Pam, Eddie and the family, while the old Victorian part in the front was used by Mrs Luckin in her later days. In between old Mrs Luckin's death in February 1974 and John's marriage, this space lay dormant.

However, the catalyst for the bed and breakfast venture at Orfold was quite amusing. Pam told Consuelo that Eddie had bought a job lot of mustard-yellow gloss paint and used it to paint the outside windows; the problem was that she hated it. Thus, Pam's first target was to pay for the windows to be repainted. Within a short time, Pam had not only paid for the repainting but had a thriving business, often sending Consuelo surplus guests in the late 1970s.

Until the mid-1980s, Orfold was predominately a dairy and arable farm. The pedigree dairy Shorthorn herd was Eddie's pride and joy and he would sometimes show and judge cattle. However, by this time, the size and breed of the herd was simply no longer financially viable. On 10 August 1985, Orfold hosted a dispersal sale and the cows were sold. Consuelo's diary entry describes Eddie *looking very sad*. After a short time, the old farm buildings were also sold and dismantled. It was the end of an era.

Eddie's other passion was his garden. His vegetable patch was worth seeing and was an exemplar. It was situated just outside the old kitchen, sandwiched between the house and the old moat, which was lined with trees giving the plot protection from westerly winds. Sitting outside the kitchen door, having a drink was a sheer delight, as Eddie did not tolerate weeds and only grew vegetables in military straight lines. It was a showcase, although some of the magic came from the extensive use of artificial fertilisers and pesticides. Often, he would exhibit flowers and vegetables at the Wisborough Green Flower Show, dropping off early in his grey minivan and returning late to avoid the crowd. In 1994, Eddie won no less than thirty-one awards at the flower show.

Although he was essentially a private man, Eddie was very

competitive. In addition to the flower show, he liked to be first in the area to cut hay or start combining. On more than one occasion, Eddie's impatience cost a water-brook's worth of hay as a late flood took it towards Pallingham Manor and beyond, much to the amusement of the Lerwills spying from the far side of the River Arun.

For many years, surplus produce was sold at the farm gate. Goods would be stacked in the porch by the other back door, near to the drive. Local horse owners would also call in to buy a few small bales of hay and straw. This was about as much social mixing Eddie could tolerate with outsiders.

Unfortunately, John's marriage ended at about the time Eddie died. John continued arable farming until his mother passed away in 2013. The farm was then sold.

Mr and Mrs Sidney Butt

One Monday morning at Pulborough Market in the mid-1960s, Berns' friend George Harding asked if he might be interested in having a caravan parked at the farm. George knew a London couple called Sheila and Sidney Butt who needed to find a new pitch for their small weekend caravan; importantly they had no children and no dog. Was Berns interested?

The small, pale-green caravan was duly installed at the top of the hill next to the bridleway. Sidney built a small annex for the Elsan toilet and a small lean-to shed.[54]

Sidney worked for one of the daily newspapers in Fleet Street and liked to escape London at weekends, driving to Sussex in his Armstrong Siddeley car. Sheila was older than Sidney, and spent a lot of time chain-smoking and plastering her face with make-up. Rhona and Angela found this amusing as Consuelo only ever used a bit of lipstick and that was usually applied as an afterthought.

In the warm summer months, the Butts came most weekends and would often have a cup of tea at the farmhouse while collecting a

[54] Elsan: a generic term for a chemical toilet.

container of water. Sometimes Consuelo and the children would visit them after lunch, often sitting outside sharing the view across to Wisborough Green. Conversations were varied and sometimes involved discussing new trends in the metropolis. One covered the subject of a new craze for an Italian dish called spaghetti bolognese.

Sheila sold its merits and told Consuelo that it was easy to cook and popular. Armed with Sheila's recipe, Consuelo got organised and cooked it for the family. Naturally, Berns was not keen due to his stomach problems and it being *foreign*. The rest of the family ate quickly having thoroughly enjoyed the new cuisine; however, within a short time several of them had terrible indigestion. In retrospect, they had probably just over-indulged or eaten too quickly but it fuelled Berns' fear of *'foreign muck'*. Sadly, this put an abrupt halt to trying foreign food at the farm.

Visits continued and then started to ease off, until one weekend Sheila announced that Sidney was having an affair and that they would be divorcing. This was a sad end to some happy times chortling away with the townies at the top of the hill.

Mr Ernest Bicknel and Mrs Biddy White

Forest Stores at Wisborough Green delivered groceries to Frithwood for about fifteen years. Usually, Consuelo would telephone her list through to the shop on Monday or early on Tuesday, ready for the delivery on Wednesday. If she forgot, Mr Spooner the manager would phone her.

Just before teatime, Ernest Bicknel would arrive in his van and carry the heavy box of groceries into the scullery. Knowing it was his last delivery of the day, Ernest would enjoy a cup of tea with Consuelo whilst checking off the items against the list and catching up on local news. Hugh remembers that the groceries came to about £8 a week in the 1960s.

Ernest was not a typical van-delivery man. He was a middle-aged, well-spoken, intelligent man who was over-qualified for his role. His clothing never varied; he wore a tweed jacket, collar and tie and washable nylon trousers. Kindness came naturally to him and he nearly always brought a bar of chocolate for the siblings to share, and greeted them with 'Hello ducks.'

Ernest was never a gossip and rarely spoke detrimentally about anybody, however, on one occasion he revealed a sad and pathetic story about a customer. Angela, aged about eight at the time, listened with intent as the tale unravelled.

Biddy White lived in a big old house called Burdocks, near Coldharbour on the road from Wisborough Green to Fittleworth. Ernest chronicled the slippery journey from a middle-aged Biddy, still capable of scratching a living, to an elderly lady unable to accept her years. Pastures had become a wasteland with towering, unkept hedges romping away, as if they were auditioning for a rewilding film, and the ramshackle outbuildings looking neglected and abandoned.

The hovel-like house was almost buried in creepers and undergrowth. The interior was cluttered and filthy, but what resonated with Angela was not this degradation, but Ernest recounting the dreadful smell of stale urine hitting his nostrils before entering the dilapidated old dwelling.

Angela realised that there was a lesson in this story for her to prepare well ahead for old age.

Mr George Neave

George Neave was Consuelo's uncle on her father's side of the family. He worked in Brighton, in an office job he detested, but stuck at it until retirement. George married Evelyn (known as Eve) and they lived in a post-First World War villa house in Portslade, near Hove. Sadly, they never had a family of their own.

Being a school holiday-boarder, Consuelo's only taste of real family life was staying with George and Eve for brief spells. In retrospect, this was probably quite an ordeal for George, who was serious and a stickler on manners and decorum, and must have found Consuelo and her siblings quite a handful. Consuelo adored the couple and was sad when Eve died of cancer just before Hugh was born. Eve's sister, Bree, then came and looked after George until he died.

Although particular, George adored the outdoor life and visiting the farm, albeit being a bit primitive. On the days preceding his visits, Consuelo would be on edge, cleaning and tidying. Held in high esteem, Consuelo wanted her favourite uncle to be proud of her growing family.

George loved the three Lerwill siblings, treating them more like grandchildren, although he was never at ease with children. When Angela was young, she was a bit frightened of this tall serious man and was reluctant to go over and kiss him when he arrived. He apparently mentioned this to Consuelo, who sensibly said that once Angela was sure of him, she would eventually treat him to a kiss. It worked.

George was keen on education and encouraged the children to study hard at school. He was keen on learning himself and when Hugh was about ten years old, started sending a weekly publication called *Look and Learn*. After reading it thoroughly, he would send it on to Hugh. This was greatly appreciated as the children did not have comics.

George was sadly missed by the whole family when he died in the mid-1970s.

Consuelo's Old Friends

People naturally gravitated towards Consuelo and she acquired friends throughout her life, often keeping in touch through letters. Nursing buddies tended to be townies and had little or no knowledge of farming life but enjoyed their summer visits. Marjorie, Hilda and Liz were nursing colleagues from Brighton, and Jean and Margaret were friends acquired from Consuelo's Horsham days.

Marjorie had a difficult marriage and a large family of wild children, who would descend on the farm and literally eat everything Consuelo laid on the tea table. Consuelo was compassionate and tried hard for several years to turn a blind eye, realising that life was hard for her old friend. The friendship came to an abrupt close when Marjorie pushed Consuelo too far on a matter concerning her eldest daughter. Consuelo tried to be kind but was not going to be taken advantage of by anyone. It was the final straw.

Hilda and Liz were older than Consuelo and visited together in the early days. With a freshly cleaned out van, Berns would collect them from Pulborough Station, having placed an armchair in the back for the second lady. The children found this amusing as it looked a bit like a throne.

Hilda was tall, quite good-looking and had a posh voice. Liz was shorter and had a stockier build. Berns called them, 'The fat one and the thin one.' They would tell the children all sorts of stories about their parents, when they were courting, including smuggling Consuelo through the window when she was late back to the Nurses' Home on more than one occasion. The children loved to hear them telling tales.

Time moved on and Hilda went to work at a home for retired servicemen where she met George. Hilda would then bring him to the farm where George and Berns became friends. On one visit, Hilda offered Berns a ticket for the Irish Sweepstake. He agreed but said he wanted the second coupon in the book. The voucher resulted in Consuelo's first fridge. Sadly, George died in April 1983.

Margaret and Jean were Horsham friends and lived in the same road, Three Acres. Margaret and Alan had three daughters of about Angela's age. As the family grew, the allure of free pony rides and a farmhouse tea meant that their phone calls sometimes came a bit too frequently at busy times but were rarely refused by Consuelo.

Jean was married to Peter, who was a successful carpet fitter and they had two youngsters, Jayne and Tim. Occasionally the two families would socialise together and the children became friends. Later in 1970, Rhona lodged with Peter and Jean whilst attending Crawley Technical College in her first year. This made leaving home for her at sixteen a bit easier.

Friends in Later Years

Over the years, many friends and acquaintances came along and helped Berns and Consuelo with various work around the farm; mostly unpaid. Other friends helped in other ways by taking Consuelo shopping or to cultural events or offering the use of their swimming pools. Although kind, Consuelo was never a *taker* and always tried to return the favour in some small way.

As the siblings grew up and left home, harvesting became particularly challenging. Friends came to the rescue. Angela's old school friends, Kay and Roger Hird were very kind and helped out for a number of years before having a family. The Arter and Wales families also helped with harvest and other tasks. Helping at Frithwood was very popular with young children.

People were good to Consuelo because she was good to them. Her natural humility, compromise, kindness and balance made her company refreshing and uplifting. In 1989, Andrew Wales took Consuelo for a flight in his plane over the Arun Valley which she loved.

Other new neighbours were supportive in different ways. Pat Hill and Graham Pratt lived at Northwood and took Consuelo on holiday to France several times. Time to relax around a warm sunny swimming pool was bliss for Consuelo. Armed with a few freezer meals, Berns could just about tolerate Consuelo's absence. Just before she returned, one of the siblings would arrive to welcome her home and tidy and clean through the farmhouse.

Nevertheless, Consuelo tried to help Pat where she could, always making herself available to help with Pat's Open Garden Days. She also gave a coffee morning in 1996 to raise money for Pat's mercy trip to Sarajevo taking clothes and supplies to the war-torn capital; she raised £180.

Jane and Michael Joseph at Woodlands were also very kind. Sometimes, the couple would take Consuelo to musical concerts at Christ's Hospital or to a theatre further afield. Once, Michael brought a beautiful piece of Thai silk back from Bangkok for Consuelo which she made into a fabulous skirt. Jane and Consuelo got on particularly well as both women were keen on botany and gardening. Many times, the two ladies would venture across Lordings Rough to show the other a botanical treasure they had just discovered. When Jane and Michael had their young family, Consuelo would sometimes babysit.

As well as support and friendship, Consuelo was fortunate, as at least three different lots of friends had swimming pools by the time they left the farm. She never took advantage of this and only ever went if invited. However, she loved the treat of a swim during the summer months, often combining it with a quick chat before returning home.

Adversane To Woodlands Lane

'When wealth is lost, nothing is lost;
When health is lost, something is lost;
When character is lost, everything is lost.'

BILLY GRAHAM (1918–2018)

Mrs Elizabeth Pinches

Frank and Elizabeth Pinches moved to Woodlands Farm in the 1960s and were Guernsey dairy farmers. Elizabeth suffered with rheumatism and did not play an active role on the farm. The couple had two children who were older than the Lerwill siblings; a son, Michael, who went to Southampton University and a daughter, Ann, who helped Frank on the farm. Apart from family responsibilities, Elizabeth enjoyed reading, current affairs, history, gardening and attending the Women's Institute in Billingshurst.

She was also a member of the National Trust and once took Rhona to Uppark, near Petersfield, probably one of the first times Rhona had explored a grand house. It was quite an adventure. Later in life, Rhona was to come across Uppark in her career at Sun Alliance, which handled the insurance claim after the extensive fire in 1989.

The Pinches had a television long before the Lerwills and were generous, allowing the children to come and watch *Compact* and *Doctor Who* on a regular basis. Frank was a great fan of *Doctor Who* and would milk the cows early on Saturday afternoons so that he could participate. It was a ritual that about four-thirty in the afternoon, the three siblings would trundle over to Woodlands and sit glued to the television. Angela can remember hiding behind the sofa to avoid watching the frightening bits featuring the Daleks.

Rhona and Angela spent happy times in Elizabeth's company.

Rhona recalls on one wet afternoon being kept amused having to fill a matchbox with as many items as possible. On another occasion, Rhona fancied becoming a journalist and Elizabeth would let her have old newspapers to read and study.

On one visit, Elizabeth's father was visiting and met Angela aged about four. He told her that he was a 'Tough old bird.' On returning home she recounted the quote as 'A tough old rook', which amused her parents.

Westlands Farm Cottage and its Inhabitants

The Willis-Thomas ladies were a mother-in-law (Tommy) and a daughter-in-law (Dorothy) duo who lived at Westlands Farm Cottage on the lane between Woodlands Farm and Adversane. After losing Ron, the two ladies eked out an existence that was simple, tending their garden and taking much pleasure from their cats and the Sussex countryside. Their cottage reflected their quaint ways and was beautifully unspoilt by modern conveniences.

Unremarkable on the outside, the house was constructed largely of brick, interspersed with some elements of Wealden sandstone. It had a rectangular layout with a chimney at each end. Looking from the front, it had a central front door and a living room on each side.

The front door opened straight into the left-hand sitting room, and immediately displayed an enormous inglenook fireplace on the far, left-hand wall. It was an extremely cold room as the chimney proudly boasted a good view of the sky through its narrowing aperture. This room was rarely used by humans or cats, although chairs were adorned with throws just so the odd cat could change its mind. To the back of this room was a primitive bathroom that had a low beam, below which one had to stoop before using the toilet.

On the right-hand side was the main living room, which was blessed with a Rayburn that acted like a magnet for cats and humans alike, especially in the winter. After passing through what felt like 'Scott of the Antarctic territory' one was welcomed by a kettle singing on the old range and a smell of coal dust and a fug of cats. With Tommy seated comfortably in her armchair, sandwiched between the Rayburn and the window and engaged in entertaining their guests, Dorothy would busy herself making the tea and getting the cake out of its tin. Spare seating frequently had to be brought in from the other room, as space was at a premium and preference was given to the cats and their paraphernalia. One intelligent cat had commandeered an ingenious position on the large shelf behind the Rayburn, well out the way of a human foot or any draught.

The garden surrounding the cottage was random in shape and had a feeling of evolution rather than design. A tall, largely unkempt hedge hugged the lane as it curved round the adjoining field, giving the ladies their privacy. Halfway along, there were the remains of an old Anderson shelter. The focal point in the front garden was a small barn built of Wealden sandstone that helped to shield the cottage from the driving wind and rain which were prevalent in the winter. However, most of the garden was to the back of the cottage.

On the far side, an old pond could just about be seen, snuggling under some overhanging tree cover, presumably used by ducks and geese in yesteryears. On the west side, was a ramshackle gate hung at a slant and used by previous occupants as a short cut to get to work on Westlands Farm. In retrospect, the cottage, its garden and its residents gave one the idea of a bygone age and of things slipping away. However, at the time the Lerwills visited, it was company and friendship that were important. The future could look after itself.

As the cottage was on Angela's normal route to secondary school, she and Consuelo would sometimes arrange to meet there after school. With a timorous knock at the front door, they were always made welcome and the four of them would chat away about local and garden news, over tea and cake. Recollections of conversations are limited. However, Tommy did tell Angela that she had been one of the first women of her generation to use a typewriter and work in an office outside the home. As Tommy was born in 1883, this would have made her aged seventeen at the turn of the century when she probably would have started work. Tommy died on 10 October 1981 aged ninety-eight and Dorothy on 2 September 1985.

Sunwood and the Treens

After Mr Paynter's death, Sunwood was sold to Mary and John Treen. They were a middle-aged couple who had a grown-up family. Looking back, they were an unusual pairing.

Mr Treen was said to be an inventor, but no one ever knew what he had invented. He was quite a tall man, slightly hunched, wore large baggy cord trousers with a belt and had a Hitler-type moustache. He was quiet and was rarely seen. He had a brother who looked similar and after a few years he came to live at Sunwood in a small caravan in the garden. Quite what he did with his time was also a mystery. Somehow, Sunwood never looked a happy house.

Mary was from a different mould from her husband. She was of medium height, had a full figure, almost butch, short grey hair and always had a cigarette in her hand or mouth. Sometimes, when concentrating, she would purse her lips, almost like she was relying on the cigarette for inspiration. Her right index finger and female quiff of hair over her brow both boasted a patina of nicotine suggesting that she smoked a good deal.

In the summer, Mary could often be found in the garden. If Consuelo and the children were out walking, they would often stop and have a chat. On these occasions, Mary would frequently be wearing a strapless top which looked as though it was made of a large tea cloth wrapped around her ample bosom, displaying a wonderful bronze suntan. With large, cumbersome breasts, Mary needed to take care when bending over in case they escaped. Her personality was brisk and feisty, almost bombastic, and a bit intimidating to the young Lerwill children.

Mary bred, showed and sold bull terriers. After buying the bungalow, a few kennels and two exercise pens were built, probably accommodating about four to six bitches. The dogs were kept on sawdust and the soiled bedding was stacked in small piles out of sight of the house, along the hedge parallel to the bridlepath. On dry days, Mary would try and burn the muck, which would smolder and release the most pungent and repugnant smell. The Lerwill siblings hated those days of reeking whiffs, as they walked or cycled past. It was revolting.

Fortunately, over the years Mary and Dorothy Willis-Thomas became close friends, and Mary would often take Dorothy shopping. This was especially important to the ageing Dorothy who had no transport of her own. Although a bit gruff on the outside, Mary was a kind soul.

Sadly, Mary died quite suddenly on 25 May 1989.

A Sadness Descends

The lane between Adversane and Woodlands Farm is about a mile long and in the early days had about six dwellings. However, during the 1960s, a fistful of sadness uncurled and unfurled, involving three households: the Pinches, the Wells and the Garbetts. A serious brain injury and two young deaths struck like lightning.

Following a fairly routine operation, Frank Pinches slipped in the cattle yard and hit his head incurring a serious bleed on the brain. He was rushed to Southampton General Hospital for urgent surgery. Fortunately, Frank survived the ordeal, but it soon became obvious that his farming days were over. The farm was sold to Ted Cripps in 1972, and Frank and Elizabeth moved to Wigmore in Shropshire to start an early retirement.

The Wells family lived, effectively, in a shack, which had originally been built as an artist's studio, probably in the 1920s. However, by the mid-1960s it was barely habitable and had a leaky roof. Consuelo had seen the bowls collecting water and empathised with the family. While Mrs Wells contended with walking along the bumpy lane with a pushchair minus one wheel with the children, her husband continued to travel in style in an old Jaguar car.

Geoffrey was the eldest of three boys, and was a likeable lad. On leaving school and getting a job, disaster struck and he died. Fortuitously, Geoffrey had taken out a life insurance policy and this helped to pay for the bungalow that now stands in the middle of the paddock.

The Garbetts lived at Westlands Farm and produced eggs in a small way, letting the adjoining land to Berns for a few years in the 1960s. The Garbetts' three children attended Arundale, a private school in Pulborough. Mrs Garbett was a fair bit younger than her husband and on occasions could be a bit snooty. When Ann, the eldest child, was about ten years old, she died of cancer. After this tumultuous event, Mrs Garbett's stiff exterior mellowed.

Strong Legs Essential

'A loud noise at one end
and no sense of responsibility at the other.'

ATTRIBUTED TO MONSIGNOR RONALD KNOX (1888–1957)

North Heath Church of England School

As Hugh approached school age, Berns and Consuelo started discussing schooling options. Their final choice was North Heath Church of England School on the A29 between Brinsbury and Codmore Hill, probably as there was a school taxi which would collect and deliver Hugh from Snape Farm, a mile away from Frithwood.

Consuelo always prepared a substantial cooked breakfast for the children, usually involving eggs. She would then bundle the children into the green van and take them to the taxi pick-up point.[55] However, once old enough, all three used their bicycles. Angela was proud of her second-hand red bike, lovingly renovated by John Croom for her fifth birthday. At the time, there were only six properties occupied from Snape: Haybourne Cottage, Northwood Farmhouse, Lee Place Lodge, Lee Place Farmhouse, one of Lee Place Farm Cottages and Frithwood, so there was comparatively little traffic.[56] Once collected, the taxi driver would continue to collect other children along Pickhurst Lane and Gay Street.

North Heath was a typical Victorian primary school consisting of two classrooms, a porch used for hanging coats and outside facilities across a small yard containing Elsan toilets. The staff consisted of two full-time teachers, Miss Wiggins and Miss Masefield, a part-time

---

[55] The lane from Frithwood to Snape was a private road which allowed Consuelo to drive without a licence.

[56] Lee Place House was then owned by the Tipladies who lived overseas and were rarely in residence.

117

school secretary, Mrs Laudenbach, and two dinner ladies, Mrs Geary and Mrs Reed.

On arrival, the children would quickly find their friends and run about until Miss Wiggins came outside with a big handbell. After forming a line, they would file into school assembly held in one end of Miss Wiggins' classroom. Younger children sat cross-legged on the floor, the older ones on chairs. Centre stage, in the front were Miss Wiggins and Miss Masefield. After the usual mix of prayers, singing a hymn or two, a Bible story and school notices, the children returned to their classrooms to start their lessons.

Around mid-morning, the two classes totalling about forty to fifty children would have a short break. During this time, they were expected to go to the toilet, drink their one-third of a pint of free milk, and run off a bit of energy. Appointed milk monitors then had to wash and dry the foil bottle tops which were collected for Guide Dogs for the Blind. In the winter, hungry blue tits sometimes pecked the foil tops for the cream below.

Hot lunches were delivered about 12.30 p.m. from Billingshurst Primary School which had a school kitchen. From about midday, the children would start to get a bit fractious and tummies rumbled. On hearing Peg's delivery van, it was action stations as the hot food was brought into the building in large aluminium cannisters and trays, and rapidly dispensed.

School lunches were bland and rarely relished. Beef stew with pearl barley was a particular problem for both Rhona and Angela as the barley was usually rock hard. At the time, children had to eat their main course to earn their pudding and go outside to play. Sometimes Rhona and Angela preferred to forgo their pudding and playtime to avoid the torment of gritty pearl barley against their teeth. One day, Rhona resorted to spitting it into her handkerchief and discreetly depositing it over the school hedge.

At about 3 p.m., school would finish and the children would pile into the taxi once more to return to Snape Farm. Usually, Rhona and Hugh wandered back along the lane with the Badun children from Lee Place Farmhouse. At Lee Place Lodge, they would either follow the track back to the farm through Northwood or, if it was dry enough, wander along the Lodge Field bridlepath. Sometimes, Consuelo might meet them with Hemp and Angela in the pram, and the party would ramble home together. The van was rarely used in the afternoons.

One afternoon, Consuelo met them at Clapper's Pond. Rhona remembers that there had been torrential rain and after arriving back from school they found Clapper's Pond flooded. Fortunately, Consuelo had anticipated the problem, and had walked to meet them with their gumboots. Ever practical, she threw them across the flooded road. They waded across and then chucked the boots back for the Badun children.

Miss Joan Masefield

Miss Joan Masefield was the niece of the Poet Laureate, John Masefield. She lived in a rented cottage on the Stopham Estate, between Pulborough and Fittleworth. Normally, she would walk to school, but sometimes used the infrequent bus service. Vanity was never part of her persona. She wore home-knitted cardigans and warm plaid tartan skirts, strictly below the knee, and flat walking shoes. Her hair was simply fashioned into a bob, often featuring a Kirby-grip each side of her middle parting keeping the odd obstinate strands at bay. She also wore thick glasses.

Consuelo called Miss Masefield 'A little quaint.' The first time the two women met was when Consuelo went to North Heath to arrange for Hugh to start school. As they sat face-to-face, Miss Masefield informed Consuelo that after leaving school, her father had given her the choice of either teaching or nursing children. She expounded that as she hated children, she felt teaching healthy ones might be preferable to sick ones. This was not quite the mantra a parent expected. However, she was an excellent teacher and the children loved her no-nonsense approach.

Miss Masefield was a good storyteller and she seemed to have a bottomless pit of tales. The stories most loved were of her grandfather's naughty parrot. As Miss Masefield sat on the edge of her chair, her legs splayed out, she would laugh and chuckle and reveal the most enormous pair of pastel-shade bloomers, which the youngsters found highly entertaining.

One story involved her grandfather employing a new governess. In the kerfuffle of the young lady arriving and being shown to her ground-floor room, the parrot had somehow been popped onto the windowsill and forgotten about, hidden from view by a drawn curtain. Some hours later, when the governess was preparing for bed, she heard some whistling and saucy comments coming from the window. On closer inspection, she drew back the curtains to find that the parrot had pecked a hole and had been spying on her. As the story unfolded, both teacher and the children roared with laughter.

Miss Masefield's first lesson was usually related to news and weather. As she was a gifted artist, she would draw a simple picture of the current weather on the blackboard. A windy day was always a runaway umbrella with its keeper hanging on. The children had writing books with a plain bit at the top and lines at the bottom. They were required to draw their own picture of the day and then write a few lines below, finishing off with patterns and colouring, but keeping within the lines. Later, Angela realised that this was all about hand–eye coordination, but at the time it was just fun.

Angela was fond of Miss Masefield and continued to keep in touch and occasionally visited her in Stopham until she died in 1991 aged eighty.

The Winter of 1962/63

Snow started falling heavily on Boxing Day 1962 and remained on the ground until March 1963. Rhona remembered waking to her world being transformed from a bustling farm into an eerie stillness. Looking around, she saw that the old barn, cart shed and hovel had been covered by a confetti of virgin snow; a white Disneyland.

On the first morning, Berns had quite a job even getting out of the house as the snow had drifted against the back door. Fortunately, Consuelo had filled the water tank the night before, but everyone had to use water sparingly as the pipes were frozen and no one knew when they might thaw.

Hugh and Rhona were not much bothered by these practicalities as they were after some fun. They sledged and played snowballs for hours on end, usually only retreating to the house to warm themselves or have a meal. Always the engineer, Hugh decided that in order to help the sledge go faster, they needed to construct a snow ramp. This was highly successful and lasted for weeks as the sub-zero temperatures continued.

After two additional days' holiday and with about eight inches of snow on the ground, the children returned to school. On the first day of term, the taxi did not arrive as the weather was so severe and many roads remained impassable. The cold gnawed hard as Hugh and Rhona wondered what to do; the intrepid pair decided to plod on to school, arriving at about eleven o'clock. Both Miss Wiggins and Miss Masefield were amazed at the siblings' pluck and courage and called them their little heroes, trudging the three to four miles in the perishing cold.

Consuelo remembered them making small foot-holes in the crunchy snow across the top of the Lodge Field. These small holes were used again and again as the pair tramped and traipsed to the school taxi with numb feet.

Getting to School

The Lerwill siblings attended two senior schools: Hugh and Angela went to the Weald School in Billingshurst and Rhona went to the Horsham High School for Girls. Officially, the County Council allocated the bus stop at Blackgate Lane. However, it was only Rhona that regularly took this route to catch the Southdown bus to Horsham. Hugh took a lackadaisical approach, often arriving too late in his teenage years to catch any bus, and meandering along the A29 with his thumb stuck out, hoping for a lift. Later Angela favoured Adversane.

Ever conscious of effort, Hugh and Angela applied the simple adage 'As the crow flies' and worked out the shortest routes cross-country. Distance-wise, Adversane was easily the better choice, but suffered from some serious obstacles.

Fanny Dryden was a spinster who had a small dairy herd of Guernsey cows at Jupplands Farm, right at the end of the lane near Adversane. Fanny's laissez-faire approach to her neighbours and stock, resulted in her ever-hungry cows wandering aimlessly along the lane looking for the odd blade of grass, and excreting teeming amounts of manure over the track, which was full of potholes. However, this was nothing in comparison to an encounter with Fanny's Guernsey bull which was to be avoided at all costs.[57] No bull is risk-free. Finally, Fanny sold Jupplands Farm for development, and the cows were no more.

With this encumbrance gone, Mr Pinches and Mr Garbett joined forces and had a concrete road laid from Adversane to Westlands Farm. This significantly improved the route for all users.

Following the sale of Woodlands Farm in 1972, there were further transformations. The farm changed from being a dairy farm, using strip grazing and electric fences to a larger extensive grazing regime, and the concrete road was extended from Westlands to Woodlands, completing the whole lane.

These improvements meant that by the time Angela went to secondary school, the Adversane route was the better choice. In the winter, she would walk in wellington boots across three grass fields to Woodlands, retrieve her bicycle and cycle the mile or so to Adversane, dumping her bicycle and boots at Southlands Farm. In the summer, when the ground was dry enough, she would bike from Frithwood through Northwood to Sunwood to connect with the lane to Adversane.

Rhona's Journey

Rhona preferred the Blackgate Lane route to catch the service bus, partly as she had Melanie Croom's company from Lee Place Lodge. It was an arduous day for any child of eleven, often leaving and returning in the dark during the winter. Melanie's company helped make it a little more bearable.

---

[57] Dairy bulls are known to be more vicious than beef bulls.

122

After breakfast, Consuelo would usher Rhona to the cart shed checking that the bicycle tyres were sufficiently hard. Once her paraphernalia was strapped onto the bicycle, she would ascend the hill towards the top gate. This was always kept shut and so had to be negotiated, if one did not want to lay the bicycle on the ground. It was awkward, but possible providing there was not too much wind. Sometimes her bicycle behaved like a drunken soldier as the wind took hold.

Once navigated, she remounted and headed at speed towards Northwood. However, care was needed on entering the wood as protruding ash roots could easily catch the front wheel and throw one off balance. In winter, the plentitude of waterlogged potholes threatened Rhona's long white socks. Once past the children's old haunt of First Tree Fort at the end of Northwood, it was a sharp turn right and a slight incline to Lee Place Lodge.

At the Lodge, Rhona would call for Melanie, who was usually running late, with her father frying eggs on the Aga range for the children's breakfasts. In the meantime, Rhona would fuss their old dog, Tweddle. Before setting off, the girls would often stuff their straw boaters in their front baskets to avoid them flying off as they raced along. The punishment for arriving at school without a boater was a detention after school on Wednesdays, something they could do without. Finally, the girls would be on their way and soon past Wablegate Field and Clapper's Pond.

With Snape behind them, the road improved as this was maintained by the County Council. After a couple of fields and past Canada Corner, the girls entered Blake Wood which stretched out for about a mile, climbing a slight incline. On their left was Stablebarn Farm, which was part of Brinsbury Agricultural College and housed the Friesian dairy herd. At the time, Bill Pollard was the cowman.

Further on to the right was Toat Farm which also had a dairy herd. Out of the woods, the countryside was more open and once more gave a good view of Toat Monument on the right. Descending the steep hill near Blackgate Farm at speed needed care as there was a sharp bend at the bottom. At last, they were on the straight run to St Richard's Cottages, where they would dump the bicycles in a gateway, leaving them unlocked until they returned later in the day.

Rhona's Walk to Adversane

Bicycles and wellington boots were two important items whilst living at Frithwood; one got you around, the other kept you dry. Although Rhona preferred the Blackgate Lane route to school, a bicycle puncture meant that she would sometimes have to walk to catch the bus, until Consuelo had made time to mend it.[58] On these occasions, Adversane presented a better choice.

There were two possible routes, across the fields through Woodlands Farm or through Northwood. Summer jaunts would take her across the fields to avoid the swarms of mosquitoes in Northwood, but in the winter, she might choose to tramp through Northwood in her trusty boots, avoiding the ruts and bogs as she found her way. At the end of Northwood, she would walk past Sunwood Farm onto the lane to Adversane.

On reaching the end of the road, she would quickly chuck her boots under the Pinches' churn stand and hurry off to the bus shelter in front of the Blacksmiths Arms. There, she would meet the Ayres siblings, from Lordings Farm, who were also on their way to schools in Horsham.

Horsham High School for 'Gals'

Rhona was the only child to pass the eleven-plus in 1965 at North Heath School. This was unfortunate, as making friends at the High School was even more difficult for the shy youngster. Although Rhona had been desperately keen to follow Berns' sisters to the Horsham High School for Girls, it came at a price; a long day, lots of homework and isolation.

Rhona's return trip was also difficult. Although school finished at

---

[58] Punctures were common when Joe Muller and Vic Newman were hedge trimming along the lane.

3.50 p.m., Rhona had to wait for nearly an hour for the next bus. Finally, she would arrive back home at the farm about 5.45 p.m. It was then a quick tea and stacks of homework.

Rhona's most enjoyable part of the day was on the bus. The single-decker bus had unofficial zones, the High School girls sat at the back and the Collyer boys sat in the front. Even the positions on the back seat were allocated; Rhona's was next to the emergency exit.

One of Rhona's first memories of the High School was Harvest Festival in her first year. It was late September and Rhona's form teacher Miss Alexander had asked if anyone could bring in some standing corn to decorate the stage; Rhona volunteered. The following weekend, Consuelo and Rhona gathered some odd bits of wheat and barley, left behind by the combine and parcelled them in an old feed bag for transportation. Once on the bus, windows started to be opened as passengers, old and young, began to complain about the pong. The smell was coming from the old feed sack which had contained a fish-meal concentrate. Rhona was somewhat embarrassed and red-faced by the time she arrived in Horsham.

In the mid-1960s, Horsham looked different. The bus would drop the children off at the Bishopric, near to the entrance to King and Barnes Brewery, before it proceeded on to the Carfax. The High School girls would then walk towards town to the traffic lights, turning right onto the Worthing Road. To the left was Manor House School playing field and to the right the United Reform Church and the offices of Bishops, the house removal company. Continuing their walk, they would pass Prewetts Mill on the left and a little further on the right was the High School.

The High School was situated in and around Tandbridge House, a big old Victorian building. Like many schools at the time, it had grown over the years with a sprawling hotchpotch of outlying buildings. One day, Rhona discovered a beautiful WC in blue and white porcelain secluded behind a closed door, which was not on public display.

At the time, the head teacher was called Dr Hoar and was an austere woman, who was only interested in 'gals' of a certain kind. Dr Hoar had never acknowledged Rhona and on her last day at school,

Rhona decided to confront her. She bravely knocked on her office door and went in. Dr Hoar glanced round with a look of disdain and said that she was busy. Rhona stood her ground and demanded a short interview.

Going Out

Going out in the evenings was a military operation for the three youngsters, largely as Consuelo did not have a driving licence and Berns was quite uncooperative. All three children devised their own strategy to cope. A good starting point was always venue location and attendees.

Permission always had to be sought for an evening out. Therefore, ascertaining Berns' mood was essential. Ask at the wrong time and the prospects for a night out could be scuppered. Berns had a standard reply *'How are you going to get there and back?'* He never seemed to realise that might be his job. With all this sorted out beforehand, the youngster had a reasonable chance of success.

Some friends' parents were kind and would help out, collecting and dropping the youngsters off either at the bus stop at Adversane or at Tanners Farm (on the Adversane to Newbridge Road) or opposite the church at Harsfold Lane in Wisborough Green. Each location required a half-hour walk home across the fields, sometimes in cellar-dark conditions.

Nevertheless, some parents like Mr Garrett, would only agree if Consuelo was at the drop-off point for collection. Supposedly, he did not want to be responsible for anything untoward happening to Angela. In these instances, Consuelo would go to bed early and set the alarm for about forty-five minutes before the due pick-up time and try to steal a bit of sleep. On the alarm ringing, she would quickly dress and melt into the velvety darkness to the rendezvous point. Meanwhile, Berns was snug in his bed, presumably awake and waiting for Consuelo and Angela to return. Sometimes his behaviour was quite unfathomable.

At other times, the youngsters would simply stay with friends, either those hosting the parties or attending them. From time to time, friends' parents would deliver the youngsters door-to-door, but this was a big ask as the farm track was not only long, (some 2.5 miles), but was rough in places with big potholes. Not something every car owner wanted late at night.

Consuelo once told Angela that she and Berns rarely slept until the youngsters had arrived home and that, on one occasion, Berns had asked what time it was. After being told that it was after midnight, Berns was cross that it was so late. Consuelo, however, just rolled over away from him and said that if he wanted the youngsters back at a certain time, he had better collect them himself.

Hydrologists in the Making

Consuelo was never a mother to worry too much about the state of the children's clothes, getting dirty or keeping dry. Her attitude was to let the children explore and, if they got wet and dirty, so what. Just change and put on something fresh and dry. Getting wet and mucky was all part and parcel of living on the farm.

Sometimes on wet afternoons, Rhona and Angela, suitably clad, would set out to play in the puddles and potholes by making small drainage channels into nearby streams or ditches, along the track in Northwood and along the lane towards Northwood Farm. Angela seems to think Berns may have suggested it as something to do that was useful. Using a strong stick and heel-trails, they might make new conduits or clear the existing gutters. These larger furrows often got blocked by twigs and fallen leaves and so the girls would often revert to using their hands on the awkward bits. Standing back and watching the water draining away was reward enough. Returning home, they always had a sense of achievement.

Messing about by the River Arun

With parents busy trying to make ends meet, the siblings quickly had to become self-reliant and able to amuse themselves. This was never a problem as there was always something to do, including messing about by the River Arun.

From the early days, Consuelo had often walked with the children by the river, instructing them about safety and possible dangers. Sometimes, Consuelo would pack a picnic, catch the Shetland pony Cockey and pop the girls on his bare back and head off for the river, with Hugh running ahead as chief scout. Consuelo had an art of making the mundane seem exciting to her brood. When Hugh was very young, Consuelo would tie him to a tree for safety, while he tried his hand at fishing with a home-made rod, using maggots dug from a muck heap.

Rhona remembers on one occasion, Berns' second sister Nance and her son Bryan coming to visit with the intention of fishing and having a picnic. Although the weather had turned wet, they went ahead so as not to disappoint the children. Within minutes, the two boys were hauling minnows out of the water at speed with their rudimentary rods. Apparently, the small fish were attracted to the surface because of the rain. The trip was a great success.

Sometimes, the family would have a supervised swim to cool off in the summer holidays. However, this came to an abrupt end when the new sewage works was built further upstream.

Frithwood Sports Day

One summer, when Rhona and Melanie Croom were still at primary school, they decided that they wanted to organise their own sports day. In addition to the two families, the Mullers from Northwood and the Newmans from Lee Place were also invited. With flat land being limited, it was decided that the piece of ground at the top of the hill at Frithwood was the best option.

Further debate and deliberation centred on the race schedule and this was duly copied out by hand. Races included boys' and girls' running, skipping, sack, egg and spoon, plus an adults' running race.

With Consuelo chivvying Berns along from the sidelines, a few bales of straw were brought round from the buildings on a tractor and trailer, and placed in two lines suggesting a race track and for seating. With clement weather, the afternoon was a great success with much laughing and joking. It was finally concluded with tea and cake provided by Consuelo.

Child Labour

Berns and Consuelo always taught the children that money did not grow on trees. From about the age of seven, they were encouraged to earn their own money from doing jobs around the farm. Apart from seasonal tasks such as carting bales and turkey plucking, all manner of jobs were undertaken. Mucking out pigs was a common chore at weekends. There was always plenty of dung to shift in one shed or another.

In addition to this, there were other jobs that required two people, such as cutting pigs, tending lame sheep, debeaking turkeys and holding fence posts for banging in.[59] Other solitary duties included patching hessian feed sacks, burning piles of paper feed sacks and baler string, creosoting numerous wooden sheds and spraying nettles with a watering can around the farm buildings.

There was always something to do at Frithwood.

Looking for a Body

In late September 1968, the family had a Danish exchange student called Auf staying on the farm. Earlier in the year, Hugh had gone to Copenhagen in Denmark with a party of students from the Weald School.

Unfortunately, the weather had turned particularly wet and the River Arun had burst its banks. By the weekend, there was a wide brown sea of swirling, seething water below Frithwood. On the local radio, a serious incident was reported at New Bridge, between Wisborough Green and Billingshurst. A car with a woman and two children had been swept away whilst being towed through the flood. The mother and one child had been rescued from undergrowth close to the bridge but the other child was still missing.

Aware that they would be unable to go to school the next day, the children decided to help look for the child. The enormity of the flood

---

[59] Cutting pigs: castrating male pigs. Debeaking turkeys: cutting the top beak back on turkeys to prevent them pecking other birds.

was soon obvious. In the flood's centre, the confident current continued, never confused of its direct course with dancing dervishes of trees and branches in its wake. Danger was all around.

Soon, the youngsters met several policemen searching for the child and offered their help. Together, they roamed along the river's shoreline until dusk, with no success. As storm clouds increased and light levels sank, the children decided to return home. The dead child was finally located in tangled undergrowth close to Newbridge once the floodwater receded.

Angela was ten years old at the time and learnt an important lesson; never to enter floodwater, however innocent it might look.

The Hot-water Bottle

Without any heating upstairs, hot-water bottles were essential in the winter. Under Consuelo's supervision, the siblings were responsible for bringing their cold bottles downstairs in the morning, but invariably these instructions were ignored. They often had to be rescued just before bedtime. As the children got older, they filled their own.

Naturally, Hugh, being the eldest, was the first to be in charge of this task. At the time, Angela was about seven or eight years old and was anxious to learn how to make Consuelo an early morning cup of tea; she was in training. On this particular morning, things had gone well; Angela had filled the kettle, laid the tea tray and had carefully taken it upstairs to her mother. Delighted with the prospect of a drink prepared by her younger daughter, Consuelo poured out the tea. Not only did it have a terrible odour, something resembling sweaty trainers, but it tasted even worse. After taking a couple of small sips, Consuelo decided she would have to admit to Angela that the tea was undrinkable, even if it did upset her. Nonplussed, she needed to make some enquiries.

Consuelo soon established that Hugh had topped the kettle with the contents of his previous hot-water bottle, which had left a residue in the kettle, making the water taste stale and rubbery. The whole family found this highly amusing and soon Consuelo's disapproval softened; she was also laughing about the incident of the hot-water bottle.

Observations on the Hoof

Unlike many youngsters growing up today, the Lerwill children probably had more in common with Laurie Lee and his world of *Cider with Rosie* than any author of their own childhood. Without much money or a mother that could drive, the sibling's world outside school was largely their home and its environs. However, this did not stop them exploring, making friends and generally getting to know their patch of the Sussex countryside, much as Berns had done a generation before. It was a time of fun, adventure and complete freedom, within the boundaries of mealtimes.

Walking to the children was not restricted to the weekends or considered a hobby; it was a means of having a life. Consuelo was also in this club as, without a driving licence, she was limited in getting out. This was sometimes a challenge, but never seen as a prison sentence, merely a temporary encumbrance. Nevertheless, a good pair of legs was essential for all members of the Lerwill family.

By the time the children were old enough for exploration, Lee Place and Northwood farms had been sold to Bill Wadey and then to Mr John Burnford. This was lucky, as Mr Burnford accepted that the trio would wander his land whether he sanctioned it or not, as if it was still farmed by their grandfather, Sidney Lerwill.

Providing the weather was fair, weekend jaunts of exploration were common. Sometimes there was a plan, but often these safaris took their own course, meandering across grass and ploughed fields alike. One winter, while venturing across Haybarn Field below Lee Place, one of the youngsters noticed some shiny, knapped flint stones glinting in the low afternoon sunlight in a ploughed furrow. Hugh quickly realised the striations on the flint were probably man-made, and instantly thought that they might be Stone Age. Over the coming days, there were several more archaeological forays and other bits were collected, including a possible arrowhead.

With interest roused, the threesome decided that their finds needed to be displayed and it was agreed that the best venue would be the disused stone-built toilet in the garden, which might become their museum. While Rhona busied herself with cleaning, Hugh found a few planks of wood and proceeded to nail them over the two holes previously used by numerous *derrières*. Next was a sign for the door, *'Keep Out, Fine of Five Pounds'*, daubed over the flaking green paint. The museum rarely had a paying visitor but the project entertained the children for several days.

After returning to school and retelling their story, and showing off their finds, someone suggested that a real museum might be interested. A letter was sent to the museum in Chichester and, a few weeks later, Consuelo received a telephone call saying that one of the archaeological team wanted to visit the site. Elated by the recognition that the arrowhead was Stone Age, Hugh reluctantly handed it over to be displayed at the official museum. It was a bittersweet end to the adventure.

Digging for Bullets

Hugh was always good at finding new things to do. Berns had mentioned to the children that the Canadian soldiers billeted in Northwood during the Second World War had used the canal bank in Green Brooks below Lee Place for target practice. The siblings and the Croom children decided to investigate.

The site was easily found as the canal bank curved in slightly at the range site. Using their penknives and sticks, the children dug into the bank retrieving lots of .303 rifle bullets. These were washed and their finds were then displayed in their museum.

Christmas Chocolates go Missing

Christmas stockings were always a simple affair at Frithwood. The children would lay out one of Berns' old socks at the end of their beds on Christmas Eve and hope for the best. They were never surprised by their findings in the morning. Apart from their main present, the stocking would contain a few home-grown walnuts, a tangerine and a few bars of chocolate.

By Christmas 1968, Angela and Hugh had swapped bedrooms, as Hugh had started college. Angela's new room was a slightly larger and marginally warmer room located over the dining room. To the side, it had a large, walk-in cupboard (used originally to store bottled fruit) which had been neglected and contained a lot of junk.

A few days after Christmas, Angela decided that she would like some chocolate and went upstairs to fetch a bar but could only find the cherry throat sweets, called Tunes. She went downstairs and started interrogating the family to see who had taken her chocolate bars. No one knew anything about the chocolates and Angela felt a bit miffed. It was a mystery.

Life moved on, and, as happened from time to time in the winter, Consuelo suspected that some mice had moved into the house, so she used some bait. One evening on returning with the milk drinks, she announced that she had just found a drowsy young rat descending a water pipe in the back scullery, and that she had dispatched it with the coal shovel and popped it into the Rayburn. Although disgusted that a rat would have the audacity to venture into the house, no one thought any more of it until Angela decided to clear out the large cupboard in her bedroom, a while later. In amongst the junk were some foil chocolate wrappings.

Assembling the evidence, the family pieced the story together and it was decided that the rat obviously had not suffered from a sore throat, as it had left the packet of cherry-flavoured Tunes.

Flora and some Fauna

Consuelo always had a marvellous ability to make the most of her circumstances. She was an exemplar for the youngsters in how to enjoy the local environment.

Apart from more land being under the plough due to the Second World War and the War Ag, the natural environment was still much as it had been a century before; the likes of Monsanto and other agro-chemical companies were still in their infancy.[60] Wild flowers and butterflies flourished, especially in those fields still under permanent pasture.

---

[60] War Ag was set up during the Second World War to increase domestic food production.

Consuelo soon started to take an interest in nature and became particularly knowledgeable about wild flowers and butterflies. Rhona inherited her passion and remembers the abundance of wild flowers in the big field (known as Seed Field) between Lee Place and Frithwood, when it was down to permanent pasture.

At that time, there was a hedge and ditch virtually parallel to the bridlepath from Frithwood to Lee Place, with a spring which gurgled a short way from the field boundary. In the springtime, Rhona remembers collecting watercress there and taking it home.

Consuelo would wash it in Milton solution to kill any flukes or bugs and then the family would often eat it in sandwiches.

Later in the season, the same field would host purple orchids and then large swathes of bird's-foot trefoil, making it look like a sea of yellow and orange. Sometimes, horse mushrooms would be collected and once inspected for maggots, Consuelo would fry them for breakfast. The best field mushrooms were always found on Lordings Rough.

Northwood also held its own richness of wild flowers in spring and early summer. As the mixed woodland started unfurling its new fresh green carpet, the floor below would also start to reveal its hidden secrets. There were a few snowdrops followed by the acid-green leaves of dog's mercury and wood sorrel, and then the delicate white wood anemones. At varying places, spotted bird's-nest and bee orchids could be found if you knew where to look, although not necessarily in the same season. Over on the far side of the wood there was a small patch of wild daffodils which never seemed to spread, but the family always visited them like an annual homage. Later, a profusion of bluebells acted like a carpet and would almost sparkle in the dappled light.

The hedgerow from Frithwood to Northwood also held its own magic with primroses, lesser stitchwort, scarlet pimpernel, assorted violets, a range of vetches and a most delicate pea grass with pink flowers. Uncut hedges would also reveal their secrets in the spring as pussy willow flowered and would brighten the murky days just before spring had properly sprung. Rhona sometimes took some pussy willow for the nature table at North Heath School. In February

134

1993, Consuelo's diary reported that the hazel catkins were the best she had ever seen.

Lordings Rough also held its treasures and over the years, the family had great pleasure taking particular note of a whole variety of butterflies. With the Ayres not using pesticides on their permanent pasture, butterflies could thrive in the varied habitats. Often, Consuelo would list in her diary which ones she had seen on her walks. In July 1987, she noted that she had seen six white admirals, one red admiral, one comma, several tortoiseshells and lots of meadow browns on just one walk. On another walk, in July 1994, she saw two small blues, one brimstone, one painted lady, one green-veined white, lots of meadow browns and gatekeepers. Although Consuelo could not boast to be an academic lepidopterist, she was nevertheless a keen amateur.

Butterflies aside, another observation Angela remembers was the number of insects splattered to death on car windscreens in the 1960s, often requiring the screens to be washed from time to time. Rarely, are there any deaths on windscreens today, suggesting that numbers of insects have drastically reduced as pesticide usage has increased.

Local Ornithology

The Protection of Birds Act 1954 meant that it became illegal to collect birds' eggs. Nevertheless, this did not deter the siblings who gathered spent eggshells for their annual collection. From an early age, the children took an interest in wild birds, often referring to their *Observer's Book of Birds*. With Consuelo's encouragement, there was always something new to spot, research and learn about.

On one occasion, Hugh and Rhona found some eggs in a nest in an old rotting tree stump in the middle of Northwood. On taking a mental note of them, they were thrilled to discover that they were the eggs of a coal tit, something new to them.

In the perishingly cold spring of 1963, another discovery was made by Berns. Whilst walking past the old derelict army jeep where the elder tree had taken over, he spotted a small nest under its bonnet. A pair of impatient wrens had been busy and had built a home. Unfortunately, the weather was still too cold and the young were all dead, huddled in a group.

Sometimes, when Berns was ploughing, the family would enjoy the sight of a desert of lapwings following the plough.[61] Quite how they knew that he was busy cutting through the rich clay soil no one knew, just another mystery. Sadly, over the years the lapwing numbers reduced and their place was taken by greedy seagulls.

For many years, swallows would regularly nest under the eaves of the house, cart shed and old stable. They were always welcome except when they messed on one's bicycle seat. Moving the bicycle was the easiest remedy. With families raised and as insect numbers waned, the hirondelles or swallows would start to fly particularly low on the wing and the Lerwills would know that Africa beckoned. However, if the conditions were right, other delights were in store.

Sometimes, a murmuration of starlings would gather over the old barn on warm autumn evenings, swirling around, forming and reforming, silhouetted against the setting sun in the west. Dusk would also host bats flying low around the old house.

Other pleasures might involve spotting a wedge of Canada geese overhead, having been alerted by their honking cries beforehand. No one quite knew their destination, but the leader always seemed to have a good idea. Large gaggles liked to glean the arable fields around Lee Place and Northwood in the autumn for shed corn left by the combine. In flight, they looked graceful but at ground level, they looked cumbersome and awkward.

From the dining-room window, the family enjoyed a whole range of bird life. As well as common garden birds, they saw the occasional green woodpecker burrowing about for ants in the lawn and pied wagtails bobbing about on the roofs of the cart shed and hovel, especially after a shower of rain. Sometimes, a jenny wren would flit in and out of Consuelo's flowerpots by the front door, but never stayed long. In late March 1974, Consuelo found a pair of wrens nesting in the ivy at the end of the garden wall.

---

[61] Also known as peewits, green plovers and pyewipes in Lincolnshire.

In spring, the teenagers found the incessant noise of baby sparrows and starlings being fed, above their bedroom window; a nuisance and a disturbance to any proposed, weekend lie-in. Other night-time interruptions included screeching owls and visiting tom cats on the prowl.

Some sightings were even quite exotic. On returning from school in the mid-1970s, Angela saw an unusual pale-green bird, near Westlands Farm. It was about the size of a mistle thrush, had a long, curved beak and a black-tipped crest. On reporting back to Consuelo, the family were baffled as to what it might be. Then, a few weeks later, a local newspaper article reported that a few pale- green hoopoes had been spotted in the area and thus the mystery was solved.[62]

Sightings of owls were always cherished. Once, Berns came in to the house quite upset that he had just found a barn owl drowned in one of the water tanks. Within minutes, the family filed outside to look at the cold cadaver. Later in June 1985, the family were thrilled when a pair of little owls decided to take up residence and nest above the blue bedroom. The busy pair often used the old bird table in the front garden as a staging post before taking yet more food to their young.

Over the years, Consuelo noted many birds she saw in the locality, many of which were spotted on Lordings Rough and brooks. On one occasion, she saw sixteen swans in Orfold brooks, on another a tree creeper, several long-tailed tits and a flock of yellow-hammers. Kingfishers were also recorded on a few occasions by Orfold Lock in February 1979 and near Streele Lake in 1994, but they were never common.

Just a few years before leaving the farm, a pair of kestrels started nesting in the ash trees near the boundary with Lordings Rough. Les, a keen amateur ornithologist, built a temporary hide so he could take photographs of the developing chicks. He came several years running and took some wonderful pictures, one of which he framed and presented to Berns and Consuelo as a thank-you present.

---

[62] Hoopoes are fairly common on the Continent and have long cultural associations with the Middle East.

The Hand Grenade Incident

During the spring of 1963, Hugh and Robert found a hand grenade in Northwood. They had been playing just beyond Crow Castle when they discovered it near a hazel clump.[63] Thrilled by the prospect of a Second World War treasure, they decided to take it back to Frithwood, placing a stick in the rusty, corroded ring. Hugh excitedly announced what they had found to Consuelo, at the back door. Calmly, she took charge and placed it outside under the filbert nut tree and forbade the children to go near it. She then sent for Berns.

Berns arrived in a terrible state, wondering what to do. The local police were telephoned and eventually a number was obtained for the bomb disposal unit at Broadbridge Heath near Horsham. Within a couple of hours, an Army Land Rover with two or three soldiers in uniform arrived ready for action.

Naturally, this was all terribly exhilarating for the children; not only had Hugh found the grenade but also something was being done about it at speed. After studying the ordnance, the soldiers had a brief conference with Berns as to where they might dispose of it. Berns suggested an area near a large dung heap on the boundary with the Crooked Tree Field.

While the explosive charge was set, the family positioned themselves standing and sitting on the garden wall for a bird's-eye view. With the plunger depressed, there was one enormous bang and the dung heap was decimated, with dung flying high into the air. It was the family's own Armageddon. They were shocked at its magnitude and quickly realised how lucky they had been.

Camping Frithwood Style

In the 1960s, Scout troops could often be seen camping in Lordings Rough and Green Brook below Lee Place in the summer holidays. One August, the siblings fancied the idea of camping themselves and so they hatched a plan.

---

[63] Ordnance left by the Canadian soldiers living in Northwood during the Second World War.

With no tent or sleeping bags, the family had to be inventive, something they knew a good deal about. For the tent, some old, small fertiliser bags were cut, cleaned and flopped over the washing line and roughly secured. Consuelo suggested that the children should make palliasse mattresses out of large, flaked-maize sacks filled with clean straw. She explained that she had seen the locals doing this when she was a child in Bolivia.

The scene was set and, as the sun was setting, the children could not wait to start their adventure of sleeping outside. Too excited to sleep, they watched the shadows of insects, dancing on the plastic roof, as they tossed and turned in the stuffy tent. After shutting in the hens, Berns and Consuelo checked the children and went to bed. However, all was not well.

Not only was it a hot night, but the children had not bargained for the constant surging tick-tock of the electric fence being used in the field close by. By about midnight, the experiment was abandoned as the children grabbed their bed blankets and went indoors.

Toys, Hobbies and Routines

Unlike most children, the siblings did not need copious amounts of toys as they had a real farm to play in. Toys were easily managed and housed in a cardboard box in the dining room. Board games, cards and jigsaw puzzles were kept on a shelf in the front door cupboard, away from the damp floor.

In bad weather, the box of farm toys was in constant use. This collection comprised a barn, lovingly made by George Ascot for Hugh one Christmas, a farmyard fixed onto a hardboard base containing a pig pen, cottage, a box of animals and farm machinery, affectionately known as *the farm things*. In amongst the wooden box were a couple of lead pigs Berns had when he was a boy. With years of hard use, the soft metal had bent and their little feet had curled over, and were no longer able to support their weight. However, with vivid imaginations the siblings still used them, pretending that the larger one was a sow lying on her side feeding her litter.

Hugh also played with an old wind-up train set given to him as a hand-me-down by cousin David; Eric and Madge's son. It had an olive-green engine, a blue railway station and bridge to complement the set.

Rhona and Angela both enjoyed playing with dolls. One Christmas, Consuelo's mother Jessie and sister Ruth gave them black baby dolls of different sizes. Ruth was a particularly good seamstress and made several changes of identical clothes for each doll, including a smocked dress and pale-blue pyjamas with white lace collars. Another valued present was a set of miniature saucepans.

When the children were young and home from school, there was a set routine. In the mornings, they were expected to entertain themselves, while Consuelo did farm work and household chores and cooked the lunch. Afterwards, they might have her undivided attention for about an hour before she headed back to work. If dry, the family would nearly always go for a walk; if wet or too cold, time might be spent around the dining-room table, tackling a jigsaw, playing a board game, bagatelle or card game such as Kan-U-Go, Happy Families or Pairs.

Sometimes, Consuelo would bring out her postage stamp collection and, while Angela played with the cats on the dining-room floor, Hugh and Rhona might copy their mother as she laid out stamps, whilst soaking others from their envelope backs in shallow saucers of water. Hugh and Rhona would diligently observe and swap stamps taking care not to damage these precious patches from faraway places.

Consuelo's interest in stamps stemmed from her boarding school days. Several of her chums were from overseas and others had parents working abroad like hers. Stamp collecting was what one did as a holiday boarder at Charters Towers School for Girls.

Whilst still young and before television, evenings were largely spent playing outside or continuing with the pursuits detailed above. It was then time to prepare for bed. When very young if time allowed, the siblings would have a bedtime story and say their prayers.[64]

---

[64] See Appendix I: Rhona and Angela's Prayers.

As the children got older, their interests diverged, each having their own particular hobbies. In his early teens, Hugh became interested in collecting cacti. His small collection grew and some were housed on the west-facing, sitting-room windowsill. On one occasion, no one had consciously noticed that one had flowered and had a dreadful aroma of old socks. Hugh's teenage feet were blamed, until the penny dropped.

Hugh was also interested in the latest technology and was often upstairs in his bedroom making crystal radio sets and crafting unusual lampshades out of old pierced food tins, covered with coloured cellophane, giving his den a mysterious, hippy feel. He also had a habit of collecting road signs such as 'Go' and 'Stop' which also adorned his room.

As they got older, the girls were introduced to sewing and knitting. In addition to sewing many of their teenage clothes, the girls loved patchwork. Both went on to make a number of quilts. Rhona also loved embroidery, making a number of cushions for friends and family.

Poor Judgement

Bored with playing on the farm, Angela and primary school friend, Sue decided to walk to Wisborough Green. On arriving at Green Brook, below Lee Place they were confronted by a wide flood. From the water's edge, it seemed shallow and innocent, and so they waded out using some large heavy cattle feeders to guide them to the river crossing on the far side.

On reaching the bridge, they should have turned home as the water swished and swirled around the structure, with ever-increasing menace. Still, they carried on. Using the open bridge gate as a support, they clambered along it as the water rushed and hurried beneath them, hardly giving a thought to any possible danger.

Two hours later, much had changed. The water was deeper and with dreary dimming light, the scene looked and felt far more ominous. Still, they carried on. They stripped off some clothing and once again used the gate for guidance whilst the whirling water gurgled round them. They then headed for the cattle feeders.

It was only when they reached the Lee Place shoreline that they appreciated the magnitude of their folly. Better to keep this adventure a secret.

The Stink Bomb

Rhona and Christine DuPont met at a young age whilst staying with their grandmothers in Bexhill. Over several summer holidays, the girls became friends and eventually Christine was invited to the farm for a short holiday.

Christine was used to city life as she lived in a flat in Marseilles in southern France, however, she seemed to adapt easily to farm life. Her stay was a great success but soon came to an end.

The DuPont family had been asked to tea. They arrived mid-afternoon and after a short walk round the farm, it was time to eat. As there was quite a crowd, it was decided that the children would eat in the dining room while the four adults could take tea on their laps in the sitting room. Halfway through the proceedings, the parents heard a kerfuffle and then several of the youngsters appeared through the front sitting-room window making funny faces.

Immediately, the adults filed through to the dining room and were met with the most dreadful smell. Hugh had let off a stink bomb under the table. This was not all, the DuPont's youngest daughter, Suzie, aged four, was plodding away at her tea. No one quite knew whether she was just ignoring or oblivious to the smell. She was not going to be put off her tucker.

After the initial shock and embarrassment, the two families quickly regained their sense of humour and everyone had a good laugh. However, Hugh was in the doghouse for a good number of days.

Getting Caught

Light twinkled through the cracks in the old door on the upper level known as the granary in Grandpa Sidney's time at Lee Place. Angela and her friend Barbara, aged about eight, were reluctant to open the upper door to guard against getting caught, although they were not doing any harm, just playing at tidying a redundant space.

A dog bark alerted them that someone was about and they peeped through the gaps to ascertain its owner. They spied a black Labrador dog and a large-framed man walking towards the barn from the direction of Haybarn. Although the girls stayed perfectly still and quiet, the dog had given them away. They would have to await their fate.

The tense silence was broken by the sound of the wooden latch being raised and then the slow, heavy plodding feet of a giant ascending the stairs. Tension mounted and Angela felt her mouth go dry with anticipation.

The man was Mr Burnford, the owner, and he quietly asked who they were and what they were doing. With heavy heads bowed and their eyes fixed on the floor, the girls briefly mumbled. They reluctantly raised their heads ready for their punishment, but, instead, were congratulated on their efforts of a job well done. With that, he turned and walked away leaving the two small girls to recover.

Hugh's Air Gun

Although Hugh was not an obvious 'hunting, shooting, fishing' type, he did have a brief foray with an air gun, following his catapult days. Naturally, he was well briefed by Berns and Consuelo about safety. This often meant that shooting expeditions took him further afield than just the farm.

Northwood was a favourite venue as apart from an old pheasant pen, the wood was neglected and there were plenty of pigeons, crows and rooks to cull. After treating Northwood like his own shoot for a time, Hugh then came across the bright idea of asking Mr

Burnford for a part-time gamekeeping job. Consuelo was consulted and gave her approval. A letter was written on her best Basildon Bond writing paper and duly dispatched. Several weeks passed with no reply and then one day, Mr Burnford appeared on the brow of the hill.

He had come to talk to Hugh about his proposal. The negotiations took place outside and from indoors the family looked on as nods and smiles were exchanged; the body language looked promising. Soon the man turned tail and was quickly out of sight. Obviously amused by the youth's initiative and cheek, he had offered Hugh the part-time role for thirty bob a month (£1.50 in today's money).[65] He told Hugh that he was well aware that he would continue shooting in Northwood, so he might as well be paid for his efforts.

On another occasion, Hugh had spotted that there were a lot of starlings congregating around Northwood Farm as the corn store was full. He also noted that quite a few were gathering on the roof of the old cart shed next to Northwood Farmhouse.

By this time, the house had been sold to Mrs Pepper, and sometimes her grown-up son visited at the weekends. With this tale, one has to imagine a posh chap of about thirty minding his own business, washing his BMW car on one side of the cart shed, and a youth of about fifteen with an air rifle on the other. Hugh fired the gun and hit a starling that tumbled off the roof on the far side, falling onto the man's head.

Naturally, Hugh ran round to fetch his quarry, only to find young Mr Pepper with blood cascading all over his, prematurely bald head. More shocked than angry, he suggested Hugh went shooting elsewhere and Hugh returned home highly amused by the whole event.

Lateral Thinking

The Lerwill siblings were always looking for ways to earn a bit of pocket money. Although Berns would pay them for doing jobs

---

[65] 'Bob' is an expression for an old shilling that is 5p in today's money.

around the farm, the hourly rate was always modest. Sometimes, earning opportunities came from unexpected places.

In the 1960s, fizzy drinks were largely sold in family size glass bottles, which attracted a refund. 'Tizer – The surpriser' was the siblings' choice, but was only bought for Christmas and birthday treats. However, the knowledge that certain bottles were refundable gave the Lerwill children an idea.

Receding floodwaters from the River Arun often carried detritus which sometimes included refundable bottles. After a flood, the trio would set off with an old bag to collect their swag. A walk from Lordings Lock to Haybarn might yield six bottles. After returning home, the children would wash them and then ask Mr Bicknel, the grocer from Forest Stores, for the refund and share the loot. Naturally, everyone kept quiet about their origin. Other one-off schemes followed.

Knowledge is one thing whereas applying it is quite another. Trips to Pulborough Livestock Market educated the siblings from an early age on how auctions worked. One day, Angela had been given an old fur coat by Mrs Muller from Northwood for dressing up. On arriving home, she quickly realised that her brother and sister were also interested in it and smelt a possible profit. With Angela standing at the sitting-room door, an impromptu auction started as her older siblings fought it out; Hugh won and had to shell out twenty-five shillings (£1.25 in today's money). Later, he cut off the sleeves and used the coat as part of his hippy apparel, wearing it as Rag King at college a few years later. This was not the only time Angela made money from Hugh.

At one of the gatherings after Billingshurst Flower Show at Great Aunt Dais's house, Hugh sold his newly acquired coconut to Angela for a paltry sum. She promptly smashed it on the garden path and offered pieces to amused uncles and aunts for threepence (1.5p in today's money), making a couple of shillings profit, after expenses. Naturally, Hugh was a bit miffed by his younger sister's initiative. However, he had other successes.

House signs were one such idea. Sometimes a load of cord wood was bought in as additional firewood. These were mainly the bark sides off larger trunks. Hugh was into calligraphy at the time and decided to make a sign for the farm. It turned out well and, after a few compliments, Hugh made one or two to order.

However, entrepreneurs are not made overnight. At about five years old, Angela had the idea of a lucky-dip box. With few customers and meagre prizes, namely wrapped dog biscuits, the venture only lasted until lunchtime and was abandoned.

Holiday at Moor Farm

Sadly, the five Lerwills never spent a holiday together, owing to time and money pressures. The nearest the youngsters got to a holiday was staying with relatives for a few days. One such break came about after a chance remark over a Sunday tea with visitors. Consuelo was always well organised and usually prepared food for such events the day before. After lunch, the couple would get the afternoon jobs done early. Once washed and changed, the family were ready to receive their guests.

On this particular day, Berns' third sister Flo, her husband Jimmy and their daughters, Craig (an unusual choice of girl's name), Sarah and Lyn, were coming to tea. Upon arrival, the guests were shown into the sitting room. Prior to having a television, family gatherings often involved playing games together. Rhona remembers playing chase, ace and rummy. Having obviously enjoyed the afternoon, Jimmy commented that it would be good to see the Lerwill children back at their home.

The Wardrop family lived at Moor Farm, part of the Leconfield Estate just outside Petworth on the road to Wisborough Green. It was a big old Edwardian house with a lake to the front, surrounded by trees. The house was built on a slight rise and was exposed to the vagaries of wind and rain.

Hugh was quick off the mark and within a few days, the trio were staying at Moor Farm. On one day, the children had a go at fishing which was a novelty for the girls as this was usually Hugh's domain. Flo took them walking into the woods behind the farm buildings, which they enjoyed, spotting a few unfamiliar plants.

On another day, Jimmy took the children over to meet his aged parents who lived at Osiers Farm, on the road to North Chapel. Jimmy's parents were Scottish and their heavy accents made it difficult for the children to understand. They met Jimmy's sister Jessie who had never married, but stayed home to look after her ageing parents. This was often the fate of the youngest daughter at the time.

The holiday was a success but soon passed and it was time to return home.

Friends That Neigh

*All horses deserve, at least once in their lives,
to be loved by a little girl.*

ANONYMOUS

Cockey's Dice with Death

Cockey, the Shetland pony, was a present given to the Lerwill children from Harry Laker's daughters when the family emigrated to Australia in the mid-1950s.[66] Hugh and Rhona were largely uninterested in riding, so Cockey's early life at Frithwood was largely one of being treated like a bullock that never went to market. He would graze and move round with a group of steers until they went off to slaughter and then he was popped in with the next batch.

On this occasion, he had gone with some bullocks to the field next to the A29 at Codmore Hill. Initially all went well, until someone telephoned to say that some animals were loose on the A29 and that a Shetland pony was injured. Berns and Consuelo immediately rang Dennis Marten, the vet and asked him to meet them at Blackgate Lane.

While Dennis was left to attend to Cockey, Berns and Consuelo gathered the cattle and put them back in the field and secured the hole in the hedge. On returning to the pony, a small group of people had assembled around the frightened animal; the vet, the car driver and now Berns and Consuelo. Dennis gave his diagnosis; the pony's life had probably been saved by his considerable fat.

From that day forward, Cockey lived at home, but was permanently terrified of motorised vehicles.

---

[66] Harry Laker was Berns' best school friend who trained as a veterinary surgeon.

148

Cockey goes to School

The Weald School usually hosted a school fete in June each year and the children were encouraged to offer their ideas and help. One summer, some farming friends, the Sizmers from Tanners Farm, were taking their old pony to the fete and suggested that Angela might like to come along, and bring Cockey.

With the Sizmers' horsebox prepared, Cockey was quickly led into the trailer, without giving him time to work out that a motor vehicle was in front. Securely tied, the party sped off to the fete. As usual, the pony rides were popular, and at the end Mrs Sizmer and Angela were tired. It was then time to head home.

Cockey, equally exhausted and somewhat annoyed at being duped into mounting the horsebox earlier in the day, decided to make a point and flatly refused to be loaded. At one point, he had two ropes behind him which were gradually pulling him forward. In order to resist, he just sat like a dog. After a lot of coaxing, he reluctantly mounted the trailer and everyone could return home.

Cockey in Old Age

Overall, Cockey lived a long, idle life at Frithwood. Nevertheless, as old age approached, he had a few health problems including intermittent periods of body lice. It was always obvious when he was infested as he would scratch away on fence posts or some bit of old farm machinery at the right height to ease his itch. It was time for the Coopers lice powder.

This was an effective remedy, but one that had an interesting odour for both man and beast. Cockey hated it, and as soon as he saw a human advancing with the delousing drum, he would trot off. Tactics changed and he was caught and then deloused, making the treatment easier. Cockey might have been old, but he still had his sense of smell.

Learning to Ride

Angela was the only one of the three children to take to horse riding. Although Berns had been a keen horseman in his youth, his priority was to provide for his growing family. He simply did not have the time to spend with his young daughter. In retrospect, this was sad.

By the time Angela was about seven years old, it was obvious that Cockey was becoming too small for her to ride. However, even at a young age, Angela was not shy and this led to a chance conversation. Whilst waiting for the school taxi at Snape Farm Cottage, Angela struck up a friendship with Miss Elwin's groom, Sarah. Recognising that Angela was mustard keen on horses, Sarah must have asked Miss Elwin whether she could teach Angela to ride, using their old pony Bessy.

After a few lessons in a field and hacking out with Sarah on a lead rein, Angela was invited by Miss Elwin to join them on their Sunday morning rides. Angela saw this as a bit of a landmark and quite liked the formality of these occasions.

First of all, she had to arrive at the stables in plenty of time to catch and prepare Bessy for her ride. In the meantime, Sarah would be finishing off her stable duties. After tacking-up the horses and leaving them ready in their stables, Sarah and Angela would join Miss Elwin in the house for a coffee before 'riding out'. In those heady days of horse mania, Angela's weekends were glued to Sarah's every word. She was a brilliant teacher and a great exemplar for the youngster. In retrospect, Miss Elwin must have enjoyed having a small girl around who hero-worshipped her groom and tried hard to be a good little girl.

Consuelo was always a stickler for manners and with Miss Elwin being one of the old-school, Angela knew that the rules had to be adhered to at all times. She may have only been seven years old at the time but she knew on which side her bread was buttered and was not going to jeopardise this opportunity.

Getting a Bigger Pony

Angela realised that she needed a bigger pony and discussed this with her mother. Consuelo advised her young daughter to save her pocket money and keep quiet. She added that any nagging might result in a straight 'No' from Berns. Angela did as she was told and within about eighteen months had accrued some £20.

In the meantime, Berns had been talking to a friend at Pulborough Livestock Market called George Harding. He had told Berns about the New Forest pony sales.

One late September day in 1968, Berns, Angela and George drove to Beaulieu in Hampshire. After parking and getting a sales catalogue, they went and had a look at the ponies in the high-sided pens. Berns always had a good eye for livestock, and as they wandered round, he took a note of those ponies that he found of interest and were being sold singly.

At the allotted time, the crowd assembled around the sales ring. Part way through the sale, a dark bay colt was led into the ring and Berns made his move and bought the foal for £24. Angela was euphoric.

The next challenge was getting the foal back from the sale. Berns made for the lorry park to talk to the drivers and quickly located a local Sussex haulier who agreed to bring the pony back to the farm for a given fee. With the carrier given the necessary paperwork, it was time to return home.

That evening, after telling Consuelo every detail of her day, Angela waited for the lorry headlights to appear over the hill, but none came. Deeply worried that her new pony had gone astray, her parents explained that the driver was probably running late and that the pony would arrive in the morning.

The next day Angela rushed home from school to find Satellite calmly chomping hay in the old stable. He was to grow into the pony that Angela had always wanted; he was kind and soft, and loved being handled and spoilt by a little girl who idolised him.

Waiting, Oh the Waiting

Although Angela now had a pony, he was only six months old and needed to be at least three years old before he could be ridden seriously. This was a hard lesson in patience. Then, quite by chance, Consuelo had a conversation with Mrs Scott which changed everything.

The Scott family lived at Harsfold Manor, about a mile away and had four children. Henrietta was the eldest and was a year older than Angela. In the late 1960s, the older children were just beginning to leave home to start boarding school and this left a docile old pony standing idle for most of the time. On hearing that Angela needed a ride, Mrs Scott immediately offered Pollyanna to Angela during term time. This was the perfect solution, and for the next couple of years most of Angela's term-time weekends revolved around riding Pollyanna.

Pollyanna Kicks Out

Generally, Pollyanna was a well-behaved and bombproof pony. However, on this day, she was obviously not feeling her placid self and kicked Angela on the leg. On collecting some hot water from the manor house for tack cleaning, Angela mentioned it to Mrs Scott who was very apologetic.

Angela had dismissed it as one of those things. The following weekend, she made her usual phone call to the Scotts. On arriving, she noticed that the pony was not in her paddock and that there were voices coming from Pollyanna's stable. Mr and Mrs Scott were busy grooming the pony. They said that Pollyanna was sorry for her previous behaviour and hoped that Angela might accept the box of chocolates in the corner of the stable. It was so thoughtful and kind.

Harsfold Fete

While Angela was a regular visitor to Harsfold, the Scotts hosted a fete to raise money for the church steeple at Wisborough Green. Mr Scott asked Angela if she could organise the pony rides and whether she had any ideas for money-making stalls. At about ten years old, Angela felt quite chuffed that an adult was asking for her input. She instantly agreed and said that she had recently seen a stall at a fete where people had to pay to guess the weight of something; what about a ram? On the day, Mr Burt, the farm manager, caught a ram and visitors were asked to pay to guess his weight. It was called 'Guess the Weight of Ronnie the Ram'. It was not a crowd stopper but raised a few pounds.

As always, the pony rides were popular and kept Angela and Consuelo busy all afternoon. They raised quite a lot of money and the two Lerwills walked home, exhausted, but pleased that they had been able to help.

The following week, the fete's success was outlined in a short article in one of the local newspapers. Angela was delighted to read her name in print and being given credit for organising the pony rides. Another thoughtful touch by the Scotts.

Swimming Lessons

Apart from Pollyanna, the Scotts had something else that was attractive to Angela; an outdoor swimming pool. In the summer after riding, Angela was allowed to use the pool.

One summer holiday, Mrs Scott telephoned Consuelo to say that they were employing a swimming teacher on Friday afternoons and asked if Angela might like to come along. She said that all the parents were 'chipping in' and that the cost would be three shillings (15p in today's money) per child, per session. Consuelo was delighted that her young daughter might have such an unexpected opportunity, from an already generous family.

The teacher was an elderly woman who separated the children into two groups; young ones who were beginners and older ones who could already swim. The little ones had their instruction first and then the teacher would move on to the older children.

One afternoon, whilst waiting for their lesson, Henrietta and Rory Scott and Angela observed one of the family dogs urinating with a cocked leg over one of the guest's towels and then nonchalantly strolling off. Naturally, the children started smirking and sniggering, then burst into uncontrollable laughter, overlooked by disapproving adults who were quite oblivious of the joke. It was their secret.

Draughty Crotch!

Although Angela was keen on anything equine, she always put her studies first. This meant that her pony Satellite was never very fit during the winter for fox hunting and could only attend for a few hours.

On this occasion, she had returned home from Harper Adams, helped with the turkey plucking and tried to fit in a bit of riding so she could hack to a hunt meet just after Christmas. The hunt was to meet at Rowner Mill near Billingshurst.

On the said morning, she was awake early and fed the pony with a few extra oats in the hope of a lively ride. After finishing off in the stable, she came indoors to change. What she had not allowed for were those extra few Christmas pounds which made her breeches a wee bit tight. Normally, she would wear her thick, old school games knickers under her breeches for warmth but she quickly realised that some skimpy hipsters would have to suffice.

Whilst mounting, her predicament became obvious. A tight under carriage whilst astride is not desirable and could have consequences. Even raising her foot to the stirrup had taken considerable effort. Fortunately, Satellite was well behaved at gates and Angela was able to lean over and open and shut them without having to dismount. Nevertheless, just before she arrived at Tanners Farm, she felt her breeches split right up the crotch!

Undeterred and determined not to miss out on her hunt, she quickly devised a plan. With friends at Tanners Cottage, she decided to ask Jenny if she could borrow her sewing kit to quickly cobble the seam, whilst standing with her breeches between her knees; time was of the essence. Stitching complete, she set off for the hunt, leaving behind an amused Jenny.

On approaching the meet, she came across a young fellow unloading his horse and, as hunting etiquette demands, waited for him to mount so that they could proceed together. Angela had come across this young imp before; a skinny, weedy runt with no backside to fill his breeches, not even any calf muscles to fill his long riding boots. Regardless, she outlined her adventure and quite expected the young chap to laugh alongside her. With no reaction, her heckles were aroused and she decided that her first impression of him had been correct, he was indeed a po-faced twit.

The hunt went well for a couple of hours and then while jumping a small tiger trap, Angela felt a great surge of cold air around her crotch as her temporary stitching gave way under the strain of her well-proportioned thighs.[67] It was time to withdraw. On returning home and giving Satellite his bran mash, Angela proceeded indoors to relay her extraordinary day to her parents.

Angela was a determined young woman and was not going to let a few extra Christmas chocolates separate her from a day's hunting.

Returning to the Saddle

During the 1970s, the Cowdray, Chiddingfold and Leconfield Hunt had a change in hunt master. The new man, Nigel Peel, was a pleasant, outgoing, friendly person. He took a shine to Berns and his old stories of Lord Leconfield in the saddle, and loved hearing about Berns' hunting past.

Over the next few seasons, the two men got to know each other better and Nigel encouraged Berns to hunt once more on his pony, Sea Mist. Over the next five to ten years, Berns went hunting on numerous occasions. Later on, Berns and Consuelo hosted at least one hunt meet per season. Sometimes, there were over fifty riders and nearly as many foot followers. Often, the point-to-point cohort of relations would arrive and help handing out the sausage rolls, mince pies and glasses of sherry, then help Consuelo clear away.

---

[67] Tiger trap: a type of horse jump.

Having Fun

'Treat others as you want to be treated.'

A FAVOURITE OF CONSUELO'S

In Times of Trouble ...

In retrospect, Berns' constitution and health were never really robust enough to be a farmer. Sometimes, his health problems involved a period in hospital. Looking back, these must have been worrying times. With Berns in hospital however, the extended family would always rally round.

This help took a practical approach and was aimed at helping Consuelo with a range of things, involving laundry, cooking and transport to hospital. Berns' sisters would decide who was doing what, so that everyone played their part. Every four or five days, an uncle and aunt team would arrive with a stack of clean laundry and another pile of tins containing edible goodies, and take away another load of washing. This meant that Consuelo could concentrate on keeping the farm ticking over.

Meanwhile, the menfolk, Berns' brother Tom, brothers-in-law Alastair, Jimmy, Stan, Paul, and cousin Eric were on-call to take Consuelo and the children for hospital visits, if time permitted.

When things were difficult, the large family rallied round and were always there to support one another.

Family Gatherings at Gwen and Alastair's

Over the years, there were many family parties of varying sizes and mixes of relations. One thing they all had in common was that they were fun and centred around good food. Many memories of family parties coalesce around Berns' eldest sister Gwen and her husband Alastair. He was an accountant by trade and had worked for Woolworths for many years, retiring from the London Head Office in quite a senior position. They were a generous couple and hosted fantastic parties, especially at Christmas.

In the 1960s, the couple lived in a wonderful, large Edwardian house in Wokingham. It had two large reception rooms and a magnificent hall with a gong. The parties usually started in the late afternoon or early evening and therefore, farm chores had to be completed early. On arrival, in their best clothes, the children quickly mingled with their cousins. It was then time to eat.

With so many people to feed, there were two sittings in the large dining room; the children ate first. The siblings all remember vividly the wonderful crackers that adorned their place settings. These were expensive and highly decorative. Angela still has a gold-coloured bracelet that she wears and has been asked on more than one occasion if it was gold. The answer being quite simple, 'Oh no, don't you know? It came out of a Christmas cracker.'

The spread was sometimes cold ham, turkey and a variety of salads prepared by Gwen, followed by a whole range of desserts brought by the aunts. With everyone fed, it was time to withdraw into the sitting room for party games and have some laughs.

The children just loved seeing the adults joining in and having some fun. Angela particularly liked a game called consequences. For this, everyone was given the name of a piece of kitchen equipment. Berns' brother Tom was always a saucepan (pronounced 'source-pehn'). A round bread board was spun and the spinner would call out the name of another utensil. That person then had to capture the board before it fell flat on the floor. If it fell flat, there was a consequence. This might involve singing a few lines of a song into the chimney. Once again, everyone had ample opportunity to snigger and make fun of the performer. On one occasion, some diluted orange squash was put in a chamber pot and kept in reserve. When cousin Barbara failed to rescue the board in time, she was blindfolded and had to rescue an old penny from the potty. Of course, when the blindfold was removed, she thought she had been fishing it out of something else! The crowd roared with laughter. Another year, cousins Craig and Sarah had been given a tape recorder for Christmas and everyone was expected to perform into the microphone.

Billingshurst Flower Show and Great Aunt Dais

Daisy, known as Dais, was Berns' youngest aunt on his mother's side; she was an Elliott. Born in 1898, she was sadly orphaned in 1907 and eventually lived with Berns' parents, Annie and Sidney Lerwill at Malham. After leaving school, she worked in Brighton for a photographer largely doing hand-tinting.[68] She was a stunningly good-looking young woman and married a rather plain man called Arthur Grainger who had money. He came from Barnard Castle in Northumberland and for many years they lived in Hartlepool.

After Arthur died, Dais returned to Sussex to live at Boundary Cottage on Station Road in Billingshurst. Slowly, a family tradition evolved whereby family members attending the Billingshurst Flower Show would congregate at Dais's house for a late afternoon tea.

Dais liked to hold court and enjoyed being the centre of attention as the family filed through, especially revelling in the gentlemen's compliments. She had a debutante quality and one could imagine Dais in her younger days in the foyer of a grand hotel parading the season's fashions for select clientele only. Her willow-like poise, meticulously tended hair, expensive perfume and twisted, silver cigarette holder gave her an air of an aristocratic character from an Agatha Christie, Poirot novel. Antique furniture adorned with expensive trinkets, a Murano glass ashtray and the odd photograph of the couple holidaying in somewhere like Capri, suitably encased in an expensive frame reflected her wealth and good fortune.

Afternoon tea was an ad-hoc affair and was served over several hours as different family groups filtered through. Tea was naturally served in bone china tea cups, and a cake stand advertised teatime dainties and sandwiches without vulgar crusts. This tea was for the more sophisticated. On fine days, some of the guests might migrate outside into the small, but beautifully kept rose garden laced with brick paths.

The country bumpkins from Frithwood had more than one feast at Great Aunt Dais's soirées.

---

[68] Before colour photography, any colour on photographs had to be hand-tinted onto the prints.

Wisborough Green Flower Show and Cricket Match

Over the years, these two annual events in Wisborough Green acted as informal family gatherings. Uncles, aunts and cousins would arrive early in order to commandeer the space for their cars in front of Forest Stores under the horse chestnut trees. Parking en masse meant that teatime treats could be easily shared and enjoyed later in the day. This location was also handy, as Berns' cousin Eileen lived for a while at Forge Cottage next to Forest Stores, which meant that the public toilets could be avoided. Prior to this, Berns' Aunt Elsie had lived on the Green in Yew Tree Cottage quite near the pavilion.[69]

Harvest pressures meant that Berns and Consuelo rarely attended but as the children got older, they would venture off on their own in search of the extended family. These sojourns were lots of fun as on the walk to Wisborough Green, the siblings discussed what teatime goodies might be on offer. With picnic rugs laid out and garden chairs strewn around, the youngsters might touch base and then explore before returning about four o'clock.

On flower show days, the Lerwills would sometimes take part in the races along with uncles and aunts. Over the years, all three siblings took part in various races including one called Round-the-Green.

Once concluded, it was time for tea. All the aunts were good cooks and each child had their own favourite delight. Angela was particularly partial to Nance's flapjacks. This was the finale of the afternoon and enjoyed by everyone as the crowd divulged who they had met and their change in circumstances, regarding largely health, wealth and family matters. Cups of lukewarm tea followed with misshaped egg sandwiches, slices of fruit cake and other treats.

With the balmy sun retreating over Petworth in the west, the various parties would then start to pack away their wares. The siblings knew it was time to head home. Upon their return, they would partake in another tea, telling their parents all about their afternoon in Wisborough Green.

---

[69] Elsie was one of the fourteen Lerwill children to grow up at Pallingham Manor.

It is sad to think that at the time, one simply took these events for granted.

Auntie Nance's Flapjacks:

> 8 oz butter or margarine
> 8 oz brown sugar
> 12 oz porridge oats, not jumbo

> * Set oven 150°C, grease 8" x 8" tin.
> * Melt fat and add sugar in saucepan.
> * Mix in oats and pack tightly in the greased tin.
> * Bake for 10 to 15 minutes until firm.
> * Cut and leave to cool in the tin.

Point-to-Point Meetings

Family outings away from Frithwood were few and far between as there was simply too much to do. Managing a mixed farm meant that there was never a really quiet period, as one peak went into another. Nevertheless, after lambing in the pole barns shortly after Christmas, there was a slight lull in March and April. This meant that the odd afternoon off could be combined with Berns' love of horses and racing.

Point-to-points are amateur steeplechase races organised by local hunts to generate revenue. Normally, horses that are entered have to have hunted a few times during the previous hunting season to qualify. As a 'thank you', local farmers who allow the hunt to run over their land are granted free car passes. This meant at least one cheap afternoon's entertainment.

Getting ready was a tactical operation. Consuelo was responsible for making sure that all the siblings were ready before Berns came indoors to change. Heaven-help anyone in the bathroom when Berns wanted to use it. She was also in charge of making a bountiful stack of sandwiches and flasks for the trip. Once ready, the children and picnic would be bundled into the back of the van and off they would go.

In the 1960s, there were about five point-to-point courses within a thirty-mile radius of Frithwood. These included, Pepper Harrow (Surrey Union Hunt), Lingfield, Midhurst (Cowdray Hunt), Parham (Crawley and Horsham Hunt) and Tisman's Common (Chiddingfold and Leconfield Hunt).[70] Tisman's was the family's favourite course but it came to an end in the late 1960s, probably because of the land changing hands. After this, Parham course started hosting more meetings for different hunts. It had good infrastructure which facilitated ever-increasing car numbers.

Tucked under the South Downs just outside Storrington, the course benefited from a small hill, where spectators could congregate to watch the entire event. This was especially important towards the end of the races, as the crowd's excitement would grow and hand gestures and shouting took over the seemingly quiet rural setting.

Invariably, the Frithwood contingent were late and so one of the first things to do after tucking into lunch was to find the gang of relations. There were the usual stalwarts; Berns' eldest sister Gwen and husband Alastair, brother Tom, cousin Jean, her children Barbara, Jill, and sometimes George, and others on a random basis. If Tom was present, locating the group was easy as his ears tended to stick out and acted like a homing beacon, especially if the party was on the hill.

Alastair and Gwen had no family of their own, and were kind to all the nieces and nephews. At point-to-point meetings, this might involve Alastair letting the youngsters each choose a horse in at least one race, which he would then back on the Tote. If it won, the winnings went to the niece or nephew. Sometimes, if there were few in attendance and a race had few runners, Alastair might back all the horses, ensuring that each child got a winner.

Occasionally, local celebrities might attend and both Rhona and Angela acquired autographs; Rhona got Jimmy Edwards' at Parham and Angela got Terry Scott's at Pepper Harrow.

Berns and Consuelo would often skip the last race to avoid the inevitable traffic queues on leaving the venue, preferring to make a

---

[70] Later merged with Cowdray Hunt.

161

quick get-away. It was then a mad dash home to all-hands-on-deck, although in reality this usually meant Berns and Consuelo rushing around tending the animals outside. The children might loaf about indoors gobbling the last of the desiccated lunch sandwiches, whilst waiting for Consuelo to lay out another tea table of food for them to devour.

Sheila's Wedding

Sheila was Flo's daughter (by her first marriage) and the eldest of Berns' nieces. Whilst nursing in London, Sheila had met Kenneth Webster, a lovely Scottish man. The couple planned to marry in June 1966. With arrangements gaining momentum, Sheila asked Berns if he could give a speech at the reception. Although terrified by the prospect, he felt that he could hardly refuse his cherished niece.

Instantly dumbfounded, Berns wondered what he had taken on, as he was an introvert. He felt petrified at the prospect of standing in front of over a hundred people. Even scribbling some notes had ended in disaster with crumpled paper and the odd expletive. He felt doomed.

One night, close to the big day, Consuelo woke to find Berns also awake beside her. Lying side by side in the darkness, she asked him what was wrong. The problem was the speech. With her usual pragmatism and wisdom, Consuelo suggested that he gave her his rendition in the dark. With the rehearsal over, the couple rolled over and returned to their slumber.

On the day, Berns delivered a perfectly adequate speech. No one was any the wiser about his previous misgivings.

Bonfire Parties

Harvest complete, the children's attention was quickly drawn to the next thing on the calendar; bonfire night. With the evenings drawing in and the chill of the odd frost, the children would prepare for the annual bonfire gathering. This consisted mainly of about twenty-five of Berns' local relations and a few school friends.

The children approached the bonfire with military precision. Preparation started early in October and as the due date approached, wood-gathering forays to Northwood increased, hauling large and small timber to the bonfire site at the top of the hill in front of the old farmhouse. Sometimes, subterfuge was used. The children would carry timber to the track and then organise themselves to use any means possible to drag the larger timber home.

After ascertaining when an appropriate vehicle might be due, such as a feed lorry or baker's van, the plan could take shape. Hugh would hide out of sight and the girls would position themselves just in front of the timber and encourage the driver to stop, asking in a sweet and coy manner for a lift back to the farm. This gave Hugh enough time to climb aboard and somehow drag the wood along the track for the short distance to the farm boundary at the top of the hill. At the gate, the girls would politely offer to open the gate, giving Hugh enough time to unhitch the logs.

Hugh was the architect of bonfire design. With largely wet lumber, it was essential that the fire drew properly to get a good blaze. Hugh's given plan was simple, a central pole onto which all the 'straights' would be leant against. This had the advantage of allowing a small cavity around the bottom of the pole to be left empty, ready to be packed with highly flammable materials on the afternoon of the party.

Consuelo's task was one of inviting relations and asking them to bring a plate of food and a few fireworks. With numbers tallied, Consuelo might consult her trusty *Woman's Weekly* magazine for seasonal bonfire-related recipes, such as toffee apples and bonfire toffee. The youngsters loved these foods having bonfire names and were convinced that they tasted better because of them.

As the deadline approached, excitement mounted and the children became obsessed with the weather forecast. Dry weather was essential if the party was to be a successful shindig. On the afternoon of the party, Berns and the children would pack the base around the pole with old baler string and used paper feed sacks ready to be lit later.

With the table set with simple fayre, guests would start arriving, parking their cars well away from the bonfire site. Once assembled, the fire was ready to be lit. Visible from Wisborough Green, motorists must have wondered whether a Spanish Armada beacon had been relit, signalling the population to ready themselves. But no, this was just a family gathering, enjoying the pleasure of a bonfire and a few fireworks followed by a simple supper before the winter set in good and proper.

These parties continued for about four or five years, until Hemp, the farm dog, escaped from the woodshed. Sadly, he was run over on the A29. At the time, Berns had sheep away from home and was convinced that Hemp had gone to check on the flock. He was a wonderful old dog, and after this tragedy, the family lost interest.

The fire had truly gone out.

Other Frithwood Celebrations

Over the years, there were lots of gatherings, from simple children's birthdays to finishing off with Consuelo's seventieth birthday party. Often, they would be family crowds celebrating birthdays, but not always.

Angela remembers her fifth birthday when a few of her friends were invited from school. The tea table was laid and the children started arriving mid-afternoon. Unfortunately, in March it was far too cold to play outside so typical games were played in the sitting room. On completion of pass-the-parcel, musical cushions and the like, the children were ushered into the dining room. After tea, Consuelo wrapped the leftover birthday cake and the children were bundled into the old green van for Berns to deliver them home. The children found the novelty of being taken home in the pig van, great fun.

Time moved on. Berns and Consuelo celebrated their silver wedding anniversary on 31 December 1975. Rhona and Angela decided to host two parties; Rhona would invite the relations to her marital home in Dorking for a buffet and Angela would prepare a dinner party at the farm for a few friends. Naturally, Angela's main course was roast turkey and it was followed by an exotic pavlova involving pineapple and stem ginger. With red candles on the table and festive decorations still *in situ*, the scene was set. Both parties went well.

After her A-levels the following year, Angela asked if she could host a party outside. She and her boyfriend at the time, John Roberts, worked hard to arrange things. Berns brought round some small straw bales and left the low trailer parked at the short end of a rectangle. This was to be the stage for Roger Hird, another school friend to use for the disco and as a table for the buffet and drinks. Berns and Consuelo were under strict instructions to stay indoors unless their help was requested. The party went well. However, over a late breakfast the next day, Consuelo asked about a couple of the guests who had apparently wandered into the house and sat with Berns and Consuelo in the sitting room. It was established that they were gatecrashers.

At twenty-one, Angela had a dinner party for about twelve friends, in the Easter holidays, whilst home from Harper Adams. That night, Berns and Consuelo were persuaded to take their hot-water bottles and an old Tilley lamp to the caravan for the night, so as not to cramp the youngsters' style. They returned in the morning clutching their bedding, looking in need of a hot drink before starting the morning chores.

The last sizeable party was for Consuelo's seventieth birthday held in 1996. Unfortunately, the weather looked changeable, but the rain held off just long enough for the lunch. Family and friends mingled, although sadly the Lerwills all knew that it would probably be the last of the big gatherings at the farm. It was another loose end tied up.

Pulborough Livestock Market

In retrospect, livestock markets were probably on the wane as far back as the late 1950s and 1960s as farms became larger and vertical integration became more commonplace along the supply chain.[71] The auctioneers King & Chasemore and a trusty gang of hangers-on,

---

[71] Vertical integration: where one company engages in two or more stages of production, e.g. producing and retailing milk.

ensured that the old market at Pulborough survived until the early 1970s. Finally, it closed after Berns' cousin Guy Lerwill moved to North Devon in September 1971.

The market was built next to the railway station, on ground now used as a small, triangular-shaped car park. This unusual piece of ground had resulted from the railway being laid onto a high embankment necessary to avoid the River Arun's floodplains. The railway travelled over the road below, via a high bridge built at an angle, resulting in two sides of the triangle. The last side was the approach road to the station. Photographic evidence suggests that farmers and growers started congregating and supposedly selling their produce just after the station was erected. With the railway being opened in 1859 and the market in 1866, one can only assume that some Victorian entrepreneur spotted an opportunity.

Fortunately, the site was fairly level but this was about its only saving grace. It was awkward to get to; up a steep bit of road, difficult for lorries with heavy loads of livestock that had to approach slowly, turn and then generate enough power to climb the steep bank, then turn in to the main gates, reverse and unload. Some animals were transported by hauliers, who would unload and then go on their way. Some farmers and dealers, such as Dennis Marten and Guy Lerwill, had their own lorries and would unload and park. Limited parking was a problem and participants often parked in King & Chasemore's saleroom car park, near the station café.

Vehicles unloading cattle usually took the space to the left-hand side of the gates as the weighing scales, cattle pens and sales ring were in that area, along with the auctioneer's office. In the middle patch, there were two rows of double pens for sheep with a raised wooden platform on which the auctioneer would perform. Over to the right, just under the railway embankment, there were more pens under a rudimentary, corrugated iron roof. These were used for young calves and pigs, and at the far end were some small cages for poultry and rabbits.

From the main road, the market could be accessed by pedestrians via one of two stairways. One was in good order, built of brick with smart handrailings whereas the other was a ramshackled affair and not for the faint-hearted, with missing stones and quite uneven in places, without any hand support. With animals weighed, graded and penned, most participants would then move off to the Station Hotel (later renamed the Water's Edge Hotel) opposite the stairways for a pint before the market bell was rung at eleven o'clock. This was always rung from the top of the good stairway and then outside the pub by Jobi, a market drover. He was a tall man with one arm who wore a brown serge coat, a pair of black, thick-rimmed glasses and a cap.

Once assembled, the business of selling would commence.

Old Market Characters

Auctions tend to attract all kinds of people; Pulborough Market was no exception. The mix of characters included auctioneers, farmers, farm managers, butchers, hauliers, market drovers and assorted others. All played their role in keeping the old place ticking over, providing enough animals arrived on a regular basis to make it financially viable.

During the late 1950s and through the 1960s, the market had a number of auctioneers, each with their own responsibility. During the 1960s, Dick Alden sold the cattle. He was a middle-aged stocky man who usually wore a tweed jacket and thick-rimmed, Ronnie Barker type glasses and spoke with quite a posh accent. Leslie Weller sold the sheep. He was a tall, well-proportioned man who had a kind smile. Berns admired the fact that he had come from a humble home, had done well, but had never taken on any airs and graces. Angela remembered him out fox hunting as a pleasant, approachable person, who always rode a large horse. Mark Monkhouse sold the chicken and rabbits, if there were any. Other market staff included David Scott-Pitcher, the market clerk, Jobi and Alf Buckman, the drovers. Mr McBride was the Meat and Livestock Commission Grader.[72]

Regular vendors and farmers included several local estates, plus

---

[72] See Appendix J: List of Pulborough Market Attendees.

large and small farmers. These comprised the Leconfield Estate (Petworth), Parham Estate, Norfolk Estate (Arundel), Godman Estate (Lower Beeding), Brinsbury College, Guy and Simon Lerwell, Bill Wadey, Vic and Clive Allen, Norman Vellacott, Jake Dallyn, Jack Puttock, Dennis Marten and Berns. They were a motley crew.

To the outsider, those farmers standing around the stock pens on Monday mornings might have looked a disparate group, but they had many common traits. Some might say they were an archetypical cluster. To others, they were loners, often insular in outlook and suspicious of strangers especially those with no agricultural credentials. Even those among them who were better off were half-admired and half-resented, as flecks of envy occasionally surfaced. It was an environment that Berns knew well and understood.

Buyers came from the south coast through to Dorking and were mostly independent butchers, several of whom still slaughtered their own animals in abattoirs at the back of their shops. Ted Cripps was still slaughtering his own beasts well into the mid-1960s in Billingshurst. For many years, Ted Cripps supported the market, often buying cattle that Guy Lerwill regularly brought to Sussex from North Devon. Then things changed and Ted Cripps bypassed the market, purchasing directly from Devon. Simon Lerwill, Guy's son, remembered that from about this time, his parents rarely bought meat from Cripps, in defiance. Nevertheless, as Cripps' sausages were about the best in the county, the odd sausage was still purchased on the sly. Berns always sold his porkers to Ted Joyce privately, although King & Chasemore always got their commission.

Some independent butchers bought in pairs. This helped to share the costs of haulage, slaughter and continuity of supply. Barry Shillingford, Barry Wood, Mr Durrant and Mr Mitchell all did this.

Hauliers were used by both farmers and butchers for transporting animals to and from market. Regular carriers included the Swabeys, a father-and-son team. Father Fred wore a cap, thick grey trousers and metal-capped boots. He was a quiet man but had a deep voice. His son David had a ruddy complexion and was well built. Simon remembered that he helped at the market with subsidy work, punching various animal's ears. Tom and Roger Green were another father-and-son team and regularly worked for Ted Joyce, the butcher. Roger had dark hair, was quiet and had a leathery, sunburnt face.

In addition to these main players, other people also attended whose businesses relied upon farming, such as fertiliser, machinery and feed salesmen. The market was a good venue to catch a number of possible customers, without having to go farm to farm. For example, Richard Gadd from Fittleworth used the market to network with farmers for his fertiliser business.

Selling usually concluded between twelve and one-thirty. It was then time for the animals to be loaded and for the drovers to wash down the pens. Nevertheless, for a select few cohorts, it was also time to gather at the Swan pub for lunch. Simon remembers that the usual suspects were his father Guy, Leslie Weller, Reg Haydon and Alex Lawson. Others might join them from time to time.

Although well under age, Simon would join them in the school holidays, stuck out of sight, but listening intently as the men chortled over farming matters. Usually, the crowd would disperse between two to three-thirty, sometimes a bit worse for wear. Simon recalled being told a story about a bale of straw being set alight in Alex Lawson's pickup as he left the Swan car park, unaware that he had a blaze raging behind his seat, as he drove through Pulborough High Street.

Ebernoe Fair

Ebernoe is a small hamlet, near Petworth about fifteen miles north west of Frithwood. On 25 July, St James's Day, the village holds a horn fair. The event consists mainly of a cricket match and a spit-roast, the finale of which is the presentation of the ram's horns to the batsman gaining the most runs. Afterwards, the roasted lamb is enjoyed by sportsmen and onlookers.

As July was slap-bang in the middle of haymaking, the Lerwills rarely attended. However, on this occasion, it was decided that they would go. With the children and picnic loaded in the old green van,

Berns turned the ignition key. Silence. After a couple of abortive attempts, he used the starting handle. More silence. A tractor was then used to haul the obstinate van up the slope to try a hill start. Still more silence. With tension rising, Consuelo interceded and suggested that they should eat their tea and give everyone (and the van) a break.

Rhona, aged about eight, and Angela, about four, found this quite exciting and asked Consuelo what they should say if anyone arrived while they were eating. Consuelo played along with the game and suggested that if they were strangers, they were to pretend that they were just out for a picnic otherwise they might think them quite mad. The little girls giggled with delight.

After eating, Consuelo persuaded Berns to try one more time. It worked and the family dashed off to Ebernoe, late, but happy.

Ebernoe Young Farmers' Club

Jean Elliott was Berns' first cousin and was married to Kenneth Grigor who farmed at Stopham, near Pulborough. Their three children (Barbara, Jill and George) were born at about the same time as the Lerwill trio and the families got on well together. Later, Barbara trained as a medical secretary, Jill as a farm secretary and George helped on the farm. By the early 1970s, Jill and George had joined the Ebernoe Young Farmers' Club and later on, asked Angela if she would like to tag along.

Young Farmers' Clubs are marvellous organisations offering, often isolated youngsters, a chance to meet and enjoy rural pursuits together. They should however, come with a warning of 'buyer beware' as they are a marriage market where unsuspecting females can be snared. Even at about thirteen years old, Angela had no intention of getting involved with a Sussex farmer's son, as she knew what might come afterwards; a lot of hard work. Nevertheless, she loved her cousins and was happy to join them.

Jill and George were well aware that Berns was not a willing taxi driver and so would often collect Angela from the bottom of Blackgate Lane. This meant a fairly big detour but they were kind, supportive and never seemed to mind. The meetings were held at Kirdford Village Hall and usually consisted of a talk from a visiting speaker about anything agricultural. The highlight for Angela however, was going to the pub afterwards with her older cousins. At the time, the Half Moon, the Stag and the Well Diggers were all popular haunts. Afterwards, the three cousins would retire to Stopham for the night.

The family lived at Stopham Manor, a beautiful Elizabethan house, which nestled in a paddock next to the old Norman church of St Mary the Virgin. Built of Wealden sandstone, the house was large but not enormous, offering plenty of living space for a half-grown family. After a long-term tenant had departed, the Stopham Estate had modernised the old dwelling and installed central heating. Nights spent at Stopham were sheer luxury for Angela, as not only was her bedroom warm but the bed was always equipped with a stone hot-water bottle lovingly filled by Jean. The mornings also brought their delights.

Upon dressing and going downstairs to the kitchen, Angela would find some of the family already assembled. Jean would be busy hovering around the stove boiling eggs and checking on the toast, while Kenneth would be sitting with his book open, reading quietly. Sometimes, Barbara's boyfriend John would be sitting at the kitchen table engaging in shenanigans with the family dog Jasper. The dog would beg and John would often smack him on the nose with a teaspoon which Angela thought was a bit mean. Jasper was undeterred and usually came back for more. George would arrive a bit later for his breakfast after finishing the morning's milking.

Getting back to Frithwood was often a bit ad hoc with a whole range of possibilities, including part-lifts, collections, deliveries, but it always happened sometime on the Saturday. Sadly, George died in his twenties in July 1980 and Angela is so grateful that she had those cherished memories of him whilst attending Young Farmers'.

Changing Environment

'Nature is painting for us, day after day,
pictures of infinite beauty.'

JOHN RUSKIN (1819–1900)

The Arun Valley

Although biased, the Lerwills always felt that the panoramic view from their top gate was one of the best in the area. One ascended the small incline from Northwood to the fir trees and originally the poplar tree, turned to the right and there it was waiting for you. In front, was a solid five-bar wooden gate, on its right a crooked oak tree with branches venturing out from about ten feet asking to be climbed. On the left, a well-tended mixed farm hedge, sometimes hand-trimmed by Berns, after forgetting to ask the hedging contractor.

Beyond the gate, the flint track continued with a grassy mound in between the wheel lines which led one's eyes over the brow to a red-brick chimney peeping out, beckoning one forward. To the left was the roof of the old Sussex barn.

Once through the gate, a pause on the brow of the hill was advisable to fully appreciate the vista. Beyond Frithwood, the Arun Valley gently undulated downwards before rising once more towards Wisborough Green about a mile away. The main landmark was the old church on its defensive mound of yesteryear, immediately behind the farmhouse. The only modern-day blight was the ant-sized vehicles moving briskly along the A272 to and from Billingshurst, just above Orfold Farm to the right. To the left of Wisborough Green and slightly to the foreground, the manor house at Harsfold, punching its weight in red brick, nestled amongst a mass of trees. Further to the left was Lowfold Farm where the Osmarstons had a dairy farm.[73]

---

[73] See Appendix E: Geographical Position of Frithwood Farm.

For anyone venturing out for a Sunday-afternoon walk, this view was a worthy prize.

Bygone Buildings and Speculation

As one matures, it is all too easy to think that change is a modern phenomenon. Fortunately, common sense tells us otherwise. When Berns' family moved to Lee Place in 1924, there were lots of clues to the past. As the Frithwood siblings got older and listened to their father's oral history, they speculated as to how these remnants might fit together.

Drawing an imaginary line from Frithwood to Orfold Aqueduct brought one to the boundary between Frithwood and Lordings farms where three oak trees stood. Largely hidden from view on the Lordings side near a gateway lay some foundation stones suggesting some sort of past construction. The Wealden sandstone indicated a building that might date back to Frithwood's time. Documentary evidence reveals that it was still standing in 1913 and consisted of two buildings, suggesting a small barn with a yard and hovel.[74] Berns had always told the children that this was his hunch and that it was probably used for overwintering store cattle.

Without mechanisation, farmers in previous years found it easier to make hay and store it locally and then bring livestock to these outlying buildings. This helped to reduce work for both man and beast. One can only imagine a carter riding one of his trusted steeds to the old yard in the wintertime and tossing hay into the overhead racks to eagerly awaiting animals. With access to an adjacent stream, beasts might have wandered in and out of the old yard for fodder and shelter. Near to these old stones lay the Wey and Arun Canal.

The Arun Navigation between Pallingham Lock and Newbridge was opened in 1787. Its original purpose was to link Chatham Docks in Kent to Portsmouth, while England was at war with Napoleon. It had a relatively short life and ceased trading commercially in 1888.

---

[74] Detail from Victorian Ordnance Survey 6 inch to 1 mile map (1888–1913), Wisborough Green, West Sussex, co-ordinates 51.014802-0.504532.

Over the vagaries of time, the old canal decayed and was in a sorry state by the 1960s with trees, scrub and reeds growing in its watercourse. However, change was on the way.

At this point, there had been four canal structures virtually side by side; a cottage, bridge, lock and aqueduct. The cottage had been built near the aqueduct and was probably accessed to Wisborough Green through Orfold Farm's track. Sometimes, in spring, a few yellow daffodils could be spotted pushing through the undergrowth in the old garden. There was also an old quince tree which Consuelo would sometimes take advantage of for making jelly. Berns knew one of the last people to live in the cottage, Wilf Milham.

He was a short man, who always wore a cap, gaiters and looked smart. On Monday mornings in the 1960s, Wilf would be seen at Pulborough Livestock Market. Amongst other things, he collected Berns' pigs for Ted Joyce, the butcher, before taking them to slaughter. Wilf was about eighty at the time which suggested that he might have lived at Lordings in the 1880s/1890s. Berns never saw the cottage, but the Victorian map, suggests that it was still standing in 1913. Therefore, one can conclude that it was lost between 1913 and the mid-1920s.

The Wey and Arun Canal Society was formed in 1970, becoming a charitable trust in 1973. By October 1995, work had started repairing Lordings Lock, largely thanks to Henry Ayres, the landowner and one dedicated canal volunteer, Winston Harwood. Winston and his terrier Trevor lived in Reading, but during the summer months spent most weekends and some holidays, camping in a small caravan parked at the site for the season. Berns and Consuelo frequently saw Winston's silhouette beavering away alone or with other volunteers during the long balmy months. Consuelo would often stop and have a chat as she stole time to walk the farm dog. Upon completion, the Canal Trust erected a plaque recognising Winston's valiant efforts.

The bridge may have served two purposes, namely to allow the towpath to change sides from south to north, and also to access the cut-off brook which was effectively a small island. On its edge, along the meandering river, stood a large established oak tree which also hid another clue to the past. Under its branches mimicking the wings of a broody hen, hid some large sandstone blocks suggesting the remnants of an old bridge, now sadly lost. One had to ask why someone would go to the expense of constructing a stone bridge at that point? Perhaps in Frithwood's early days, this might have been the route to Wisborough Green.

Turning left, from the bridge along the canal through Green Brook one came to the track leading to Lee Place along a steep track. Until the late 1960s, there used to be a red-brick, humpback bridge over the canal leading to the farm. By the time the Lerwill siblings were older, it was in a poor state of repair and impractical for modern farm machinery. It was sadly demolished in the late 1960s by Joe Muller and Vic Newman. The new Harsfold Canal Bridge was rebuilt and opened in 2020 to a different design.

Just above the bridge, on the left-hand side, there used to be a cottage with its own well. It was still standing when Berns' parents, Sidney and Annie Lerwill took possession of Lee Place Farm in 1924. The woman who lived there helped Annie in the farmhouse. After that family left, it was demolished by Colonel Helm, the landlord. Then, all that remained was the outside toilet, in which Berns used to house his hens, whilst a schoolboy. Only a few daffodils remained. Without any obvious purpose, one can only speculate and question why a cottage would have been built so close to the canal and a fair distance from the farm buildings at Lee Place?

Following the towpath beyond the steep bank, one passed a sharp bend to the left into Torey Brook and then on to Haybarn. Just below the old farm buildings,[75] there had been another river bridge, canal bridge and cottage by the canal.[76] This old river bridge would have linked Haybarn to Shipbourne on the road to Bedham. The original canal bridge was replaced at some point by an ugly concrete structure, until the swing bridge was installed in 2005.[77]

A family who had a long association with Haybarn were the

---

[75] See 'Asset Strippers', pages 187–188.
[76] The current footbridge over the River Arun dates from about 1989.
[77] The swing bridge was originally on the Leeds and Liverpool Canal at Keighley, West Yorkshire.

Stepneys. Berns' sister Pam remembered Haybarn Cottage as a two-up two-down stone dwelling which may have been built at the time of the canal. Still living at the cottage in 1952, John Stepney, aged eighty-six, remembered working on the barges going along to Newbridge in the 1880s.[78] Once the canal ceased trading in 1888, the Stepneys stayed in the cottage but got their living from local farm work.

During the 1920s and 1940s, Jack Stepney worked for Tom Lerwill, Berns' uncle, who farmed at Northwood Farm. Jack and his wife had two sons, John and Henry, and two daughters, Eddy and Lizzy. Mrs Stepney worked in the farmhouse at Northwood carrying out cleaning and laundry. Sadly, the old cottage was demolished probably during Mr Burnford's ownership. By the mid-1960s, all that remained of any human habitations were a few clumps of snowdrops and daffodils buried in the undergrowth.

Northwood Farm also had its ghosts, as behind the current buildings there had been a number of farm cottages bordered by the Cricket Field and Eighteen Acres. Berns remembered that the cottages were in a terrible state after the Great Depression of the 1930s, hardly boasting a flake of paint. One had been occupied by the Murridges who, according to Berns' sister Pam, lived like animals and were always cadging food from Tom and Dorothy Lerwill. One son had married one of the Stepneys' daughters. The cottages were subsequently demolished, probably after the estate was divided and sold in 1949.

Prior to the big house being built at Lee Place, there had been another house. Although well before Berns' time, he suggested it was a period building which had been destroyed by fire. A plaque on Lee Place House today suggests that it was completed by 1910, however, the Victorian map suggests that the previous house was still standing in 1913. The map also confirms that the farm was then called Lee Farm, not Lee Place Farm. It would appear that the new, more imposing house was built to the back of the original site and that the word *place* slipped into its name. After all, the word *place* would have

---

[78] *West Sussex Waterways*, P. A. L. Vine, 1985.

given the new Edwardian house a greater feeling of grandeur and status to its owner Colonel Helm.[79]

The new house was built with a flat garden at the front finishing with a conifer hedge mounted on a raised platform, a sort of ha-ha. Angela wondered whether the stone from the old house might have been used to build the supporting wall beneath.

Other buildings at Lee Place date from this period, including the farmhouse, the red-brick farm cottages and the lodge on the drive to Lee Place House. The farmhouse was probably built around 1922, as the Connolly's builders found a scrap of wood in a wall with this date scribbled on it whilst doing refurbishment work in the 1970s.[80] Originally, Lee Place Farmhouse had been the Estate Bailiff's house. The current red-brick bridge over the Arun below Lee Place may also date from this period, as in Colonel Helm's time it would appear that Wisborough Green was the main way in and out.[81] Angela remembers being told that one of the reasons that the Helms had moved to Lee Place was because they had friends in Wisborough Green.

Adversane also saw at least two significant changes; the increase in traffic on the A29 and the loss of the old blacksmith's forge to the left-hand side of the public house near the bus stop. With no carthorses left to be shod, Mr Carley became a plumber, and was often tinkering away in the old building, as the children waited for their school buses. The forge was demolished around 1970 when the pub was renovated.[82]

This account only scratches the historical surface and would perhaps be a task for an enthusiastic researcher to explore at a later date …

---

[79] The Helms sadly lost two sons in the Great War. In the late1960s, Lee Place House was owned by two elderly sisters called O'Brien. They told Consuelo that sometimes they had seen the ghost of a First World War officer in full uniform. Perhaps this was one of the Helms' sons.

[80] The then owners.

[81] There is no evidence of a bridge on the Victorian map.

[82] Mr Carley was the last blacksmith at the Adversane forge.

Second World War Connections

At the sale of Lee Place Estate in 1949, the farms at Lee Place and Northwood were bought by Bill Wadey, a builder from Billingshurst. After refusing to transfer the farm tenancy to Berns' elder brother Tom, the writing was on the wall. Upon Sidney Lerwill's death, the tenancy would cease. In 1960, Sidney died and after thirty-six years, the family had to move. Widow Annie, Tom, Pam and her husband Paul, and their son, Philip moved to Commonlands Farm in West Chiltington.

By the early 1960s, the farms had changed hands again, and were bought by Mr Burnford (formerly Beinstein) who lived at Borough Farm near Codmore Hill. He was very much a hands-off sort of farmer. One can only imagine that he had fled Germany in the 1930s as the Nazi's intensified their hatred of all things Jewish and civilised.

He employed a number of men: Reg Mills, Vic Newman and Joe Muller were the longest serving. Mr Ignat Baduns and Mr David Asphar also worked for Mr Burnford but for a shorter period of time. Reg was the farm manager and lived at Borough Farm. Vic had been in the RAF during the Second World War and worked as a tractor driver. He lived in the farm cottage nearest Lee Place Farmhouse with his lovely wife Jackie and their black Labrador Tim.

Joe was German and was only sixteen when the war began in 1939. He was forced to join the Luftwaffe and was shot down over the English Channel and became a POW. He was sent to the USA where he helped to dredge the Mississippi river until after the war. Eventually, he married Marie and the couple came and lived in the old farmhouse at Northwood with their Alsatian dog Rex. Some years later, they moved into a newly built bungalow at Northwood. In addition to being a tractor driver, Joe was an extremely gifted craftsman who could turn his hand to just about anything.

As neither Marie nor Jackie had children of their own, they enjoyed the Lerwills' visits. Both ladies were good cooks and would often bring out some tasty offering. Rhona and Angela were frequent visitors, enjoying the undivided attention of either lady.

Mr Baduns was the last man to milk cows at Lee Place. He had four children who were a similar age to Hugh and Rhona. Elaine, the youngest girl, became a close friend to Rhona and the two still keep in touch to this day.

Mr Baduns was Latvian, and although Latvia was neutral during the war, the country became embroiled once the Russians arrived fighting the Germans alongside them. Mr Baduns was taken prisoner and was marched across Europe, eventually settling in England. After the war, he worked on a farm in the Weybridge area where he met and married Doris, an ex-land girl.

With borders realigned after the war and alliances changed, Mr Baduns found that he was unable to visit or even communicate with his family under Soviet rule, afraid of probable reprisals. Years passed and it was not until he was in his sixties that his son involved the Red Cross family tracing service. Records showed that his brother and sister had both died during the war, but his sister's daughter was keen to meet the family. The reunion took place and his niece duly showed Mr Baduns his parents' graves. Contact continued until Mr Baduns died, but without the Latvian language skills, the family has once again drifted apart.

Mr Asphar was Maltese and served in the Merchant Navy during the war trying to get supplies to Malta. In the mid-1950s, he came to England and met Ann, his wife, whilst working at the Meteorological Office before engaging in farm work. They briefly lived next door to Vic and Jackie Newman at Lee Place, with their four young children, Christine, Karen, Peter and Simon. After Mr Asphar developed serious health problems, they moved to Southwater. Christine has written some of her memories of Frithwood in 'Other People's Memories'.[83]

In addition to these connections, the Lerwills also had more direct wartime associations with a German POW. Walter worked and lived at Lee Place and after the war kept in touch with Berns' brother Tom. Walter's farm in Germany was effectively split in two by the divide but fortunately his house and farm buildings were on the Western

---

[83] See pages 198–200.

side. For many years, Walter did not see family or friends beyond the barrier.

From time to time, he visited the UK and the Lerwill family. Consuelo records an evening meal at the Well Diggers attended by several members of the extended family, including Flo, Jimmy, Tom, Jessie, Gwen, Alastair, Walter and his family in 1981. Walter had fond memories of his time with the Lerwills at Lee Place.

Opening Up

Until the mid-1960s, there were relatively few walkers or horse riders in the area. However, change was on the way. One day, the family noticed two horse riders descending the hill, a man and a young woman. They halted just above the garden gate as if they were medieval lieges waiting for a serf to come and relieve them of their mounts. Berns went to investigate.

The man said that he was Mr Shippam of Shippam's Pastes in Chichester and that he was on a mission to reopen old bridlepaths in the area. He spelt out that he was not happy that the bridlepath was wired off at the top of the hill. Berns explained that they were the first riders through since they had moved there some ten to fifteen years before and that they were welcome to use the two lower gates to continue their ride over towards Lordings Rough. They left muttering under their breath with an air of superiority.

Time moved on and a few others started to use the lower gates and then one day a group of ramblers arrived and knocked on the front door. Berns was out at the time and so Consuelo, with Hugh at her side, discussed the wire barrier. The leader brandished his wire cutters and said that they intended to cut the wire and reinstate the right of way. Miffed by their pomposity and arrogance, Hugh hurriedly followed them trying to stop the destruction but had no luck. He got quite angry and used a few expletives, stating that his father would be furious when he got home. It was to no avail and the fences were cut.

A week or two later in the parish news section of one of the local newspapers, a report from the Rambling Club reported that they had been verbally accosted by a youth at Frithwood Farm using a lot of bad language. Fortunately, there were no names.

With this, Berns eventually asked Joe Muller to make two hunting gates and these were duly installed. The march was on for strangers to infiltrate Frithwood's sacred ground.

Additions and Subtractions

While Colonel Robert Helm was the custodian of the Lee Place Estate from about 1914, there were many changes. In addition to some building projects, his wife was responsible for planting a number of trees. However, after their departure, there were various subtractions, including some hedgerows.

Along the new drive to Lee Place House, Mrs Helm planted two rows of horse chestnut trees, under-planted with daffodils. Sadly, the left-hand row was lost after the estate was sold in 1949. She also planted a single fir tree in each of the farm cottage gardens at Lee Place, one of which had a severe pruning by an over-zealous farm worker and subsequently looked quite strange. The other grew into a magnificent tree. A number of trees in and around the farm buildings at Lee Place, called the Park, were sadly lost over the years. She also planted a few poplar trees in Hog Field along the green lane to Haybarn, close to an old pond on the Lee Place side of the track.

Just the other side of the top gate at Frithwood (in the Lodge Field) on the brow of the hill stood a number of fir trees in a rough line with a poplar tree at one end; these were also planted by Mrs Helm. On the crest of the small hill, the poplar tree was a landmark for miles around for many years and the siblings loved to spot it when driving out and about. Sadly, this was lost in the Great Storm of 1987.

In the mid- to late 1960s, farming practices were changing and increasingly larger equipment was being used especially for arable work. Lee Place and Northwood farms had effectively merged and become an arable unit. The cosy hedges that had once protected lambing ewes and overwintering cattle became costly to maintain and inconvenient for modern cultivation. This meant that old, possibly ancient hedgerows, were discarded and burnt.[84] This greatly upset the Lerwills. Sadly, this devastation was happening all over the country at the time.

One such hedgerow was parallel to the bridlepath from Lee Place Lodge to Frithwood on the Wisborough Green side. This hedge split West and East Hilly Fields from Seed Field. Along this well-kept hedge were a number of walnut trees, probably planted by Mrs Helm. Nuts were often collected and on one occasion in the early 1970s, Consuelo and Angela dug up two walnut seedlings and transplanted them into the vegetable patch at the farm.

Another change was a large bomb hole, which Hugh remembered in Wablegate Field. It was close to the rue towards the corner.[85] Hugh remembered it being some three to four metres deep. It was filled in by Joe Muller and Vic Newman in the 1960s to aid the use of arable equipment.

The Great Storm, October 1987

Rain had been falling for several days and the rivers were starting to flood. Angela had business in Crawley the next day and planned to stay overnight at the farm. On approaching Five Oaks at about six o'clock, her car phone rang. Consuelo explained that Clapper's Pond was badly flooded and that she needed to backtrack and stay with her sister Rhona and husband, Roy, near Dorking.

With the children Alice and Justin cosy in bed, the three adults talked of the night ahead and their feeling of foreboding. As they mounted the stairs, the rain thrashed against the windowpanes, the wind howled and sped ever faster around the outside of the old cottage. Things looked ominous.

In the early hours, Justin, aged four, awoke and, frightened by the shenanigans outside, opted to cuddle close next to his father in the double bed. The two sisters made tea, retreated upstairs, and sat and

---

[84] Since the Second World War it is estimated that half of Britain's hedgerows have been grubbed out.

[85] Rue: a small stream running through a narrow copse.

looked out at the raging storm. Cradling their mugs, they pondered over the power of nature. Their view outside was a silhouetted affair with only shades of black. In the maelstrom, they saw mature trees a little distance from the house reminding them of Miss Masefield's drawings of out-turned umbrellas on windy days at North Heath School. Then, all of a sudden, a great gust of wind forced a large ash tree to fall, crashing to the ground not far from the cottage. Rhona and Angela were shocked, although not surprised.

In the morning, the true extent of the storm became apparent as the media started reporting the magnitude of the damage. Several more trees had fallen around the cottage at Mid Holmwood. No one in the house attempted to go to work.

The sisters tried telephoning the farm, but the lines were damaged. By mid-afternoon, Consuelo rang from a neighbour's house. She outlined that they were well but that there had been quite a lot of damage. A turbulent flurry of wind had swept across Seed Field, caving in the window of the corn store and ripping off a large part of the asbestos roof. One largish piece had flown over the loose boxes and landed in the farmyard; others were scattered like a bomb blast. The grain in the shed was ruined. Tiles were missing off the old barn and cart shed. She also said that the poplar tree and a few of the fir trees at the top of the hill had fallen, and in the garden, a Bramley tree and the prunus had blown over. In addition to this, there were some fourteen trees of varying sizes blocking the track through Northwood, as well as countless others either completely flat or lying propped against each other.

It took about ten days for the electricity and the telephone to be reconnected and many months for the debris and insurance claims to be settled. It had been a night to remember.

Disappearing Dairy Cows and Churn Stands

The second half of the twentieth century saw huge changes in UK agriculture. Dairy farming was one such example. In Angela's younger days, she could remember Berns saying that dairy farmers were lucky as the Milk Marketing Board (MMB) provided a monthly cheque and a guaranteed price. With pressures from the European Union regarding market competition and the continuing move towards bigger units (note the industrial word), many dairy farmers were either getting out or becoming larger.[86] From some twelve dairy farms within a two-mile radius of Frithwood in the 1960s, only a couple remained in 1997, when the family left Frithwood.[87]

Bigger units meant that churns became impractical and the MMB instigated an enormous shift in favour of bulk-tanker collection. However, churn stands remained for a number of years as small landmarks and beacons of a bygone history. They were dotted everywhere and made from a variety of materials.

Lee Place Farm's churn stand was by Lee Place Lodge, where the lanes met. At Adversane, there were two churn stands nearly opposite each other. One was just outside the gate of Southlands Farm owned by the Voices. The other, used by the Pinches, was near to the telephone box and constructed of old railway sleepers. Lordings Farm also had one slightly projecting onto the road.

After years of disuse, many were lost, but some can still be seen adorned with pots of flowering annuals, giving a clue to the past history of some gentrified farmhouse sold off to wealthy outsiders seeking the rural idyll.

Gateways

Gateways were also changing as machinery got larger and fewer in number. In the 1960s, farm machinery was still relatively small and could usually manoeuvre through the old wagon gateways. With machinery getting bigger however, these gaps were too narrow to use and there was a trend to widen the openings and install double

---

[86] Over the past twenty years, dairy cow numbers in Britain have halved and dairy farms reduced from around 30,000 in 1995 to 12,000 today, although production has stayed stable.

[87] The families (and farms) are as follows: Osmarstons (Lowfold), Luckins (Orfold), Ayres (Lordings), Voices (Southlands), Myrams (Steepwood), Pinches (Woodlands), Padfields (Mill House), Dallas (Tote), Brinsbury School of Agriculture (Stablebarn), Guy Lerwill (Pallingham) and Burnfords (Lee Place).

metal gates, often with padlocks. Access from field to main roads also reduced as it became too dangerous with increased traffic levels. It is all too easy to think that the countryside stays still, but it evolves over time just like any environment.

Changes South of Wisborough Green Church

Fortunately, Wisborough Green has not encountered mass development, unlike some villages nearby. Sadly, some old buildings have been lost, others renovated, new houses squeezed into vacant plots, roads widened, hedges grubbed out and pavements extended.

Over time, Harsfold and its surroundings have seen a number of changes. After the Second World War, part of the manor house was demolished, reducing it in size and making it more conducive for modern family use. The current porch is a relatively new addition, bought in Ireland by its current inhabitants, Rory and Jane Scott. Regrettably, part of the old coach house in the stable block, halfway along the drive, collapsed in the 1970s/1980s whilst being used to store grain, because of the sheer weight. Luckily, the impressive tree-lined drive remains and gives a wonderful display of daffodils in springtime.

Fortunately, the beautiful period farmhouse at Harsfold with its pond, island and bridge has survived largely intact. With changing land management however, the old timber-framed farm buildings became obsolete, sadly fell into disrepair, and some of them have now disappeared.

The old farmstead was built adjacent to the farmhouse with a large Sussex barn, cattle yard and hovel with tiled roofs to the back of the picturesque house. On the lane which peters out to the bridlepath leading towards the River Arun, there was another smaller barn with an open-sided hovel and yard, hugging the trackside, amongst the majestic oak trees which still stand. Next to the relatively modern brick dairy parlour stood a cart shed with an upper floor and an outdoor stairway. There was a small track in between the buildings which led towards the brooks and a view of Orfold Farm, with a duck pond on the right-hand side.

Along the lane towards the village, there used to be a single-storey wooden chalet built on the left-hand side, next to the pond. For a time, it was used by one of the Scotts' relations as an art studio. Further, on the left and to the back of the farm cottage on the lane is Harsfold Copse. In amongst the trees lay a small field which was once the home of another barn largely hidden from view. Angela remembers sheltering in it while a storm blew over, whilst out riding the Scotts' pony, Pollyanna. Sadly, this old barn has also been lost over time.

Back on the lane and crossing Simmonds Bridge, the vista reveals a good view of the church on the mound. Two gateposts, perhaps once signalling a boundary of some sort were in the vicinity of a house on the right and an old barn on the left. The two had been known as Bennetts Farm in Victorian times. By the 1960s, the old place had been split; the right-hand side belonging to the Scotts at Harsfold and the small barn and paddock on the left-hand side to the Osmarstons at The Elms. Both buildings were in a poor state by the mid-1970s, the old barn being the subject of arson and the ugly house empty for many years. In the 1980s, the house was bought by Mrs Peel who fully renovated it.[88]

Just above this house there was a small field owned by the Scotts. This became the site of the village allotments and also housed the Scout hut, which was built from second-hand materials that had originally come from the demolished POW camp at Billingshurst.

By the early 1960s, vehicle numbers had increased to such an extent that it was positively dangerous to walk along the A272 from Harsfold Lane to The Elms without any verge, let alone a pavement. The authorities must have decided that a number of issues needed addressing: widening the road, extending the graveyard into the paddock adjacent to the church and providing a pavement from the village pond to the front of the church to the new estate at Glebe Way.[89] The first residents, the Cooper family, moved into 1 Glebe Way in 1969.

---

[88] Mrs Peel was Nigel Peel's mother, the local hunt master.
[89] Glebe Way was built on the former ground of the rectory.

Further along the A272 towards Billingshurst, a small farmhouse used to stick out and force the road to bend. This was demolished to straighten the road at about the same time. It was in the vicinity of the current sewage works.

No doubt there have been lots of other changes, but these are just a few observed by Angela.

Asset Strippers

In the late 1970s, Mr Burnford put Lee Place and Northwood farms on the market. Fortunately, Joe Muller and Vic Newman kept their jobs but moved to Borough Farm; Mr Burnford's other property at Codmore Hill.

Local landowners were contacted to see if they were interested in buying any adjacent land. Ted Cripps bought the Crooked Tree Field and Five Acres, Brinsbury bought the two fields behind Northwood. Berns was offered East Hilly Field on the west side of Frithwood, but declined. The rest was auctioned in Pulborough on 15 November 1978 and bought by a Mr Carr from Eastbourne for some £506,000.

It was bad enough that the Carrs were not local farmers and that they swarmed in with big machinery and tackled the arable work with no regard or love for the old place. After all, it was just another profit-centre in West Sussex to them, but worse was to follow.

The first Angela knew of the momentous event was when Consuelo wrote to her at college. Consuelo explained how the Carrs and their team had arrived at dawn one Saturday morning and started to demolish the old farm buildings at Lee Place. David and Jean Brooks, who lived at Lee Place Farmhouse, immediately tried to reason with them and made numerous telephone calls to anyone they could think of to try to have it stopped. Nevertheless, without the buildings being officially listed, the destruction continued.

By the time Angela came home from Harper Adams for the Whitsun holiday, there were only skeletal remains standing at Lee Place and Haybarn. The Lerwills were bereft at the desecration. Angela even wrote to the local paper voicing her opinion. Walking round the old remains deeply saddened the family, especially when

Angela and Consuelo spotted the resident barn owl at Haybarn on a nearby tree looking forlorn and forgotten.

What seemed ironic is that the Weald and Downland Museum from Singleton had approached Mr Burnford some years before wanting to buy the old buildings at Haybarn. They were especially interested in it as it had two cattle yards attached to the main barn making it very unusual. Thinking he was doing his bit for conservation, he declined ...

Unfortunately, there were other examples of asset stripping; two old buildings belonging to Brinsbury have also been lost. There used to be an old barn nearly opposite the farmhouse at Northwood. Positioned on the opposite bank above the stream, it was a landmark. Another small barn and yard halfway between Snape and Canada Corner on the east side has also disappeared.

Being small and without a nearby house, it would appear that these sorts of old buildings can easily be cashed in on and smudged out of existence without many questions being asked. Sad, but probably true.

A House Through Time

The piece below is designed to give an insight into how the old farmhouse at Frithwood changed over time from unloved to much loved, to then becoming a gentrified weekender and financial investment.

1949 ... Imagine that you are a time traveller. Blindfolded, your hands cautiously explore, finding stony outcrops to the left and right, of differing heights at about chest level, a gateway in a wall perhaps. With sight restored, your view is of Frithwood.

The Elizabethan farmhouse has a brick chimney, just off-centre, a red-tiled roof and is built of Wealden sandstone. The autumn light suggests warmth but the black Second World War utility paint covering the door and casement windows give the house an austere feel. It reminds you of an aged widow, still wearing some of her past finery but with a dribble of egg yolk on her lapel; sad, but proud.

A grassy patch separates you from the house, maybe once a lawn. In the matted sward, a few bricks poke through at a jaunty angle; a path begging to be recognised, leading to a long-handled Victorian boot scraper adjacent to the front door.

Long-term, loving tenants were what Frithwood needed. Enter Berns and Consuelo.

1981 ... Standing in the same gateway, you notice many changes. A freshly painted garden gate stands before you, robustly shielding a well-tended and loved garden from passing livestock.

Once a sad old widow, the house is now a happy, gracious host able to welcome any caller. Partnered with Consuelo, they make a relaxed pair. With a large established wisteria rambling over the front of the house, it looks as though the odd differences between the house and garden have been ironed out. They are friends once more.

The window frames have been repainted with cream gloss and the front door, although still black, exudes a confidence it once lacked. No longer intimidated by 'them next door', the old girl can now boast her credentials of a repointed chimney and a new roof, meaning that she can flex in any storm. Surrounding her, a beautiful garden abounds with plants gathered, swapped, and grown from cuttings and seed. Dedication, patience and love exudes from every bloom. She is back in the land of the living ... and loving.

2019 ... You are now visiting Frithwood for the last time. The old farm has had two owners since Berns and Consuelo left in 1997. The Van Prague family was the first and modernised it extensively. Down came the hotchpotch of buildings. Out came the Rayburn in the inglenook fireplace and the lovingly tended garden. In came new windows, a contract gardener, central and underfloor heating. A typical cover to any nondescript box of fudge from Devon. To some people, this was a good outcome but to the biased Lerwills with nearly fifty years of history and memories, this was a benign interpretation of the country idyll.

Once up to scratch, the investment was sold for a tidy sum. Another family wanting a weekend retreat arrived, seeking every urban amenity but with a view. The only full-time residents were a few rabbits living near the old cart shed and no resident dog to keep them at bay. Without the beautiful garden and with the wisteria sliced in half, the old house now looks sterile and frigid. The burglar alarm is the only thing shining bright, advertising that there might be something worth stealing. It seems that the days of unlocked doors and everybody being welcome are sadly over.

Old Age Descends

'Whatever begins, also ends.'

SENECA (4 BC–AD 65)

The Decision to Move

Although Berns and Consuelo's lives were largely buried away from the hustle and bustle of the modern world, old age was descending. As far back as 1986, Consuelo was trying to persuade Berns to think about moving.

Sometimes, action follows a shock. Within a short period of time, his close friend (Mac Steele), neighbour (Fiona Scott) and Berns' eldest sister (Gwen) were all dead. Coming in close succession, one can imagine Berns wondering who might be next.

Mac died of lung cancer. Although retired, Mac and Alma were still living in the old farmhouse which they had bought from the County Council some years before. Alma would need to move to something smaller. This might well have played on Berns' mind, wondering how he or Consuelo might cope in similar circumstances.

Fiona Scott from Harsfold Manor was next, leaving Donald alone and ailing in the big old manor house. One could easily imagine Donald feeling lost without Fiona.

Berns may also have been shaken by Gwen's sudden death. Although well into her eighties and seemingly well at the time, the abruptness of Gwen's death shocked the extended family.

All three deaths happened while Angela and her husband Brian were living in Cyprus. Angela decided to act. She wrote two letters, one to Berns' doctor and one to her father. In the letter to Berns, she outlined what may happen if they left it too late to sell the farm as a couple. It was time to quit and have a few years of not worrying about money and enjoying a few luxuries such as central heating.

A letter was drafted and addressed only to Berns. Recognising the writing, Consuelo asked Berns about its contents, surprised that it had been just directed to him. He replied 'Oh, the usual.' Later alone, she read the letter but even then, the couple never spoke about its contents. It would appear, however, that Berns' *'little grey cells'* were activated as while they were at a Christmas supper party at Northwood a month or so later, he let it slip that he intended selling Frithwood in the New Year. This was the first Consuelo had heard about it.

Angela would like to think that her letter might have acted as a catalyst but one could never tell with Berns. He was, after all, a man of few words but deep thoughts.

Where are They Now?

Sadly, Berns died within a year of leaving the farm in 1998 and Consuelo in 2013.[90] Hugh and Angela live eight miles apart on the edge of the Cotswolds and Rhona in Amberley, West Sussex.

Although different, they have all inherited a love for the countryside from their father, a fondness of gardening from their grandma Jessie and an intelligent curiosity and inquisitiveness from their mother.

All three consider themselves privileged and proud to have been raised at Frithwood. They were the lucky few ...

---

[90] See Appendix K: Ten Things Angela Loved about her Parents.

Other People's Memories

*⁗The funny thing about truth,
everyone seems to have their own version.⁗*

Carlos Wallace (1883–1963)

Recollections of an Employee (Julian Moores)

Julian was a farm student during 1962/63.

Winter of 1962/63

On 26 December 1962 at around 22.00 hours, snow began to fall across the south of England which proved to be the start of one of the coldest and longest periods of freezing weather ever recorded in the country. By the night of 27 December, the snow had fallen to a depth of 10 cm and on 29 December a blizzard driven by gale-force winds piled snowdrifts as high as any hedge in its path. The road to Frithwood Farm was quickly blocked all the way to the main Pulborough Road and so began one of the most challenging and bitter winters ever experienced.

Food for the animals on the farm was limited but fortunately a good supply of hay from the previous year was stored in the big barn next to the house. However, concentrate mixes were in relatively short supply and a scheme had to be devised to get the ingredients from the main road to the farm some miles inland. Southern Counties Agricultural Trading Society (SCATS) lorries were eventually able to get to the Codmore Hill turning and a trip to rendezvous with their vehicle on the old grey Ferguson, complete with flatbed trailer, was necessary to collect these essential food supplies.

The extreme cold posed some problems with the feeding and especially the provision of water to the stock. The breeding turkeys in their long, triangular houses known as arks, had small water troughs which froze readily in the constant sub-zero temperatures and had to be regularly thawed and refilled on several occasions during the day. Gradually a feeding routine for all the stock fell into place, but most of the mainly dark, overcast days were taken up with repetitive tasks to keep the stock comfortable and well fed.

By the end of January, there had been no respite from the sub-zero temperatures and the wildlife was starting to show signs of distress. Wood pigeons, usually plump and indomitable survivors, were dying of hunger and cold as the natural food gleaned from the farmland was covered in a thick layer of snow and frozen into the soil at temperatures down to -15°C.

Banner headlines hit the local papers as each day brought further hardships to people and transport. 'Diesel fuel freezes in municipal bus tanks – services disrupted!' trumpeted one local paper. 'Hungry foxes kill bullock in Godalming!' cried another treading a fine line between truth and reality. The sub-zero conditions lasted throughout January and February when even the sea began to freeze and daytime temperatures rarely exceeded zero degrees centigrade.

The subterranean well at Frithwood never faltered throughout the whole of this time drawing water from deep below ground and filling the house tank and various other receptacles on the farm. This single source provided both washing and drinking water for humans and animals. The small dew pond near to the Nissen hut must also have had a source of below-ground warming water as only on the coldest of days did it show a layer of ice over the surface. Lean wildfowl, mallard, moorhen and on one occasion, a water rat made their way to this moderately warm oasis in the middle of the freezing desert. These creatures, emboldened by their pursuit of available food, lost their usual shyness and would allow a relatively close approach for observation.

The Nissen hut was the nerve centre for the mixing of rations. It contained an old hammer mill and mixing unit together with the storage for the ingredients used in the manufacture of the various feeds for the animals, the pigs being the largest consumers. With the presence of so much stored grain, mids and maize came the inevitable presence of the local rodent population chewing the sacks and pilfering the grain which fell to the floor.[91]

---

[91] 'Mids' is short for middlings which is a husk layer on wheat grains, which Berns used in rations for sows.

Around the adjacent pig pens, concrete paths had been laid at various times and where the substrate had not been consolidated the opportunistic rats had excavated a maze of tunnels with various pop holes. If one was to wait quietly for a few minutes, a head would appear and scan the surrounding area before the whole rodent would emerge and scamper to the grain store for replenishment, bouncing across the hard-packed snow with ease.

During February 1963, the South was again consumed by blizzards and icy winds and it seemed as though the dreaded grip of this prolonged winter would never end. Heavy clothing was mandatory with at least two vests, long johns, a light sweater, a heavy sweater and a top coat. Head gear was, of course, the balaclava, famed for saving the soldiers' ears from cold and frostbite at the Battle of Sevastopol in the Crimean War. Gloves were an absolute necessity as without them your fingers immediately froze to the water troughs and bowls as you cleaned and refilled them.

On one occasion, the wind was so ferocious that the snow was blown through the gap under the bedroom window, and in the morning stood in a small pyramid on the floor. During the day, the temperature stayed so low that the hot-water bottle left on top of the bed had frozen solid by nightfall.

On one particularly moonlit night around 8 February, I watched, hidden in the shelter of a haystack adjacent to a small patch of kale, as several hares and rabbits, driven by hunger, came to feed on the small bits of brassica poking through the crusted snow. The biting cold and constant quest for food had made these creatures less wary than normal and they grazed, unaware of my presence, quite peacefully together. Having my gun with me, I fired at one of the hares and to my surprise two animals dropped to the shot – some welcome fresh meat for Consuelo's kitchen. Having shown them off indoors, I hung them out of reach high in the cart shed, no deep freeze required, they were frozen stiff by morning.

As the bitter cold dragged on throughout February, people wondered how this would end and when. Temperatures as low as -22°C had been recorded in January and no respite had been felt for ten weeks. But by 4 March a mild southwesterly flow of air reached the country and the thaw began. By 8 March we could see grass without snow for the first time for several months and the coldest winter for 200 years had at last relaxed its grip. A forced lockdown of some twelve weeks meant only the children venturing to school had left the precincts of the farm.

In the big barn next to the house the hay had lasted well and been sufficient to feed both sheep and cattle throughout the winter. On pulling out one bale I noticed what appeared to be a round, ball of feathers but on closer inspection I found it to be a cluster of twenty-three tiny wrens who had huddled together to seek warmth from each other but had, in turn, perished through extreme cold and hunger.

Castration Time

Every litter of pigs has a mixture of boar and gilt piglets and at a few days old, the boar piglets had to be castrated to prevent fighting amongst the litter as they were weaned and fattened together.[92]

At Frithwood, this procedure would commence by separating the whole litter from the sow. Coaxed with a scoop of food, the sow would nonchalantly waddle outside, accompanied by any escapee gilt piglets. The boar piglets were then caught and castrated.

Bernard would produce a scalpel and some salt water to act as a douche to flush any blood away. Each piglet was held between Bernard's knees and a cut was made revealing a tiny testicle which was removed and the spermatic cord cut through with the scalpel. The process was repeated for the second testicle. Squealing loudly, the piglet would be doused in the saline fluid and placed outside to its ranting mother. Each animal was done in turn until they were all returned to the sow.

Hemp the dog was the chief beneficiary of the whole operation as he would sit patiently outside wherever the castration was taking place. With a deft flick of the hand, Bernard would toss the tiny sweetbreads over the door and Hemp, with the precision of a much-practised dog, would snatch the morsel in mid-air and swallow it with delight.

Within a few days, the wounds had healed over and the piglets resumed their natural exuberance playing together as though nothing had happened.

---

[92] Gilt: young female pig.

The Hand Grenade

On a bright April morning with a fresh breeze blowing, two small figures descended the sloping track towards Frithwood farmhouse. One of them, Hugh, held at arm's length before him a straight stick, and balanced on the end of the cane was a small, compact rusty metal object. The other smaller figure proceeded a few paces behind visibly unsure as to the prudence of this adventure.

'Look what I've found!' Hugh said, thrusting the object proudly towards me.

Hugh was holding a stick which was supporting a rusty round pin attached to a Number 36 Mills Bomb, known affectionately in the military as a 'Pineapple Grenade' due to the cross-grooving on the casing.

The stick, together with the bomb, was handed over and gently placed in a bucket half-filled with soil. Bernard had arrived on the scene and showing concern for the find enquired as to what sort of damage it could do if it were to explode.

'Probably flatten the farmhouse if it goes off here,' I replied.

'What should we do with it?'

'Army bomb disposal, call them!' I said, feeling a sense of authority in knowing the correct procedure and looking forward to the possibility of a massive controlled explosion on the farm.

The bomb disposal unit was called and the bucket containing the grenade moved to a respectful distance from the farmhouse. After an hour or two, the squad of four men arrived in a long wheelbase Land Rover and proceeded in an unhurried, but efficient way to prepare the offending grenade for detonation.

A hole was dug next to a dung heap a good way from the house, a charge prepared and attached to the bomb. The hole was refilled and a wire was brought back from the grenade to the vehicle where it was attached to a detonator. When everything was checked for the third time, one of the soldiers pushed the plunger and a mighty explosion followed, immediately throwing a huge amount of soil and dung high into the air.

Hemp the dog, normally fearless but frightened by gunshot, had sensed the impending chaos and had disappeared. He returned two days later.

Hugh was duly cautioned to leave any further finds of a military nature where they were in Northwood and not to bring them back to the farmhouse for inspection.

As in many parts of West Sussex, Canadian and American troops were billeted in readiness for D-Day and some were obviously less than careful with their armaments when they left for the landings.

Recollections of a School Friend (Christine Asphar)

Christine lived at Lee Place in one of the farm cottages for a short time in the mid- to late 1960s and became friendly with Angela.

I was nine to ten years old, recently moved with my family to a new, very rural home and started attending the local primary school. A taxi collected me and other children from the lane, returning us after school – including Angela. We got to know each other, she offered to let me ride her pony called Cockey, and to help muck out his stable and have tea, giving me instructions how to walk to her home, along the lane and through the woods. She mentioned a gate, but where was the house? After some hesitation, and not seeing an alternative, I walked through the gate, and as the track descended, a very old house came into view. I self-consciously made my approach to the front, and was met by a smiley, kindly lady, Consuelo, Angela's mum. She made me feel instantly at ease, and went to find Angela.

Frithwood Farm holds really happy memories for me. It was a beautiful home, where I was always made to feel welcome. I was told where the short cuts were to get there quicker. There was Angela, who tried patiently to teach me to ride, and how to muck out the stable; there was Cockey, stubborn, who moved when he wanted to and not when the rider did, his tummy nearly reaching the ground; there was Rhona, Angela's older sister, very grown up, very regal; there was Hugh, Angela's older brother, with long hair, maybe one of those hippies mentioned in polite society in hushed tones, very mysterious, exciting, playing wonderful music. Then there was Consuelo, so welcoming, who made wonderful teas, with home-made butter, jam and scones, unfailingly kind, encouraging and interested in me; there was Bernard,

198

an archetypal farmer, a true man of the earth, rooted, saturnine, not one for small talk. Sometimes he teased me and smiled at me, that was like the sun coming out on a dull day.

Over the time I lived there, Angela and I spent a lot of time together. I was taken out on trips with the family, Bernard telling us a joke and everybody seemed to understand, except me. I joined them after tea sometimes to watch TV, and watching the Marty Feldman show. I recall sleeping over, playing with Angela with her tea set, making cheese on toast and using far too much cheese. I remember when the River Arun burst its banks one autumn, and Hugh and Bernard racing to the river with ropes because someone was thought to be in peril but there wasn't anyone.

One time when Frithwood Farm and neighbouring houses were completely cut off from the outside world by a flood, we didn't go to school. For several days a tractor had to bring in supplies and the post. And best of all, when the river burst its banks and then froze solid in the winter. We had our own skating rink. An abiding memory is of Angela dreamily and elegantly skating, singing 'Hey Jude' to herself. Another memory is of taking our dolls to the floodwaters and making them fall in, and rescuing them just before they drowned, then taking them home to get them warm and dressed in dry clothes.

I remember the flowers Consuelo grew in front of the house, how beautiful the house looked in the summer, the two sets of stairs in the house with a narrow corridor in between, the medieval table in the dining room which dipped in the middle, the outhouse at the back and the orchard behind.

Frithwood Farm was my second home, and I really wished it was my home. I loved feeling included by the family. I loved exploring the country around with Angela or on my own, with the river and the disused canal which had silted up, and an island in a tributary – I used to scramble on and feel safely hidden in nature. There was also the walk to Wisborough Green, spending time with Henrietta, Angela's friend, on the way there, and swimming in her pool.

I remember Lee Place Farm as being mysterious and foreboding, like Wuthering Heights; the barn near our home in which I and other children had the best time jumping from stacks of straw bales onto soft *deep beds of loose straw. I have never forgotten the fun and excitement of that one day.*

Frithwood Farm is a jewel in my memory, and I have called on the above remembrances often during dark times since.

Recollections of a Grandson (Justin Theobald)

Justin Theobald was Berns and Consuelo's only grandson, born in 1982.

Sundays with Grandma and Grandpa

It felt like most Sundays were spent at Grandma and Grandpa's. As a child, the forty-minute car journey felt like a real adventure. There was a turning off the A29, just after the café which had an old helicopter which we used to stop to play in. The turning that led towards the farm was mainly a single-lane track with lots of blind corners. I lost count of how many wing mirrors Dad lost off his car. I also recall some journeys were scarier than others when the road would flood near Pat's house. Dad would drive through the flood and nearly always get water on the electrics so the car would conk out! We would have to wait for the battery to dry with Dad revving the car or even getting out to push and jump-start the car to get it going again.

When we arrived at the farm, we drove past chicken runs on the left, sheep in the fields to the right, cows and ponies in the paddock behind the farmhouse. We were always met by the excited farm dogs, who lived outside and who greeted us with barking and wagging tails. Lassie and Gemma were the first dogs that I can remember. They were both brown-and-white collies. I remember that Gemma was my favourite as Lassie was a bit old and grumpy. The dogs sometimes had puppies. I have lots of fond memories of playing with the puppies in one of the old pigsties. After Lassie passed away, they kept a black-and-white puppy called Kate. They also had a farm cat called Sixpence who had lots of kittens; our first pet cat was one of those kittens and we called her Tigger. My uncle and auntie also had two of her kittens to take to their farm in Devon.

I recall one time that I was left in the car on my own whilst Mum and

Dad unpacked the car. I climbed into the front seat but trod on the handbrake which made the car creep forwards. Thankfully, it rolled into a dip in between the new and old stables which meant no harm was done.

We would always be greeted by Grandma at the front door asking why we were late. We were then ushered into the dining room for a Sunday roast, with Grandpa at the head of the table looking towards the window onto the front garden. I used to sit to Grandpa's left. However, because Grandpa always used to tickle my knee by squeezing them, I soon retreated to the other side near Grandma. I was then far enough away from the knee squeezer.

It was here that Grandma taught me lots of things including how to lay a dining table and table manners such as not to have your elbows on the table.

Grandma made the best roast dinners. There was always an amazing spread of food. Grandpa would always carve the meat at the table. After sharpening his carving knife, he would portion the meat onto the plates. We were then allowed to help ourselves to the vegetables, often home-grown, from separate dishes. Grandma would also make her own Yorkshire puddings which were simply the best. I soon learnt not to fill myself up too much with the main course as Grandma would always make a delicious pudding, usually a crumble with custard. The filling of the crumble would depend on the season. My favourites were strawberry, rhubarb and apple. After a meal, I always used to enjoy a drink of water from the tap which came from the well in the garden.

Once lunch was concluded, we would always take the dogs for a walk, in preparation for tea. We used to walk across the fields towards Michael and Jane's home and then to the river and canal where we would play Poohsticks over the bridge. We would then loop round past Lee Place and back to the farm. Occasionally, we would do a different walk and look at the plane hangars where one of the Pink Floyd band members lived at Streele Farm.

In the summer, we would play cricket in the paddock, ride the ponies (Satellite was brown and Sea Mist was grey), have tractor and trailer rides on the hay bales. Before it got dark, we would walk the cows back to the barn, shut in the chickens and turn the electric fence on to protect them from the fox. One winter, maybe at Christmas time, I also remember learning to play chess with Uncle Hugh and Uncle Brian. I also recall Grandma letting us scrape out the mixing bowls prior to teatime treats being popped into the oven.

Sometimes, I was allowed to invite a friend with me. After lunch, we would be allowed to go off and play. We were always told to not climb on the hay bales in the barn or go too far. However, we always played in the hay bales and probably went too far! My friend Alan remembers spending hours looking for a water spring in the nearby field, exploring the barns. He said he can also remember the smell of home-made jam, running over the hill, dodging the cowpats and spending a night in the caravan. I also recall throwing chunks of sand at rats that would run around the rim of the barns.

We would often see hot-air balloons and microlights fly over the farm. One day, we were so excited as a hot-air balloon landed in one of Grandpa's fields. We raced to greet them. As there were no mobile phones in those days, the people had to use Grandma and Grandpa's phone to call to be collected. Whilst they were waiting, my sister and I were lucky enough to be given a hot-air balloon ride. This was the first time that I realised that I was scared of heights.

At teatime, we would all resume our normal seats at the dining table to enjoy the second feast of the day. The milk, butter and cream for the tea was from the farm's house cow. Home-made scones, jam, shortbread biscuits and an assortment of other goodies were also on offer.

Once we had eaten our tea, it was then time to return home. I remember jumping out of the car to open and close the top gate and looking across the Lodge Field in the summer to see the most amazing sunsets of the round orange, glowing sun setting in the west. Each time we went home along the lane, another adventure unfurled all over again.

Holidays at the Farm

During the summer holidays, we would stay in the blue caravan at the top of the hill, near the entrance gate. Before we could move our things in, we would first have to spend what felt like hours cleaning out all of the dead flies. Mum, Dad, Alice and I would then spend a few nights sleeping on top of the hill. Sometimes my sister Alice and I were left at the farm while our parents worked. We then had rooms in the house, although when I was very young, I slept on a camp bed in my grandparents' room.

From memory, the mornings would always start with Grandma, Alice and I letting the chickens out with the dogs running free. The dogs loved to run rings around the chicken arks whilst we would collect the eggs. We would then take the dogs around the field before meeting Grandpa in the cow shed where he was milking the cows. Grandpa taught me how to milk the cows and I remember it feeling and also smelling disgusting as the cows would have done fresh cowpats.

Grandma had lots of friends nearby. I remember Jane and Pat both fondly as they were so welcoming. Grandma would take turns to walk us across the fields to their houses where we would swim in their swimming pools. On a hot summer's day, this was great.

I also remember the calves being kept as bullocks before being taken to market. One was called Blackie and he would always run out of his shed to greet me at the gate so that I could stroke his nose and behind his ears. He was a friendly chap.

During the Easter holidays, it was usually lambing season. Unfortunately, there were always a few lambs who were shunned by their mums. However, this led to the lambs being kept in the pigsties which meant we could bottle feed and cuddle them. As a kid, this was like a dream come true. We named one male lamb, Sam the Ram. Even when Sam had grown and was in the field, I still remember calling him, and he would run over to me so I could make a fuss of him. The inevitable market day came for the lambs, which thankfully I did not fully understand when I was a child.

The farmhouse seemed big, especially when you are a kid. It had two sets of stairs. I remember playing hide-and-seek with Alice and it would always take some time as there were so many places to hide. Other recollections include hard, coarse toilet paper, Grandpa listening to the radio and reading his Farmers Weekly and me trying to get a tune, any tune from an old hunting horn.

Christmas

Christmas was always good fun at the farm, although I remember being very frustrated that we had to wait until after lunch before we could open our presents.

Grandma would prepare an amazing Christmas lunch (I think this was always on Boxing Day), which was followed by a home-made Christmas pudding. I remember that I preferred crumble but I wanted the Christmas pudding as Grandma would always include a number of 20p pieces wrapped in foil, which we could keep if found in the pudding. Sometimes other relatives would join us.

After lunch, I would race into the front room where the Christmas tree was, with all the presents underneath. Alice and I would then sort all the presents out into piles for everyone, in front of the fire. This had to be done out of the way of the TV as Grandpa would be watching the horse racing. Grandpa would get extremely excited and animated watching the horse racing which I found hilarious.

Once the presents were opened, we would then play games. One game that I remember is where someone would choose a letter and then you had to think of rivers, countries, places and the like that began with that letter. You would only get a point if you had chosen something that no one else had on their list. Scrabble, Monopoly, draughts, and a lot of chess were also played.

Grandma always made sure that we kept a list of who got us what presents to enable us to write thank-you letters to everyone who had given us a gift.

It is not until now, when I am reminiscing, that I realise how lucky I had been as a child.

Glossary

Acre
The area of land a man and two oxen can plough in one day, covering about ten miles.

Bale grabber
Agricultural implement attached to the front of a tractor with numerous hooks used to snatch small or large bales of hay or straw for loading onto a flatbed trailer.

Bale sledge
Sledge attached to a small baler to collect bales ready for stacking.

Beet pulp
By-product of sugar beet crop, rich in calories.

Brindle
Brown-and-white coloured sheepdog.

Brooder units
First housing for young poultry chicks.

Buck rake
Farm implement attached to rear of tractor for carrying things.

Candling
Process using light to establish egg fertility.

Caruncles
The loose bumpy skin on a stag turkey's head and neck that can be bright red or blue around the face. In the breeding season, it becomes engorged with blood.

Cubbing
Hunting and killing young foxes.

Cutting pigs
Castrating male piglets.

Dagging
The removal of mucky wool from a sheep's fleece to prevent fly strike.

Deadstock
Farm machinery and equipment.

Debeaking
Cutting the top beak of a turkey to prevent it pecking other birds.

Desert of lapwings
Collective noun.

Dipping
Submerging sheep in a pesticide mix to prevent fly strike.
Dressed or trussed bird
Gutted poultry ready for the oven.
Egg crocks:
Large, wide-rimmed earthenware pots used to preserve eggs in the past. Springtime gluts of eggs were preserved using a technique called *water-glassing* utilising a hydrated lime solution (1 oz per quart of water) in these pots.
Front-end loader
Similar to a buck rake but at the front of a tractor.
Fly strike
Occurs when flies lay their eggs in dirty, wet fleece largely around a sheep's posterior. If left unattended, maggots can kill a sheep.
Flushing
To prepare ewes for mating.
Green lane
Lane with hedges or fences each side but without a hard base.
Gilt
Young female pig.
Hand tinting
Used to colour black-and-white photographs prior to colour photography.
House cow
Cow kept to provide milk for the farmhouse.
Humus
Organic matter essential for soil fertility.
Gaggle of geese
Collective noun.
Lactation
The process of milk production.
Mischief of mice
Collective noun.
Permanent pasture
Pasture which is rarely, if ever ploughed.
Piece rate
The price per unit paid to a worker.
Pig wire
Livestock fencing made of wire with a square pattern.
Rough plucked
Plucked birds but not gutted.

Rue
  A small narrow wood with a stream running through it.
Settling up
  To conclude a debt.
Snood
  A flap of skin that hangs down over a stag turkey's beak.
Scours
  Agricultural term for animal diarrhoea.
Tiger Trap
  A cross-country horse jump.
Wedge of geese
  Collective noun.

Acknowledgements

Thanks are due to everyone who has contributed to this book in any way. You know who you are, but perhaps special mention should be made to my sister Rhona Hoy; brother Hugh Lerwill; nephew Justin Theobald; husband Brian Swinyard; cousins – in particular Simon Lerwill; good friends Christine Asphar and Julian Moores for their invaluable help and assistance in making this a reality. Thanks are due also to Shirley Bridgen, Amanda Ford and Anne Thompson for their important help in editing and proofreading the draft.

Afterword

Helping others has always been close to Angela's heart. She is currently helping a small school in Burundi. Established by a refugee friend in collaboration with UNICEF, the school has been operating for several years. However, the day-to-day expenses are the responsibility of the Burundi Education Foundation charity.

If you have enjoyed this book and you have it in your heart to either give a one-off or regular donation, it would be well-received by these poor children. Even a small sum of just £5 will pay for a teacher for a day.

Please donate online to:

- Burundi Education Foundation
- Metro Bank
- Sort code: 23-05-80
- Account number: 22665655
- www.burundieducationfoundation.org.uk/donate

Appendix A:

Family Group Sheet for William Lerwill

Husband: **William Lerwill**
Date of Birth   7 March 1855
Marriage   23 April 1878
Death   21 September 1916
Father   William Lerwill (1806–1885)
Mother   Mary Rawle (1812–1877)

Wife: **Eliza Jane Blackmore (aka Ida)**
Date of Birth   19 November 1858
Death   12 July 1927
Father   John Blackmore (1827/8–1899)
Mother   Jane Herepath (1827/8–1915)

Issue 1:   **Florence Mary Lerwill (aka Betty)**
Date of Birth   28 May 1879
Marriage   September 1915
Death   24 November 1915
Spouse   Lee Napper

Issue 2:   **William John Lerwill**
Date of Birth   9 December 1880
Marriage   1913
Death   31 May 1966
Spouse   Lena Maud Gatley (Died 23 August 1974)

Issue 3:   **Walter Sidney Lerwill (aka Sidney)**
Date of Birth   4 November 1882
Marriage   April 1910
Death   29 January 1960
Spouse   Mary Annie Elliott (aka Annie or Nan)

Issue 4:	**Mabel Alice Lerwill (aka Mab)**
Date of Birth	25 February1884
Marriage	1916
Death	1961
Spouse	Ralph Nash

Issue 5:	**Thomas Henry Lerwill**
Date of Birth	1885
Marriage	7 October 1913
Death	9 May 1954
Spouse	Dorothy Esther Woodhams (1887–1969)

Issue 6:	**Alfred Edward Lerwill**
Date of Birth	1887
Marriage	1911
Death	25 April 1954
Spouse	Nellie May Collins (aka May 1886–1972)

Issue 7:	**Ida Priscilla Lerwill**
Date of Birth	1890
Marriage	1921
Death	19 August 1973
Spouse	George Elliott

Issue 8:	**Hilda Gertrude Lerwill**
Date of Birth	1892
Marriage	Spinster
Death	1967

Issue 9:	**Frances May Lerwill**
Date of Birth	1893
Marriage	1920
Death	Unknown
Spouse	Benjamin Joyce

Issue 10:	**Violet Jeanette Lerwill**
Date of Birth	1896
Marriage	1918
Death	1963
Spouse	Felix Crawford (born between 1893 and 1895)

Issue 11:   **Frank Victor Lerwill**
Date of Birth   May 1897
Marriage   Unknown
Death   1983
Spouse   May Foster

Issue 12:   **Elsie Irene Lerwill**
Date of Birth   25 May 1898
Marriage   1921
Death   22 February 1978
Spouse   Ronald Collins

Issue 13:   **Doris Beatrice Lerwill**
Date of Birth   1900
Marriage   Unknown
Death   1987
Spouse   Jack Sale

Issue 14:   **Percival George Lerwill**
Date of Birth   31 August 1903
Marriage 1   1933
Spouse 1   Leah Garrett (divorced)
Marriage 2   1939
Spouse 2   Joan Caroline Hearn (aka Babs)
– Date of Birth   26 April 1921
– Death   22 June 1977
Death   May 1981

Appendix B:

Family Group Sheet for Walter Sidney Lerwill

Husband: **Walter Sidney Lerwill (aka Sidney)**
Date of Birth   4 November 1882
Marriage   April 1910
Death   29 January 1960
Father   William Lerwill
Mother   Eliza Jane Blackmore (aka Ida)

Wife: **Mary Annie Elliott (aka Annie or Nan)**
Date of Birth   1887
Marriage   1910
Death   27 February 1964
Father   Thomas Howe Elliott
Mother   Ann Rocket

Issue 1: **Gwendoline Violet Lerwill**
Date of Birth   28 December 1911/12
Marriage   12 June 1940
Death   9 December 1996
Spouse   Alastair Grigor

Issue 2: **Nancy Elliott Lerwill**
Date of Birth   20 June 1913
Marriage   23 March 1940
Death   24 June 1998
Spouse   Stanley Swain

Issue 3: **Thomas Sidney Lerwill**
Date of Birth   6 July 1915
Marriage   Bachelor
Death   21 February 1986

Issue 4:   **Florence Mary Elliott Lerwill**
Date of Birth   6 November 1916
Marriage 1   February 1938
Spouse 1   Eric Walter Goodall
Marriage 2   1 February 1947
Spouse 2   James Craig McClung Wardrop
Death   25 November 2007

Issue 5:   **Bernard Walter Lerwill (aka Berns)**
Date of Birth   15 November 1918
Marriage   31 December 1949
Death   29 August 1998
Spouse   Dorothy Consuelo Neave (aka Consuelo)

Issue 6:   **Pamela Lerwill**
Date of Birth   30 September 1920
Marriage   12 June 1954
Death   10 August 2020
Spouse   Paul Anthony Kahane

214

Appendix C:

Family Group Sheet for Thomas Howe Elliott

Husband:	**Thomas Howe Elliott**
Date of Birth	1862
Marriage 1	19 April 1884
Spouse 1	Ann Rocket
Marriage 2	(Between 1901 and 1907)
Spouse 2	Mrs Lister
Death	17 December 1907
Father	John Elliott (1829–1889)
Mother	Elizabeth Anne Howe (1831–1887)

Wife 1:	**Ann Rocket**
Date of Birth	1858
Death	23 November 1901
Father	Unknown
Mother	Unknown

Issue 1:	**John Rocket Elliott**
Date of Birth	1884
Marriage	1907
Death	Unknown
Spouse	Katie Beatrice Penn (aka Kitty)

Issue 2:	**Thomas William Elliott**
Date of Birth	4th Quarter 1885
Marriage	29 April 1910
Death	4th Quarter 1954
Spouse	Annie Alice Eliza Tingley

Issue 3:	**Mary Annie Elliott (aka Nan or Annie)**
Date of Birth	1887
Marriage	1910
Death	27 February 1964
Spouse	Walter Sidney Lerwill (aka Sidney)

Issue 4:   **Emily Elliott**
Date of Birth   1890
Marriage   1913
Death   1972
Spouse   William Rhys Thomas

Issue 5:   **Alfred George Elliott (aka George)**
Date of Birth   2 June 1895
Marriage   1921
Death   1975
Spouse   Ida Priscilla Lerwill

Issue 6:   **Daisy Elliott (aka Dais)**
Date of Birth   1898
Marriage   Unknown
Death   1977
Spouse   Arthur Grainger

Issue 7:   **Charles Elliott**
Date of Birth   Unknown
Death   Died young

Appendix D:

Schedule of Sale

That Valuable Freehold Detached

PICTURESQUE SMALL FARMHOUSE

WITH ABOUT

33½ Acres of Land

AND KNOWN AS

"Frithwood." Lee Place, Pulborough.

FRITHWOOD

PULBOROUGH, SUSSEX

Situate to the East of and adjoining Lot 2, possessing all the charm of ancient Sussex, with its original old oak and chimney corner, and, whilst the present occupier has done much to install modern necessities, the old-world characteristics have in no way been interfered with.

An article in " The Wanderer " in its Christmas 1948 number states:

"This charming XVI century Farm House, tucked away in the folds of the hill, whose slopes gently unfurl their beauty to reveal the silvery waters of the Arun wending its way gracefully towards the sea, may be said to present the perfect combination for living life pleasantly. Unequalled are the extensive views to the South, Chanctonbury Ring, to the far distant North, Leith and Box Hills."

SCHEDULE

No. on Ord.	Description.			Arable.	Pasture.	Sundries.
114	Pasture	...	...		13·800	
115pt.	Pasture	...	...		17·000	
115a	Pasture	...	...		1·148	
116	Pasture	...	...		10·762	
117	Pasture	...	...		14·130	
127a	Arable	...	...	14·406		
130	Pasture	...	...		17·077	
131	Pasture	...	...		14·582	
131a	Pair Cottages		...			·451
132	Garden	...	...			·221
132a	Lane ...	...	...			·210
133a	Pasture	...	...		·632	
134	Arable	...	...	10·489		
135	Canal ...	...	...			3·029
134a	Rew ...	...	...			·610
136	Pasture	...	...		11·438	
143	Buildings, etc.		...			1·148
145	Arable	...	...	19·243		
149	Arable	...	...	5·137		
960	Pasture	...	...		10·856	
961	Pasture	...	...		5·491	
961a	Pasture	...	...		2·826	
961b	Pasture		...		·390	
962	Knobs Crook Cottage	...				·483
972	Pasture	...	...		8·934	
				49·275	129·066	6·152

SUMMARY

Arable	...	...	49·275
Pasture	...	...	129·066
Sundries	...	...	6·152
			184·493 acres.

Let to Mr. W. S. Lerwill with other lands on a weekly Michaelmas tenancy at a rent apportioned to this Lot for the purposes of sale at £175. One of the Lee Place Cottages is in hand and will be offered with

POSSESSION ON COMPLETION.

See Conditions Nos. 15, 16 and 17 as to rights-of-way.

Rateable Values: House £6.   3 Cottages £14.
Total Rates for the Half-year ending 31st March, 1949, £6 15s.
Land Drainage Rates: Owner's Rate 16/5.   Occupier's Rate 4/8.

Outgoings:
   Apportioned Annuity or Rent Charge £15 per annum.
   Tithe Redemption Annuity £4 14s. 6d. per annmun.

Appendix E:

Geographical Position of Frithwood Farm

Appendix F:

Layout of Farm Buildings

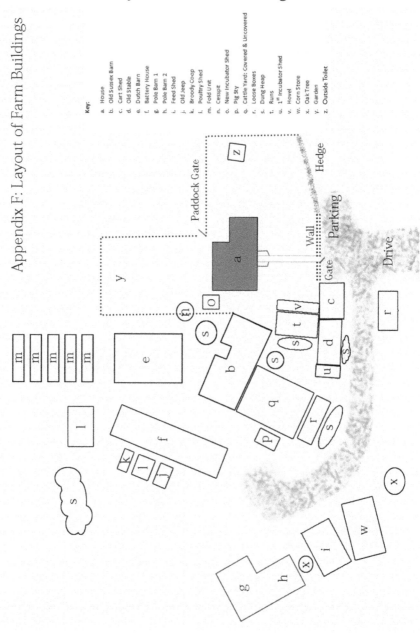

Key:

a. House
b. Old Sussex Barn
c. Cart Shed
d. Old Stable
e. Dutch Barn
f. Battery House
g. Pole Barn 1
h. Pole Barn 2
i. Feed Shed
j. Old Jeep
k. Broody Coop
l. Poultry Shed
m. Fold Unit
n. Cesspit
o. New Incubator Shed
p. Pig Sty
q. Cattle Yard: Covered & Uncovered
r. Loose Boxes
s. Dung Heap
t. Runs
u. 1st Incubator Shed
v. Hovel
w. Corn Store
x. Oak Tree
y. Garden
z. Outside Toilet

Appendix G:

Architectural Description of Farmhouse

[Written by John Roberts, BA (Arch), DipArch, RIBA, ARB]

The house is a typical three-unit (or three bay) lobby entry house with an internal axial chimney stack and back-to-back fireplaces that heat the two main ground-floor rooms (parlour and kitchen) and an unheated room which, if I recall correctly, you can see used to be divided into two. Probably one would have been a pantry (usually fitted with wall-mounted shelves and a brick or stone plinth on which items were placed to cool) and the other a buttery (often used to store home-made ale). This style of house, built with a chimney stack, was the successor to the yeoman's open hall house (which had no chimney and was open to the rafters in the main living space or hall and dated from the 1400 to 1500s). This became common throughout the country from the 1590s onwards. Obviously, it could have been built in the early 1600s so technically you could describe Frithwood as late sixteenth/early seventeenth century.

Appendix H:

Favourite Sayings and Expressions

- A fly in the ointment
- A stitch in time saves nine
- A watched kettle never boils
- Absence makes the heart grow fonder
- All hands to the tiller
- All quiet on the Western Front
- All the time you live under my roof …
- Almost scared to use it … *(reference to using coal)*
- Always look on the bright side of life
- And so on and so forth
- Ants in your pants
- As keen as mustard
- Bake up
- Better late than never
- Birds of a feather flock together
- Born in a barn?
- Bosom pals
- By hook or by crook
- By Jove
- By the bye
- Can't see the wood for the trees
- Charabanc
- Chinwag
- Clear the decks
- Confined to barracks
- Count your blessings
- Creaking gates last the longest
- Dear as poison
- Do you follow?
- Do you get my drift?
- Don't count your chickens before they have hatched
- Don't kick someone while they're down
- Don't put off until tomorrow what you can do today
- Don't tar them all with the same brush
- Down in the dumps

○ Each to his own
○ Early to bed and early to rise makes a man, healthy, wealthy and wise
○ East, West, Home is best
○ Educate a girl and you educate a family
○ Everything comes to he who waits
○ Fair crack of the whip
○ Famous last words
○ Frog in your throat
○ From the horse's mouth
○ Goose chase
○ Half-full, not half-empty
○ Hanky-panky
○ Heavens opened
○ Hell for leather
○ Hell's bells ... *(popular with Joan Croom)*
○ Hold your horses
○ Hollow legs
○ Home, James, and don't spare the horses
○ Honesty is the best policy
○ How the mighty have fallen
○ I would love to be a fly on the wall
○ Ideas above your station
○ If walls could talk
○ It's better to have loved and lost than never loved at all
○ It's no use closing the stable door after the horse has bolted
○ Jack of all trades, master of none
○ Keep your pecker up
○ Kill two birds with one stone
○ Knee-high to a grasshopper
○ Laugh and the world laughs with you, cry and you cry alone
○ Look after the pennies and the pounds will look after themselves
○ Make do and mend
○ Making ends meet
○ Manners maketh man
○ Many hands make light work
○ Money doesn't grow on trees
○ Muck out ... *(Jill Scrase's reference to house cleaning)*
○ My goodness
○ My word is my bond
○ Necessity is the mother of invention
○ Needs must
○ Never say never

- No flies on him/her
- No peace for the wicked
- Nosy parker
- Not enough hours in the day
- Oh, what a wallop
- Old blighter
- One good turn deserves another
- Only got one pair of hands
- People who live in glass houses shouldn't throw stones
- Perishing thing
- Pinch and a punch for the first of the month
- Play it by ear
- Plough your own furrow
- Pull up your socks
- Put your pride in your pocket
- Rally round
- Rascals
- Red sky at night shepherd's delight, red sky in the morning shepherd's warning
- Remember your friends on the way up as you may pass them on the way down
- Scratch lunch
- Snap out of it
- Still waters run deep
- Success breeds success
- Take us as you find us
- Talk the hind legs off a donkey
- That's a turn up for the book
- The grass is always greener on the other side
- The lion's share
- The pen is mightier than the sword
- Time flies
- Time waits for no man
- To get cracking
- To grin and bear it
- To hold the fort
- To make hay while the sun shines
- To rub one's nose in it
- To take the bull by its horns
- Toodaloo!
- Treat others as you would like to be treated yourself
- Up at the crack of sparrows

- Up with the lark
- Waste not, want not
- We eat to live, not live to eat
- We'll see …
- Well, I'm jiggered
- Wheat from the chaff
- When in Rome do as the Romans do
- When the cows come home
- Where there is a will there is a way
- Where there is muck there is money
- Wing and a prayer
- Wiser in hindsight
- World and his wife
- Yes! *(favourite retort of Berns)*
- You can lead a horse to water, but you can't make it drink
- Your word is your bond

Appendix I:

Rhona and Angela's Prayers

Rhona's prayer mantra was:

God bless Mummy and Daddy,
Hugh and Angela,
Grandma and Grandpa,
Nana and Auntie Ruth,
Aunties and Uncles,
All my cousins and kind friends
And make me a good girl forever and ever.
Amen

Angela's prayer mantra was:

Matthew, Mark, **Duke** and John
Bless the bed that I lie on
Four corners to my bed
Five angels there be spread
Two at my head
Two at my feet
One at my heart
My soul to keep.

Appendix J:

List of Pulborough Market Attendees

Auctioneers:
Dick Boxall
Dick Alden; Cattle
Leslie Weller; Sheep
Mark Monkhouse; Chicken and rabbits
Jim Pearce; Understudy, then went to Shrewsbury or Hereford

Other Staff:
David Scott-Pitcher; Clerk
Jobi; Drover
Alf Buckman; Drover

Hauliers:
Fred and David Swabey
Tom and Roger Green
Wilf Milham
Stuart Woods
John Tiller; Driver for Woods

Vendors:
Leconfield Estate; Mr Mac Andrew, Manager
Parham Estate; Mr Gordon Duke, Manager
Norfolk Estate; Arundel
Godman Estate; Mr Percy Powell, Manager
Brinsbury College; Mr Reg Haydon, Manager
Clive and Vic Allen
Bill Ayling
Riv Batchelor
Jake Dallyn
Ernest Ayre
Mrs Freddie Izaat
Mr Johnson
Alex Lawson
Guy Lerwill
Bernard Lerwill
Dennis Marten

Bob Myrham
Stephen Osmarston
Tom Rusbridge
John Ryden
Mr Strudwick
Norman Vellacott
Bill Wadey
Bill Woodbridge

Buyers/Butchers:
Roger Clark; Rudgewick
Fred Clay; Yapton Abattoir and Shop
Ted Cripps; Billingshurst
Godfrey Dormand; Dorking
Bob Durrant
Highland; Lancing
Martin Harriet; Dealer
Jack Humpheys; South Coast
Ted Joyce; Arundel and Littlehampton
Geoff Mitchell; Partridge Green
George Pearce; Horsham
Paul Reeves; Billingshurst, Horsham and Roffey
Barry Shillingford; South Coast
Whittear; Horsham Abattoir
Barry Wood; South Coast

Private Cattle Dealers:
Follett; Dorking
Lade; Cranleigh

Other Attendees:
Alan Borman; Farm Manager, Coombelands Farm
Bill Ford; Farm student
Richard Gadd; Fertiliser Sales
Harry Hawkins; Knackerman
Reg Johnson; Leconfield Estate, Shepherd/shearer
Eddie Salter; Salesman for brewer's grains, stock feed, potatoes
John Sherlow
Frank Smith; Salesman for Sadlers Grain and Feed
Roger Smithers; Farmer and haulier
John Steel
Tony Tidy; Salesman for Ford Tractors

Appendix K:

Ten Things Angela Loved about her Parents

Dad:
- ✓ Loved my mother, even more than Frithwood
- ✓ Loyal
- ✓ Perseverance
- ✓ Hard-working
- ✓ Never promised things he could not deliver
- ✓ Excellent judge of people
- ✓ Did not care what others thought
- ✓ Ploughed his own furrow
- ✓ Took people as he found them
- ✓ Good stockman

Mum:
- ✓ Loving
- ✓ Kind
- ✓ Thoughtful
- ✓ Hard-working
- ✓ Well-organised
- ✓ Intelligent
- ✓ Fair
- ✓ Optimistic
- ✓ Resourceful
- ✓ Pragmatic

The Author

Angela Lerwill was born in Rustington, West Sussex, in 1958 and grew up on her family's farm near Wisborough Green. After her formative education, she attended Harper Adams Agricultural College graduating with a Higher National Diploma in Agricultural Business Administration and Marketing. She then established her own market research business and later gained a Bachelor of Science (First-class Honours) degree with The Open University.

Travel has featured strongly in Angela's life. Since spending a working holiday in Australia and New Zealand as a student, she has visited most corners of the world.

She now lives on the edge of the Cotswolds in Gloucestershire with her husband Brian Swinyard, a retired civil servant. Angela continues to keep herself busy with helping numerous refugee and asylum-seeker friends, and raising money for good causes and charities. During the Covid-19 pandemic she started writing this book, which recalls memories of her idyllic rural childhood.

Ingram Content Group UK Ltd.
Milton Keynes UK
UKHW012352120523
421672UK00003B/46

9 781789 633399